ARCHAEOLOGY AND CREATED MEMORY
Public History in a National Park

CONTRIBUTIONS TO GLOBAL HISTORICAL ARCHAEOLOGY

Series Editor:
Charles E. Orser, Jr., *Illinois State University, Normal, Illinois*

A Continuation Order Plan is available for this series. A continuation order will bring
delivery of each new volume immediately upon publication. Volumes are billed only upon
actual shipment. For further information please contact the publisher.

ARCHAEOLOGY AND CREATED MEMORY
Public History in a National Park

Paul A. Shackel

University of Maryland
College Park, Maryland

Kluwer Academic/Plenum Publishers
New York, Boston, Dordrecht, London, Moscow

Library of Congress Cataloging-in-Publication Data

Shackel, Paul A.
   Archaeology and created memory: public history in a national park/Paul A. Shackel.
     p. cm. — (Contributions to global historical archaeology)
   Includes bibliographical references and index.
   ISBN 0-306-46177-3
   1. Archaeology and history—Harpers Ferry National Historical Park. 2. Harpers Ferry
National Historical Park—Antiquities. 3. Harpers Ferry National Historical
Park—Historiography. 4. Harpers Ferry (W. Va.)—History. 5. Harpers Ferry (W.
Va.)—Antiquities. 6. Harpers Ferry (W. Va.)—Historiography. I. Title. II. Series.
F249.H2 S52 2000
975.4'99—dc21

                                              99-055382

ISBN: 0-306-46177-3

©2000 Kluwer Academic/Plenum Publishers, New York
233 Spring Street, New York, New York 10013

http://www.wkap.nl/

10 9 8 7 6 5 4 3 2 1

A C.I.P. record for this book is available from the Library of Congress

Printed in the United States of America

For
Barbara J. Little

Preface

This archaeology of Harpers Ferry provides an example of how interest groups create their own memory and define a usable past. Archaeology can either bolster public memory and tradition, or it can help contradict the status quo by providing an alternative past. The archaeology presented in this book performs the latter. It explores how the memory of Harpers Ferry's wartime and Victorian eras developed at the expense of labor and working class histories. The archaeological interpretations confront time-honored historical views of the past that have been perpetuated by historians and archaeologists and reinforced for a long time by the National Park Service. The archaeology presented here acknowledges more inclusive histories, and it allows us to provide alternative voices to a past.

Understanding how memory is created requires knowing the political, social, and economic circumstances in which histories are created. For instance, in the case for understanding Harpers Ferry's Victorian history, it is necessary to explore the national context of the town's redevelopment after the Civil War as well as the context for the creation of the town's histories today. Interestingly, there are many similarities between the late 19th and the late 20th centuries. People in both eras faced great social and economic challenges with many citizens fearing the future, evoking traditional value rhetoric, and distrusting a new alien population. H.W. Brands (1995:3) points out that in the 1980s and 1990s, the common political discourse is that liberalism is embedded in the national capital. Liberalism is soft on crime, encourages higher taxes, and is hostile to traditional American institutions. In the 1880s and 1890s the rhetoric consisted of traditional values, the way of life of the American farmers. They considered the capitalist, centered in East Coast industrial cities, as the enemy. These powerful centers developed at the expense of the South and the West.

While the late 20th century produced a populism of Rush Limbaugh and Pat Robertson and the Republican Right, the 1890s saw the emergence of Mary Lease and Tom Watson, both vocal proponents of the Populist movement (see Brands 1995:186–191), and the Populist Left. In both eras racism played a major role. The 1896 Supreme Court decision for *Plessy* v. *Ferguson*, legitimized racism and Jim Crow legislation through the infamous charade of "separate but equal." Affirmative action legislation of the 1950s and 1960s was being dismantled in the 1990s, and legislators justified this action by claiming affirmative action was an over-correction to the racist legislation from over a century ago.

A historical archaeology of 19th- and 20th-century Harpers Ferry serves as a good example of how people—facing social tensions—manipulated history for their own social, economic, and political means. It is a phenomenon that is not limited to Harpers Ferry, a national park, the United States, nor any specific to a period. The manipulation of historical consciousness occurs every day at many nationally significant sites.

Harpers Ferry became a popular tourist town in the post-Civil War era and even today there is a revived interest in the town. Deciding which history to interpret to the visiting public helped to transform the town into a nationally significant site. It was part of a larger attempt by many new entrepreneurial Americans whose power structure was increasingly being threatened by lower-class laborers and a new immigrant population. They created a past that was heroic, an era when one did not question loyalty to a higher structure. They recalled a time when issues like racism and labor did not threaten the established hierarchy. Reclaiming an idyllic past helped to control and stabilize the present hierarchy.

Harpers Ferry, situated at the confluence of the Shenandoah and Potomac rivers (Figures 1 and 2), is best known for its Civil War and antebellum histories. It was the host to John Brown's raid; one of the first two United States Armories developed there; and the town played a strategic role in the Civil War. When I initially read the 20th century histories of Harpers Ferry, I came away with two conclusions about the town's post-bellum history. First, the town had only a military history during the Civil War, commemorating the deeds of the "great men," such as Stonewall Jackson. The lives of citizens who were dramatically affected by the conflict are absent from these stories. Second, after the Civil War, Harpers Ferry stood battered from an intense military occupation. Domestic structures lay in disrepair, stripped of their former architectural elegance. Only a few walls remained of the armory, a place that once contained some of the nation's most celebrated industrial advancements. Many townspeople who fled during the war never returned to rebuild, and only minor attempts were made to reindustrialize the town (Barry 1988 [1903]; Writer's Program 1941; Roberts 1960; Smith 1977). But, in fact, Harpers Ferry did become a thriving Victorian town.

I find it intriguing that most of these histories of Harpers Ferry generally stop just after the Civil War. It is easy to come away with the impression that the town reached its economic zenith in the 1850s and 1860s and virtually disappeared after the war (except Gilbert 1984, 1999). Some historical and archaeological overviews also reinforce the former

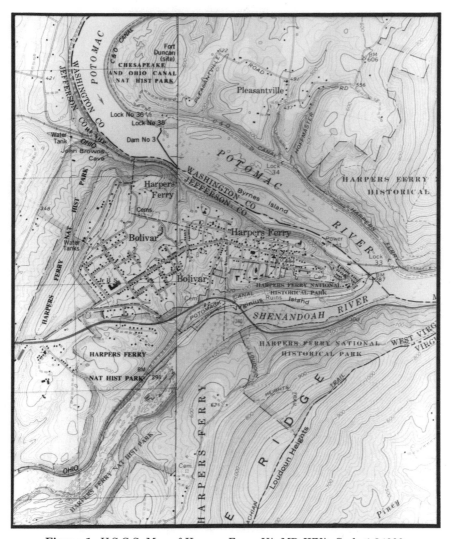

Figure 1. U.S.G.S. Map of Harpers Ferry, VA.-MD.-WVA. Scale 1:24000.

National Park Service policy that operated under the assumption that the town should be commemorated only because of the strategic role it played during the Civil War (Gardner 1974; Hershey 1964; Snell 1960a, 1960b, 1973).

Certainly the town reached an industrial peak in the 1850s, and it did play a strategic role during the Civil War. The dramatic story of Stonewall

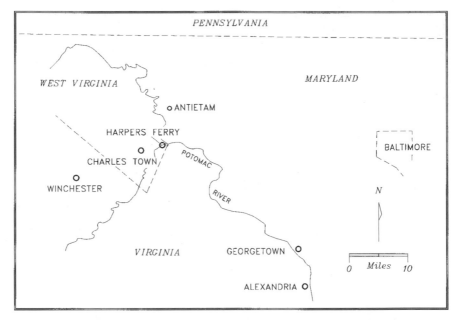

Figure 2. Location of Harpers Ferry. (Drawn by John Ravenhorst)

Jackson's siege and capture of the town has become a major interpretive thrust of the National Park Service (Hearn 1996; Frye 1987; Oates 1970; Shackel 1996; Smith 1977). A museum in Lower Town is now dedicated to this event. However, recent archaeological excavations in Harpers Ferry's commercial district provide information about the town's domestic life during the Civil War. The archaeology also furnishes some of the most substantial Victorian assemblages in the East Coast for a small industrial town (Halchin 1994; Shackel 1993, 1994). The archaeology has awakened a history that was dormant for over a century.

The histories of Harpers Ferry's Victorian era, until recently, have been almost nonexistent. After the war, Storer College was founded in Harpers Ferry for the education of former enslaved people. The town also held the second meeting of the Niagara Movement, precursor to the National Association for the Advancement of Colored People (NAACP), in 1906. Small water-powered industries were revitalized and became a major employer for Harpers Ferrians. The town became a major regional tourist attraction from the 1880s through the 1920s. Why people have ignored Harpers Ferry's postbellum history, I believe, is an interesting and powerful story—not because the postbellum histories have been omitted, but rather because the question of how and why local memory obscured the town's postbellum history from text and memories are intriguing (see for instance Sider 1996:48–83; Cameron 1996:91–97; Montgomery 1996:98–102). The material culture record from archaeological excavations lends significant support for interpreting a Victorian town history suppressed for decades.

While historians of the Civil War are always interested in studying strategic points in battles and war, they often apparently ignore the impact of the war on civilian life and the creation of public memory. For instance, Yugoslavia suffered dramatically during its civil war in the mid 1990s and more recently in the late 1990s. Historians and news agencies quickly reported the chaos, bloodshed, and military maneuvers. Ever since a fragile peace has been established, we hear very little about the rebuilding of the country. The heroics of war overshadow a very different form of heroics.

Like the Bosnians, and more recently like the Kosovo Albanians, the residents of Harpers Ferry faced a desolate homeland, with destroyed dwellings and the loss of family and friends. One of the stories of Harpers Ferry's heroic past is the courage and persistence of its residents in rebuilding their homes and in making the Victorian town a thriving community. It is a story that has often been overlooked in favor of other industrial or war-related histories. Although this book is about the archaeology of domestic life during the Civil War and Victorian Harpers Ferry, I hope it challenges us to view the history and effects of war, and the notion of heroism, in a very different way. This phenomenon is not specific to Harpers Ferry; other towns and historic sites have had their pasts manipulated as well (for example, see Lowenthal 1985, 1998; Loewen 1995). The story of Harpers Ferry that is told is determined by which memory we choose to interpret. I believe this story can include the way humans struggle, persist, and overcome the odds to rebuild a new life in a desolate land. This is a story that is long overdue.

Acknowledgments

During my tenure at Harpers Ferry National Historical Park, there were many archaeologists who made the program a success. I am indebted to them for their hard work and professionalism. They include Ellen Armbruster, Janet Blutstein, Anna Borden, Brett Burk, C. Gary Butera, Karen Coffman, Vikki Cornell, Susannah Dean, Gwyneth Duncan, John Eddins, Diane Fenicle, Benjamin Ford, Mark Goleb, Jill Halchin, Nancy Hatcher, Jean Harris, Jill Harris, Deborah Hull Walski, Marcy Jastrab, Kenneth Kulp, Eric Larsen, Michael Lucas, Erika Martin, Mia Parsons, Kelly Passo, Amy Peters, Devon Pyle, John Ravenhorst, Andrew Schenker, Tina Schutts, Dennis Scott, Jennifer Shamberg, Priscilla Smith, Kimberly Sprow, Nancy Turner, Frank Walski, Dave' Warren-Taylor, Susan Trail, Anna-Marie York, and Cari YoungRavenhorst. The archaeology program also had a strong volunteer program, and I am grateful for the efforts of Allan Alexander, Sandra Anderson, Daniel Ballas, Jason Beard, Howard Beverly, Hilary Chapman, David Christy, Jeffery Cogle, Douglas Dammann, Carolyn Gates, Theresa Grob, Logan Johnson, David Larsen, Katrina Larsen, Ryan Levins, Guian McKee, Stephanie McSherry, Thomas Neff, Bob Newnham, Janina O'Bien-Trent, Anne Marie Parsons, Jane Rago, Marcia Robinson, Douglas Sause, Karl Smart, Jack Smith, Mary Beth Williams, and Terrie Wise. It was also a pleasure working with and receiving feedback from the park's historian team: Patricia Chickering, Michael Jenkins, Mary Johnson, Stan Bumgardner, and John Barker. The cultural landscape team consisting of Maureen Joseph, Perry Wheelock, and Steve Lowe, provided considerable input into this project.

Susan Winter Trail served as the original principal investigator for the Harpers Ferry construction project that began in 1989, and I commend her efforts for beginning this research project. John Ravenhorst provided the Autocad drawings, and Cari YoungRavenhorst produced some of the photographs. Frank Schultz-DePalo provided guidance in facilitating the curation of artifacts, and Bruce Noble gave helpful feedback. Nancy Hatcher helped me locate unpublished manuscripts and photographs.

The following people provided expertise and advice through the course of the project and I appreciate their assistance: Joanne Bowen, Gregory Brown, Charles Gunn, Paul Mullins, Karl Reinhard, Irwin Rovner, and Linda Scott Cummings. I draw upon their specialization and synthesize their results for this book. I am especially grateful for the hard work and dedication of Brett Burk, Linda Scott Cummings, Deborah Hull-Walski, Eric Larsen, Michael Lucas, Irwin Rovner, and Frank Walski for their synthesis of complex data sets that I use. Their efforts, which are found in many archaeological technical reports of Harpers Ferry, are greatly appreciated. Mark Warner provided me with several references to *The Bee*; I appreciate his sharing this information.

The archaeology project could not have proceeded without the strong commitment of Park Superintendent Donald Campbell. Members of the park's administrative staff were also very helpful; they include Peggy Smallwood, Gayleen Boyd, Julie Johnston, Rita Mihalik, Ann Shuey, Judy Coleman, Joyce Howe, Kay Kenney, and Dori Lent. Special thanks to Facility Manager Richard Fox and Grounds Foreman Dennis Ebersole for providing staff and equipment throughout the excavation process.

Stephen Potter, chief archaeologist for the National Capital Region (NCR), National Park Service, provided helpful technical oversight throughout all phases of this program. NCR staff archaeologists Marian Creveling, Deborah Hull-Walski, Robert Sonderman, and Matthew Virta also provided assistance for archaeology projects. Many people, especially Laurie Burgess, provided valuable feedback while I wrote this manuscript. I also appreciate the fine copy-editing work performed by Barbara Merchant.

Part of my research was performed while I received fellowships from the West Virginia Humanities Council and the Winterthur Museum. I truly appreciate the assistance that I received from Neville Thompson while I used the library facilities at Winterthur. I also appreciate the assistance of Deborah Hull-Walski, Collections Manager, Department of Anthropology, Smithsonian Institution.

I appreciate the helpful guidance and suggestions provided to me by Chuck Orser and Eliot Werner. Barbara Little read several drafts of this manuscript. She gave encouragement and suggestions throughout the writing of this book.

Contents

SECTION II REBUILDING HARPERS FERRY AFTER THE WAR

Tables and Figures

Tables

Figures

Introduction
Harpers Ferry: A Place in Time

A BRIEF HISTORY

After the bombardment of Fort Sumter and after Lincoln's call to raise 75,000 troops, Virginia seceded April 1861 from the Union. Seizing the armory and arsenal at Harpers Ferry became a major objective for the Confederacy. Lieutenant Roger Jones, stationed at Harpers Ferry with 50 regulars and 15 volunteers, feared that an advancing force of 360 Confederates would capture the town. Before these forces arrived on April 18, 1861, Jones set fire to the federal buildings and abandoned the town. The arsenal, along with 17,000 guns, was destroyed, although the townspeople, in an attempt to salvage their livelihood, saved the machinery. The Confederates shipped the armory machinery to Richmond, Virginia and Fayetteville, North Carolina where they used it to make arms for the Confederacy (Noffsinger 1958:45–46; Hearn 1996:56).

During the Civil War, Harpers Ferry changed hands eight times. Most residents left town. The armies seized abandoned houses and used them as quarters for troops. Both armies destroyed parts of the town in retaliation for attacks. The civilians who remained experienced shelling and sniper fire. The war destroyed the armory establishment and most of the private industries.

After the Civil War, Harpers Ferry stood as a shell of its former self. Houses were damaged. Only the walls remained of the United States Rifle Works that once contained some of the most celebrated American industrial advancements, including the birth of the American Manufacturing System, or interchangeable parts. Democratic Conservatives, who controlled the business community, believed that the region needed to industrialize and to develop its mineral resources. They established many committees to attract industries to the former armory sites along the Shenandoah and Potomac River shores. Entrepreneurs equated this new era in America industry with progress, and potential growth seemed limitless. The business community in Harpers Ferry subscribed to this ideology, and they strived to attract industry to help rejuvenate their town (Fenicle 1993). Redevelopment did not occur until the Democratic Conser-

1

vatives took control of the town's politics toward the end of Reconstruction, in the 1870s. They then carried out their program.

The Bollman Bridge, originally under construction before the Civil War, was rebuilt and completed by 1870. It enabled people and goods to pass over the Potomac River from Baltimore into Harpers Ferry. Across the new wrought iron structure "trains rumbled into town, discharging passengers at the new depot, or unloading freight at the siding with noise and commotion that regularly interrupted the quiet of the community" (Gilbert et al. 1993:3.77). Harpers Ferry became an important depot as the Baltimore & Ohio Railroad expanded to Wheeling, West Virginia, Pittsburgh, Pennsylvania, and other western cities in the 1870s and 1880s. The Chesapeake and Ohio Canal also resumed operations and entrepreneurs shipped coal, wheat, flour, lumber, and corn through Harpers Ferry to the port of Georgetown. The canal reached its commercial peak in the mid-1870s (Gilbert et al. 1993: 3.78–3.80) although the railroad played a major role in the town's economy through the 1920s.

Harpers Ferry's commercial district initially struggled to redevelop in the 1870s. Disastrous floods in 1870 and 1877 accelerated the deterioration of Lower Town Harpers Ferry. They were more devastating than those in the past because of regional environmental deterioration. Timber along the Shenandoah Valley had been harvested or burned during the war. The high waters carried topsoil down river, leaving large quantities of mud throughout Harpers Ferry's commercial district. This added burden meant that the town needed an extraordinary amount of energy and money, more than ever before, to make it economically viable again. Without the aid of the federal government, who once had an interest in manufacturing weapons in town, residents had a greater financial burden to clean up the town.

Joseph Barry (1988 [1903]:164), a local historian, commented on the 1870 flood:

> The very streets in many places ploughed up, as it were, and chasms many feet in depth were made in the road bed. Every house on the south side of the street, from the market house to the Island of Virginius was either entirely destroyed or badly injured.... Some 70 houses in all were either entirely demolished or rendered uninhabitable ... in many instances, the very foundations obliterated.

Two years later William Cullen Bryant (Bryant 1872) described the town as:

> still more sleepy and dilapidated than its normal condition. The recent war stunned it. Then came the disastrous flood of 1870.... Pass where you will, there are evidences of the desolation left behind by these two occurrences [the war and the flood]. And the people of Harpers Ferry have very naturally lost heart.

Many buyers who purchased government lands in the town's commercial district at the 1869 government auction after the closing of the armory filed applications for abatement. They claimed they had paid inflated prices and that their new, flood-worn property had lost considerable value. They based their bids on the prospects of a rumor that a Washington politician would reindustrialize the town immediately after the war. This rumor never came to fruition. An act of Congress on June 14, 1878, allowed purchasers of lots to apply for abatement. Twenty-nine purchasers, who had originally paid a total of $39,755 for their properties, had their sales abated to $9,668.35. Other government sales in the 1880s disposed of the remaining government lands in Harpers Ferry and a new optimism reigned in Harpers Ferry (Snell 1979).

Water power had been the catalyst for much of the industrial growth before the Civil War. Steam power gained importance in the United States during the 1870s and 1880s, as its fuel costs decreased. Water power became perceived as inadequate, unreliable, and therefore more expensive. As a result, Harpers Ferry never regained the many water powered industries it had during the 1840s and 1850s. In the 1870s and 1880s, however, outsiders from the North took advantage of the opportunity to re-exploit the Shenandoah and the Potomac's water power for flour, pulp, and paper milling (Gilbert 1984, 1999).

Virginius Island was purchased by two Ohio entrepreneurs, Jonathan Child and John McCreight, from longtime resident Abraham Herr. Herr's flour mill had been destroyed by Confederates during the Civil War, and he decided to reinvest his capital elsewhere. Child and McCreight reestablished water powered industry by converting an old cotton mill into a flour mill. The extensive development of the Baltimore & Ohio Railroad allowed them to reach larger markets, and they operated a profitable business for over a decade. Although the flour mill was damaged in the 1870 and 1877 floods, Child and McCreight did not give up heart. They refurbished the mill and some workers' houses. The industrial community operated at full potential in less than a year (Gilbert 1984; Joseph et al. 1993; Johnson and Barker 1993).

After the war, the older prominent town families lost considerable influence, while a new middle class of businessmen, merchants, and their families gained control of the town's finances. Families like Quinn, Decaulne, Ames, Conway, Walsh, and McGraw either constructed or rehabilitated worn-torn structures for businesses, boardinghouses, restaurants, and domiciles (Gilbert et al. 1993:3.74–3.75).

By the 1880s citizens in what was known as Lower Town developed and rebuilt the main business district on Shenandoah Street. A two-block corridor was filled with commercial establishments, giving the town a character of a bustling and profitable commercial district (see Shackel and Winter 1994). Economic expansion and optimism were fueled by Thomas Savery's purchase of the armory grounds and the rifle factory site in 1884. He first constructed a paper mill on the armory grounds along the Potomac. By 1890, he had completed a pulp mill on the rifle factory site along the Shenandoah (Gilbert 1984). Savery spent most of his time as an absentee landlord, living in Delaware. Harpers Ferry, which once contained dozens of industries catering to the local and regional population, now contained only several specialized water-powered enterprises that catered solely to regional and national markets.

There were those who felt optimistic about the town's growing economic success. Although the flour mill no longer operated in the 1890s, and the economic situation looked bleak, others took a chance and joined Savery in industrializing the town. In 1895, a Harpers Ferrian, James McGraw, built a brewery to join his bottling works that began operating on the north bank of the Shenandoah River. He called it the Harpers Ferry Brewing Company. It continued to operate under several other ownerships in town until 1942 (Hull-Walski and Walski 1994).

Since the town's reindustrialization never reached the prominence of the antebellum armory era, many Harpers Ferrians took advantage of the growing trend in America—the birth of tourism. The town exploited its history, its national icons, and its natural resources to attract visitors (Joseph et al. 1993; Shackel 1995, 1996:3–4).

In 1880 the railroad built an amusement park on 20-acre Byrne Island in the Potomac River beside Harpers Ferry (*Spirit of Jefferson* 6 July 1880; Gilbert et al. 1993:3.90–3.91). Tens of thousands of visitors came to Island Park each summer by rail. Boardinghouses, hotels, restaurants, and bars overflowed between Memorial Day and Labor Day.

Tourism, to some extent, replaced large-scale industry as the town's major economic base, although some industries remained profitable into the 20th century. The town prospered until the floods of 1936 and 1942 washed away bridges, and a new bridge and highway system bypassed the town in the 1940s (Gilbert et al. 1993).

By the 1940s, only a few structures were occupied in the Lower Town area. Since the main highway no longer came through the center of the town, and fewer tourists visited, it became difficult to resurrect the community. Water powered industry had abandoned the area, although people still came to see the Civil War sites and John Brown's Fort (no longer on its original foundations, but on the Storer College Campus), and admire the area's scenic beauty. In 1944 President Franklin D. Roosevelt signed legislation to create a national monument at Harpers Ferry. A decade later the National Park Service became caretakers of the monument and in 1963, it became a national historical park (Shackel 1996:57–58).

REINVENTING HARPERS FERRY'S HISTORY

Harpers Ferry thrived as a tourist and small industrial town from the 1880s through the early 20th century. It was rebuilt with prominent Victorian architecture, consisting of stone and brick buildings. Twentieth-century histories, including recent ones, developed a scenario that portrayed the Victorian town as a shadow of the prewar town. Rather than recognizing its economic rebirth, town histories mourned the loss of the United States Armory and celebrated its role in the Civil War.

This attitude is obvious in a 1903 folksy history of the town (Barry 1988 [1903]) and in the Work Project Adminstration's (WPA) Great Depression Writer Program's (Writer's Program 1941) community history. The Writer Programs, a depression era government-funded project, developed local histories for many American communities in the 1930s. Many researchers based their syntheses on local research and oral accounts, and these community histories were designed in part to encourage tourism. In 1941, the Writer's Program described Harpers Ferry as

> war-battered and flood damaged, is but a relic of the thriving village that before the War between the States centered about the government armory and Hall's Rifle Works and seemed destined to become an important industrial town. . . . [O]nly the memory of the early industrial activity remains. Residents find employment in the Baltimore & Ohio Railroad shop at Brunswick, Maryland, four miles away, in near-by quarries, and in the small retail shops of the town. (Writer's Program 1941:224–225)

Although tourism declined significantly during the Great Depression, Harpers Ferry retained some regional and national recognition. In the WPA history, it was noted:

> In the summer, tourists-service enterprises blossom along the main thoroughfares; tourist homes, closed during winter months, reopen; and post card and souvenir vendors are busy. Nearly every citizen considers himself a volunteer guide, and a few charge small fees for conducting the sightseer up the natural stone steps, past the Harper House to Jefferson's Rock and John Brown's Fort. During winter months the town's folk return to their quiet round of church suppers, bingo parties, knitting circles, and occasional trips to the movies at Charles Town or Martinsburg. (Writer's Program 1941:225)

The Writer's Program also described the area known as Virginius Island. Virginius Island was always privately owned and it provided support services to the armory and the local population. Some industries, such as the flour mill, had regional markets. The locals called the island "Herr's Island," named after the first person to consolidate ownership of the entire island in the 1850s. Abraham Herr and his family lived in the industrial community that he created, keeping a close watch on the workers' daily activities. Herr built and maintained workers' housing (Halchin

1992; Johnson and Barker 1993; Joseph et al. 1993). Herr also enabled smaller entrepreneurs to rent or lease the water-powered industries he owned on Virginius Island. Many of these smaller industrialists served the local Harpers Ferry area.

In 1867, Herr sold the island and industrial rights to the two Ohio entrepreneurs, Child and McCreight, who later sold it to the absentee industrialist from Delaware, Thomas Savery. Savery's pulp mill provided jobs for Harpers Ferrians from about 1890 until 1935. When the 1870 flood destroyed many smaller Virginius Island industries, Harpers Ferry lost most of its small-scale commerce that catered to the local population. People inhabited the island until the 1936 flood destroyed the last remaining inhabitable structure (Halchin 1992; Johnson and Barker 1993). In the WPA history, it said:

> Herr's Island, once the site of an industrial village called Virginius, is a desolate, deserted 13-acre island in the Shenandoah River containing flood- and war-battered ruins of an earlier era. Virginius, which then included a sawmill, tannery, oil mill, and 12 dwellings, was established by the Virginia assembly in 1827, but remained essentially a part of Harpers Ferry. Hall's Rifle Works, a part of the Government Armory, also stood here, and the place thrived through the War between the States until the flood of 1870, which washed away or wrecked most of the buildings. The flour mill of Abraham Herr, for whom the island was named, escaped damage in this flood and operated until 1887, but subsequent floods destroyed it and the few remaining buildings. (Writer's Program 1941:234)

Although Child and McCreight purchased the island from Herr in 1867, and operated a flour mill until 1887, Herr is recognized in the WPA history as owning and operating the flour mill in the postwar era. Thomas Savery owned Virginius Island from the 1890 through the 1930s, and like Child and McCreight, he was an outsider. None of the postwar Virginius Island owners revised the small scale commerce that catered to the local population. Instead, their businesses focused on regional and national markets. They did provide the community hundreds of unskilled jobs.

Savery continued to served as an absentee owner; for a period in the 20th century his son managed the operations in Harpers Ferry. Thomas Savery's absentee ownership deprived the town of any form of paternalism that locals may have found in Herr's ownership, and to some extent during Child and McCreight's tenure. Herr lived on Virginius Island and became part of the community. He eventually purchased additional property and became the sole proprietor of the island. Unlike Herr, who maintained dwellings for his workers, Savery rented out houses to anyone who would pay the rent. He did very little to maintain these structures (Halchin 1992; Johnson and Barker 1993). Even today, the industrial island, called

Virginius by the National Park Service, is still called Herr's Island by many locals. A resident of the island during the 1910s and 1920s gave a recent oral history, in which she drew a map, naming the island as "Hairs [sic] Island" (Figure 3) (Farmer 1995).

RECLAIMING HARPERS FERRY'S HISTORY

There is an emphasis on Harpers Ferry's antebellum and Civil War histories as well as a conspicuous absence of Child and McCreight, and Savery from the WPA's industrial history of Harpers Ferry. This phenomenon, masking a class history, is well documented in other communities. For instance, Sider (1996:48–83) describes a worker's history of resistance and strikes in Lawrence, Massachusetts as having been repressed by community memory. In this mill community, the Strike of 1912, euphemistically called the "Bread and Roses Day," was branded by the Catholic Church as having been instigated by the most "unsavory immigrants" (quoted in Sider 1996:52). Supervisors and managers intimidated strike leaders in the factory throughout the remainder of their lives. Later, community leaders focused on the strike, rather than the working condi-

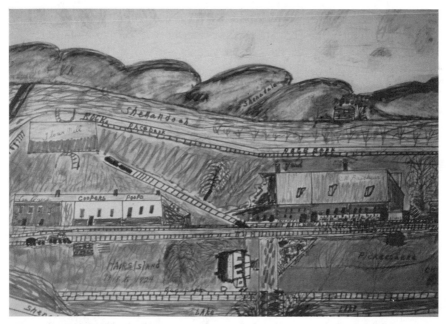

Figure 3. Late 20th-century perception of early 20th-century Virginius Island as drawn by former resident, Mrs. Edna Brashear Farmer.

tions, the reason for the strike. More important, the testimony of the factory working conditions by a 14-year-old girl in front of Congress, were also suppressed from historical consciousness (Cameron 1993, 1996).

The histories of Harpers Ferry tend to be about prewar industry and the "great men" of the Civil War. Therefore, there are some similarities between what Sider (1996) found at Lawrence—the suppression of working class histories, and at Harpers Ferry—the suppression of postbellum working class histories. Based on my understanding of the Virginius Island's historical description, I assume that the WPA history relied significantly on many selective written and oral accounts of the town since class consciousness is nonexistent in their writings. I find it compelling that the Writer's Program does not mention the subsequent owners of Herr's property (Child and McCreight, and Savery). Especially since Savery operated the pulp mill along the Shenandoah River until 1935—about the same time the WPA was researching the town. A power plant developed by Savery on the Potomac River continued to generate electricity for the area until 1991. Harpers Ferrians, comprising mostly of merchants and working class families, created their own history. They chose to delete the latter owners from their nostalgic memory of industry in the "good old days." The postbellum industrial owners were outsiders, from the north, and did little for the working-class families, except to pay low wages for their labor and take their rent money. These postbellum owners failed to revive the small scale industries that served the local population. The special paternalism of the early armory days, including Herr's occupation, is long remembered and cherished by locals, especially at the expense of the postbellum era (see Barry 1988 [1903]; Smith 1977).

Histories continued to be written in the middle and late 20th century that conveyed the town had its most glorious and significant history in the 1850s and 1860s (Smith 1977; Moulton in Drickamer and Drickamer 1987; Hearn 1996). The myth perpetuated that industry no longer existed in Harpers Ferry much after the Civil War, and the idea became entrenched in the National Park Service custodianship of Harpers Ferry. Many 1950s through 1970s histories of Harpers Ferry sponsored by the National Park Service ignored the town's Victorian history, and the conditions of everyday life during the Civil War. If historians mentioned the town's postbellum history, it was an afterthought, or footnote (for example Everhart 1952; Noffsinger 1958; Snell 1958, 1973, 1979). A 1960 history on Harpers Ferry described the town in its postwar years. The author, Bruce Robert (1960:n.p.), noted:

> After the war homes had been rebuilt by some of the former inhabitants of the town, but many "Ferrians" had to move away forever. The town, like a badly crippled soldier whose injuries leave him unable to compete in a post-war world, became a permanent casualty of the Civil War.

> So it happened that Harpers Ferry slipped out of the America of commerce and industry and into the stream of history.

When the National Park Service came to town, it subscribed to this version of history. The organization began an ambitious program to restore the community to the 1859–1865 period. Part of this enthusiasm may have been generated by the park's preparation and participation in the Civil War centennial. Much like other national shrines (Williamsburg, Monticello, and Mount Vernon), the national park developed under a policy that encouraged time freezing. They restored the built landscape to a particular period of perceived importance. For Harpers Ferry it was the Civil War era. While an abundance of architectural and archaeological evidence suggested that a Victorian town once thrived in Harpers Ferry, the National Park Service administrators decided in the 1950s to remove any sign of postbellum architecture and ignore its Victorian history (Gilbert et al. 1993). An April 25, 1954 letter between National Park Service officials explains the condition of the town:

> As you intimate, the place is a slum. Its qualifications are chiefly historical rather than architectural. Its appeal is sentimental rather than historical or aesthetic. Still there is an attractive aura of decay and ruin which it would be a pity to mar by a rash of restoration. (Letter, Fritz to Pete 25 April 1954)

The service did not follow these recommendations. By the late 1950s many post-Civil War era structures were removed and restorations had begun for the preparation of the Civil War centennial celebration (Shackel 1996:5).

Archaeology Supporting the Myth

It is not surprising that much of the early archaeology in Harpers Ferry was done to support the prominence of Harpers Ferry's antebellum era. Archeologists have worked in Harpers Ferry National Historical Park since 1959, rediscovering the community's rich cultural and industrial history. Most of these excavations, until recently, have concentrated on the early and mid-19th-century gun manufacturing industry and supporting commerce. The earliest archaeology was done at the arsenal, the structure that John Brown hoped to seize and capture weapons to supply newly freed slaves (see Cotter 1959, 1960). Edward Larabee (1960a) excavated several trenches during the summer of 1960 and found the walls of the arsenal building (Figure 4). He also did the initial excavations on Halls Island and found some foundations belonging to the United States Rifle Works (Larabee 1960b, 1961, 1962).[1]

Figure 4. Excavations at the new arsenal in Lower Town Harpers Ferry conducted by Edward McMillian Larrabee, September 5, 1959. (Courtesy, Harpers Ferry National Historical Park)

In 1964 William Hershey (1964) performed excavations around the Lockwood House. The site was the original location of John Hall's domicile. Hall is credited with perfecting the development of interchangeable parts. The purpose of the excavations was to find outbuildings and graves related to the Civil War. Archaeologists found Victorian era features related to Storer College were found, but they only kept a sample of these artifacts since, at the time, this era was not considered archaeologically significant.

David H. Hannah (1969) produced the first cultural resource assessment on Virginius Island in the mid-1960s. In 1966–1968, he directed a Job Corps project to uncover the foundation walls of the large cotton mill that operated in the prewar era. The National Park Service conducted testing around the Shenandoah Canal wall, an antebellum feature, as part of an expanded restoration effort (Mueller et al. 1986). And in 1986, archaeological staff monitored additional construction activities around an antebellum foundry tailrace (Frye and YoungRavenhorst 1988).

In the 1970s and 1980s, there were major excavations done around a set of buildings, known as the Wager Block, in the Lower Town commercial district. The work identified major archaeological features in preparation for architectural and landscape renovations planned to restore the town to the Civil War period. Archaeologists did not consider materials dating from the Victorian era as significant because the period fell outside their scope of work (Gardner 1974). Other excavations on this block followed, providing information regarding building's functions (Blee 1978) and furnishing a more diachronic assessment of the cultural resources (Pousson 1985). Additional work along the northern side of Shenandoah Street in the commercial district occurred within several commercial dwellings (Seidel 1985).

ARCHAEOLOGY AND OVERTURNING LOCAL MYTH

Archaeology has recently made significant inroads toward producing a more class conscious and accurate history by contributing to the town's postbellum history, the focus of this book. A major survey effort documented the rich and diverse 19th-century cultural history found on Maryland Heights (Frye and Frye 1989) and Loudoun Heights (Winter and Frye 1992). This survey identified resources dating from the early 19th century through the early 20th century. In the early 19th century, both Maryland and Loudoun Heights served as major charcoaling areas, although these heights are best known for their strategic role in the Civil War. The area was later inhabited with small farmsteads in the postbellum era.

The Harpers Ferry community has always enshrined its glorious industrial past. As much as archaeology serves to glorify Harpers Ferry's industrial past, it can also function as an equally powerful tool in overturning the myth that the industrial past is the only history worth recognizing. In summer 1989, I directed the National Park Service excavations in Lower Town Harpers Ferry that were done behind a set of building known as the old master armorer's house, and behind another set of late 19th-century buildings commonly called "flood buffers." These Victorian buildings survived the 1950s redevelopment of the town because the National Park Service surmised that they served to protect in times of flooding the antebellum structures found downriver. A central goal of the most recent archaeology project was to focus upon the everyday lives of residents who lived, prospered, struggled, and worked in this commercial district area. Excavations took place at stores, dwellings, and a boardinghouse (Figure 5).

The armory's master armorer occupied one of the dwellings next to

Figure 5. Excavations occurred behind these urban lots prior to restoration. The large complex with sheds and outbuildings (left) was constructed and occupied by the McGraws in the latter part of the 19th century. It was later inhabited by the Dorans in the early 20th century. The single house with a rear addition (right) was occupied by the Hursts from the late nineteenth century. (Drawn by Laura Simpkins, Denver Service Center. Courtesy, National Park Service)

the flood buffer circa 1820–1859. Only sparse historical documentation exists on the war, postwar, and recent habitation, but it is known that two of Harpers Ferry's most prominent Victorian entrepreneurial families—the McGraws and the Dorans (1893–1907)—occupied the buildings and operated a boarding house. Mrs. Stipes also ran a boarding house (1862–1865) on the same property during the Civil War. The presence of these residents and their contributions to the commercial development of the town's Civil War and postbellum history became harder to ignore when the archaeology team uncovered several large deposits dating to their occupations. These assemblages are one of the most abundant late 19th-century deposits yet identified in Harpers Ferry (Shackel 1993b; Burk 1993a, 1993b, 1993c; Hull-Walski and Hull 1993, 1994; Larsen 1993, 1994; Lucas 1993, 1994). The materials provide an interesting comparison to an entrepreneur's household, the Hursts, who lived on the adjacent lot. The assemblages illustrate the differences in material wealth and health conditions between classes of people in an industrializing society.

All of this information provides new insights into the everyday lives of the wartime and late 19th-century citizens of Harpers Ferry and suggests some of the challenges they faced every day. These new archaeological interpretations have made significant contributions to Harpers Ferry's history. This information is now shared with visitors on some daily tours, and it is reinforced by a new permanent exhibit that showcases the town's history, incorporating both antebellum and postbellum pasts. What is more important, the exhibit goes beyond the "great men" histories, and major industrial developments: It tells the story of workers and their families within the context of the development of a Victorian tourist town.

When I first came to Harpers Ferry in the 1980s as a visitor, I was told by park interpreters that the town was destroyed during the Civil War and it remained a ghost town until the National Park Service acquired it. The National Park Service recycled the myth of the WPA history, and other early and mid-20th century accounts of the town. There were virtually no Victorian structures remaining, so the National Park Service used the existing landscape created by their 1950s restoration policy to justify their interpretations. Their version recalled a time when industry thrived before the Civil War and highlighted the strategic role the town played during the insurrection. Nothing was mentioned about how citizens coped with the war, how they struggled to resurrect the town, and how they recreated a viable economic center in the decades following the devastation of the war.

Despite new and changing interpretive strategies, the impression of a town without a working class postbellum history lives on today. A recent Civil War history of Harpers Ferry notes; "Today, the only buildings standing in the Lower Town are those preserved by the National Park Service. What six years of war destroyed and man rebuilt, the flood of 1870 swept away forever" (Hearn 1996:290).

A class conscious historical archaeology of Harpers Ferry can only enrich our national heritage and increase awareness of an era that has been traditionally overlooked. The existence of a Victorian working-class and tourist town is slowly being embraced by the National Park Service's interpretive programs. Although this era is not mentioned in the park's enabling legislation, it is now a major theme in a new permanent archaeological exhibit in Lower Town. Archaeology has contributed to overturning the myth that Harpers Ferry was not an economically viable town after the Civil War. Like the Phoenix, the town rose from its ashes and became a notable regional center that lasted into the 20th century.

This book contains seven chapters that tell the story of a working-class town that capitalized on significant historical events. Working-class families and middle class and upper class elite from regional centers intermingled in the streets of Harpers Ferry. Small industry, such as a pulp mills, brewery, paper factory, and knitting mill comprised the town's economic base. Historical sites and an amusement park helped to create a seasonal tourist trade.

Chapters 1 and 2 contribute to Harpers Ferry's Civil War history. Events such as the destruction of the United States Armory and the siege and capture of Harpers Ferry created the ruins that contributed to the memorialization and commodification of the town's history. While the "great men" histories have become central to the park's interpretation of this significant place, these chapters provide the often neglected story: a history of working-class people. Archaeology supplements and at times contradicts some of the major histories of the town. Archaeology allows us to examine the creation of memory and shows us how these memories have been controlled to support a particular group.

Chapter 3 provides a national and regional context for post war Harpers Ferry. Chapter 4 is placed in the context of late 19th-century social, political, and economic developments in the United States. The chapter outlines the development of an entrepreneur's household (the Hurst family), who lived in Lower Town Harpers Ferry, the center of the town's commercial district. Although tourist activities did not directly occur on the Hurst property, James Garland Hurst became deeply involved in the town's revitalization and tourism movement. An examination of this household furnishes information about the Hurst's Victorian lifestyle. Surprisingly, the archaeological information provides contradictory information on what Hurst proposed for a cleaner and more sanitary town, and how he actually lived his life.

Chapter 5 looks at workers and their relationship to one of Harpers Ferry's more prominent postbellum industries—the bottling works and the brewery. The founding of the bottling works (1880s) and the brewery (1890s) coincides with the town's new economic growth and enthusiasm during the Victorian era. The archaeology provides an account of working conditions and labor unrest among these unskilled workers.

Boarders lived adjacent to the bottling works and next to the Hurst household. Chapter 6 provides an overview of Victorian working-class households and the development of boardinghouse establishments in the United States. Historical information shows that the McGraw–Doran boardinghouse operated from the 1890s into the 20th century, but we do not know who actually lived there. These transients probably worked in the knitting mill, paper factory, or brewery. The historical and archaeological record provides information on how this group of people—working class households who worked in small factories—survived in this tourist town.

Chapter 7 provides a summary and some conclusion on the everyday life in Harpers Ferry during its Victorian era. Much of this information is placed in the larger context of the development late 19th-century Victorian life.

From the Victorian era through the early National Park Service occupation, the town's Civil War and industrial histories have been interpreted at the expense of other histories. Social, political, and ideological factors play a significant role deciding which histories should be presented to the public. Much of what is interpreted about Victorian Harpers Ferry provides new insights into daily life of this era.

NOTE

1. For a complete bibliographic listing of archaeology reports on Harpers Ferry, see Little (1995).

"All About Us Was the Wreckage of the Fighting"

Harpers Ferry During the War

INTRODUCTION

The stories of the Civil War in Harpers Ferry often portray the feats of the "great men." This phenomenon is not particular to either this town or this event. Commanders, many of them graduates of West Point, wrote their accounts of battle situations and conditions. These narratives are included in the *Official Records* (USWD 1880), a document that has been widely published and circulated. The *Official Record* is still a main documentary source used in contemporary histories of the Civil War. Occasionally, soldiers' letters have been preserved, and they provide an additional perspective of the war. They are also valuable accounts for reconstructing a history of Harpers Ferry (see for instance Ball n.d.; Drickamer and Drickamer 1987).

The story of the Harpers Ferry's Civil War era is dominated by Stonewall Jackson's capture of the town. It is an event that is often presented to the public by the National Park Service and Civil War historians as the most significant incident of the war in Harpers Ferry. There are, I believe, other stories that need to be told about wartime Harpers Ferry in order to provide a more balanced view of the town's history. These histories include the accounts of civilians who withstood this crisis (see for instance, Letter, Frederickson 1863; Letter, Griffith 1864; Letter, Shewbridge 1861) as well as those who came back to rebuild the town. Integrating these perspectives with the present history of Harpers Ferry, which is dominated by the accounts of the *Official Record*, can only provide a deeper and richer contextual story of the town.

THE EFFECTS OF WAR ON DOMESTIC LIFE IN HARPERS FERRY

Harpers Ferry stood in the national limelight from the time of John Brown's raid in October 1859 to the end of the Civil War in 1865. After the Confederate forces bombarded Fort Sumter on April 12, 1861, Harpers Ferry soon felt the repercussions. For the duration of the war, Harpers Ferrians confronted both armies, suffered through looting of their homes, saw their houses and businesses destroyed, and lost their livelihoods. Those townspeople who stayed in Harpers Ferry faced four years of military occupation. The archaeological record provides valuable information on the impact of the Civil War on civilian life.

On April 18, 1861, Governor John Wise ordered the Virginia militia to take Harpers Ferry (Murfin 1989). Lieutenant Roger Jones, stationed at Harpers Ferry with 42 men of the United States Mounted Rifles, did not receive aid from the local militia. Only 12 armory employees, fearing the loss of their livelihoods, agreed to help the lieutenant defend Harpers Ferry and the United States Armory (Hearn 1996:52–53). Outnumbered by 360 advancing Confederates, Jones set fire to the federal factory buildings and abandoned the town (Letter, George Mauzy to J. H. Burton 19 April 1861) (Figure 6). The townspeople, in an attempt to salvage their livelihood, saved most of the armory's machinery (*SoJ* 4 May 1861:2).

The fire caused some damage to the musket factory on the Potomac River, but the rifle factory on the Shenandoah River escaped harm. More than 4,000 guns remained in useable condition. During the next two months the Confederates used the existing factory and machinery to their advantage by employing armorers loyal to the secessionist. The employed them

Figure 6. The burning of the United States Arsenal at Harpers Ferry, 10 P.M., 1861. (Courtesy, Harpers Ferry National Historic Park, HF-533)

until funds ran out (Letter, J. Shewbridge to D. Shewbridge April 23, 1861).

Without a regulated economy or a steady source of revenue, Harpers Ferrians turned to alternative strategies to survive. On April 23, 1861, a townsperson remarked:

> Sharp traders splintered wood or cut up bits of rope, selling it at hefty prices to green recruits as bona fide scraps salvaged from John Brown's gallows. A few ladies turned to prostitution, . . . whiskey smugglers made the most money but also ran great risks, as the business was strictly forbidden by military commanders on both sides. A few citizens, both male and female, earned favors by acting as spies. (Hearn 1996:58).

Stonewall Jackson, commander of Harpers Ferry in April and May 1861, fortified Maryland Heights in early May with about 500 Kentuckians and Virginians while the construction of the Block Houses on Loudoun Heights was underway (Frye and Frye 1989:56).

The *Richmond Dispatch* noted the construction of primitive wooden huts and a 200-foot-long wooden stockade (Figure 7). The *Alexandria Gazette* reported that a "laboring force of negroes" performed much of the work on the Maryland Heights (Frye and Frye 1989:56). A soldier wrote

Figure 7. Stockade and camp of the Kentucky Regiment. (Courtesy, Harpers Ferry National Historical Park, HF-533)

that the "heights are being fortified perfectly . . . and within a few days Harpers Ferry will be a point which all creation cannot take—not but impregnable. Let Abraham make the most of that" (*Register* 24 May 1861:2).

Marylanders complained that Virginia soldiers "forcibly entered private houses, seized personal property, and insulted and threatened "unoffending citizens" (Frye and Frye 1989:54). Property was destroyed on Maryland Heights and boarder residents perceived this act as an invasion (Frye and Frye 1989:55). Angry protests by the Maryland governor led Virginia's governor to promise full and liberal compensation for any property damage caused by Virginia troops (Frye and Frye, 1989:55).

Nevertheless, former Virginia senator, James Mason, claimed Virginia had the right to occupy and fortify the heights. He remarked:

> [Maryland] remains one of the United States, a power foreign to Virginia, and in open avowed hostility to us. Occupying her territory, therefore, is only occupying territory of the enemy; nor is it invasion in the proper sense of the term, because occupation is defensive and precautionary only, and not for aggression, and will cease as soon as the enemy withdraws from Maryland. (quoted in Frye and Frye 1989:55)

General Joseph E. Johnston assumed command of Harpers Ferry on May 24, 1861, and declared Harpers Ferry "untenable" (Memorandum, by Johnston, USWD 1880:881). Since more than 300 gunmaking machines in the armory still functioned, the Confederates dismantled them and shipped the equipment to Richmond, Virginia, and Fayetteville, North Carolina (Hearn 1996:56). When word came on June 13 that 2,000 Federal troops were nearby, Johnston ordered the immediate evacuation of the town. On June 14 the Confederates set fire to the armory buildings. They destroyed the railroad bridge that crossed the Potomac River, then withdrew from the town (Murfin 1989). Most Harpers Ferrians abandoned the town; only a few families stayed behind to take their chances.

A citizen, Davis Strother (1861:9), wrote that after the Confederate evacuation many displaced families returned to town with wagon-loads of furniture. The armory superintendent's house stood open, locks broken, furniture removed, with papers, letters, and other possessions littered all around the place. People scavenged whatever they could from the building (Strother 1861:11).

Harpers Ferry existed in a demoralized state.

> Not only were the government buildings ransacked for plunder, but the abandoned houses of the citizens shared the same fate. Even women and children could be encountered at all hours of the day and night loaded with booty or trundling wheelbarrows freighted with all imaginable kinds of portable goods and household furniture. (Barry 1988 [1903]:109)

Confederates from Baltimore and part of the 2nd Mississippi regi-

ment under the command of Colonel Faulkner entered Harpers Ferry on
June 28, 1861, and ruined the rifle factory and the Shenandoah bridge.
They also pushed Baltimore & Ohio railroad cars along with engine no.
165 onto the ruins of the Potomac Bridge, which they had destroyed two
weeks earlier. The troops also wrecked the nine United States Rifle Factory buildings on Hall's Island (Barry 1988 [1903]:105–106).

On the fourth of July a lively skirmish erupted across the Potomac
River between Confederate cavalrymen and the 9th New York Regiment.
Two Federals and one Confederate soldier were killed. After the vollies
ceased and the troops retired, a prominent Harpers Ferry citizen, Frederick
Roeder, walked to the train station, assuming the fighting had stopped.
Union sniper fire struck him, and he was mortally wounded. Roeder, a
German immigrant, had an established business on High Street in the
town's commercial district. Ironically, he supported the Union and de-
plored slavery (Barry 1988 [1903]:107–108).

Harpers Ferry stood desolate (Figure 8). On July 21, 1861, Union
forces occupied the town. Their presence did not leave a favorable impression among the inhabitants. Joseph Barry, a local historian, reported that

Figure 8. A desolate Harpers Ferry. United States Armory grounds at Harpers Ferry at
the beginning of the Civil War, July 20, 1861. (Courtesy, Harpers Ferry National Historical
Park, HF-223)

troops continued to loot and rob the town, much like the Confederates did previously. They "helped themselves to most of what was left by the rebels" (Barry 1988 [1903]:109).

By the end of July, Robert Gould Shaw, who later received fame for leading the 54th Massachusetts Regiment in their attack on Fort Wagner, spent time in Harpers Ferry. He wrote that "everything about the place looks as if a set of barbarians had been through here" (Shaw in Duncan 1992:119).

Shaw also wrote about his period of convalescence in a townperson's house:

> The house I have been staying at is a building of logs, has two rooms on the ground-floor, and (I suppose) one up-stairs, and is inhabited by Mrs. Buckle, four children, a fat black woman, and myself and a man. We two sleep in the dining-room, I on a bed, and he on the floor. Where the rest are stowed, I don't know; but as I hear strange sounds overhead at night, and deep breathing and snoring, as of a fat pig, in the kitchen, I think Aunt Betty, the black woman, is in the latter uncomfortable hole, and the rest above . . . Mrs. B. is very neat and clean, and cooks me nice rice puddings, and Aunt Betty brings me flowers, and washes my clothes. . . .

By the end of August most of the Union troops had left Harpers Ferry. Only companies I and K of the 13th Massachusetts remained on Maryland Heights through October to watch Harpers Ferry and its shore-line. Federals would occasionally patrol the town and would sometimes encounter parties of Confederates lurking in the area (Barry 1988 [1903]:112). While stationed on the heights, Union soldiers continued to shoot at targets in town. Joseph Barry (1988 [1903]:112) writes that the

> gallant 13th kept up a constant fire on the few inhabitants of Harpers Ferry, suspecting or affecting to suspect them of being rebels. Everything that moved about the streets they shot at vindictively. The appearance of even a mullein leaf swaying in the wind elicited a volley from these very vigilant guardians of the nation, and it was lucky for the place that they were indifferent marksmen, else it would have been wholly depopulated.

Federal troops abandoned Maryland Heights at the end of October 1861, and between August 1861 and February 1862, the town was largely unoccupied by either Union or Confederate troops. Both entities would send nightly scouting expeditions to the area and skirmishes often erupted in or around town, making life uncertain for the citizens who remained. Townspeople had to live in total darkness in the night because Union sharpshooters on Maryland Heights would fire at any moving target they could see. Confederate scouts patrolling in the area also kept the town in a state of terror (Barry 1988 [1903]:116).

Annie Marmion, a resident, wrote that "most people know the meaning of Blockade. To the Village of Harpers Ferry as to other places it meant threatened starvation, but it also meant desolation inconceivable" (Marmion 1959:6).

Abraham Herr, proprietor of Virginius Island and operator of a flour mill on Virginius Island, had part of his enterprise made inoperable by Federal troops. They did not want the flour mill operation to fall into the hands of the enemy. He was in the process of giving 20,000 bushels of wheat to Federal troops when Confederates interrupted this transfer. A four-hour skirmish ensued, involving roughly 1,100 men, that resulted in a total of five killed and 20 wounded. Union troops recovered the dead, and the commander reported that he found them "stabbed through the body, stripped of all the clothing, not excepting their shoes and stockings, and left in perfect nudity" (USDW 1880 V:242). Colonel Geary wrote:

> One was laid in the form of a crucifixion, with his hands spread out and cut through the palms with a dull knife. This inhuman treatment incensed my troops exceedingly, and I fear its consequences may be shown in retaliatory acts here after. (USWD 1880 5:242)

One day later, "the enemy in citizen's dress came secretly to Harpers Ferry . . . " They found Herr repairing his machinery "and burned Herr's [flour] mill" (USWD 1880 5:242–243). They toppled some of the mill's walls, an act Joseph Barry called "a monument of vandalism and a reproach to civilized warriors" (Barry 1988 [1903]:116).

On February 7, 1862, another skirmish erupted between the two sides. As the Union scouts retreated across the Potomac river, one scout was killed by Confederate fire. A detachment was immediately sent across the river to Harpers Ferry and destroyed a set of buildings between the railroad bridge and the armory along the Potomac River facing Maryland Heights. Confederate soldiers had often concealed themselves in these buildings and harassed Federal soldiers on the Maryland shores. Generally, "all that winter—'61-'62—Harpers Ferry presented a scene of the utmost desolation. All the inhabitants had fled, except a few old people, who ventured to remain and protect their homes, or who were unable or unwilling to leave the place and seek new associations" (Barry 1988 [1903]:121).

Union troops moved back into Harpers Ferry during the night of February 22. A soldier from the 15th Massachusetts described the reoccupation of the town: "The streets are thronged with troops constantly arriving . . . " He described Harpers Ferry as a "ruined town with its burned and shattered buildings . . . [The town] was entirely deserted by its former inhabitant . . . " (quoted in Hearn 1996:93). Nathaniel Hawthorne wandered through the former armory grounds and later described it as "a waste of shapeless demolition. Heaps of gun barrels rusted in the rain. The brightest sunshine could not have made the scene cheerful, nor taken away the gloom from the dilapidated town . . . [I]t had an inexpressible forlornness" (Hawthorne n.d.).

The railroad bridge was rebuilt, and the first locomotive in nine months crossed into Harpers Ferry on March 18, 1862 (Snell 1960a:50). This event, along with the presence of "many civilian strangers who daily arrived to visit friends in the army, threw a new life into the town. . . . [C]itizens returned to their homes, now comparatively safe, and accumulated snug little fortunes in providing small luxuries for wearied soldiers and their friends" (Barry 1988 [1903]:122).

Protecting the railroad, a lifeline for the Union army, was essential for Northern military success. Therefore, the Union army created a railroad brigade and placed its headquarters in Harpers Ferry. On March 29, 1862, General McClellan appointed Dixon S. Miles to lead the brigade. Most of the Federal troops in occupied Harpers Ferry were new, and undisciplined. Miles often complained about the lack of battle-ready soldiers under his command.

Because of his mission to protect the railroad, Miles gave little attention to the fortification of Harpers Ferry. Although he constructed an earthwork across Camp Hill, it was surrounded by higher and more strategic positions, such as Maryland Heights, Loudoun Heights, and Bolivar Heights, which left this fortification vulnerable to enemy attack. General Wool urged Miles to construct a block house at the highest point on Maryland Heights, but Miles failed to act on the general's request (Frye 1987:14).

In September 1862, Stonewall Jackson attacked Harpers Ferry. Under Jackson's command Major General Lafayette McLaw and his seasoned troops took Maryland Heights, the highest point surrounding Harpers Ferry. A combination of poor leadership and miscommunications among Union troops assisted McLaws' efforts. The Federals had no choice but to surrender. While carrying the white flag, the brigade was still fired upon by some Confederate artillery from the heights. Miles was mortally wounded. On September 15, the Confederates captured 73 pieces of artillery, 10,000 small arms, 200 wagons, and 12,500 prisoners. It was the largest United States surrender prior to World War II. A military investigation of the surrender found that Miles' actions "amounting to almost imbecility, led to the shameful surrender of this important post" (quoted in Hearn 1996:190).

After the surrender, Jackson marched toward Shepherdstown and left A.P. Hill in charge of processing the captured Federals in Harpers Ferry. Hill paroled prisoners by having them sign papers that stipulated they would not fight again until they were exchanged. Enlisted men surrendered their weapons, but officers were allowed to keep their sidearms. Runaway slaves were recaptured in an attempt to return them to their former plantations.

Colonel Trimble of the 60th Ohio Volunteer Infantry Regiment had several freed slaves who worked as servants and teamsters. He appealed to Hill to allow these former enslaved people to accompany his troops into Maryland, rather than sending them back into slavery. A.P. Hill agreed to Trimble's request, and he gave each person a pass. A Confederate cavalry squad stationed at the Potomac crossing bridge stopped the blacks, and, though Trimble showed the guards the passes issued by Hill they refused to allow the blacks to stay with him. Trimble pulled out his revolver, and held the Confederate commander at gunpoint, until his entire infantry, including the blacks, were safely across the river (National Park Service n.d.:13).

The next day Hill withdrew from Harpers Ferry to join Lee and Jackson at Antietam. The Confederates destroyed the Potomac bridge during their withdrawal. After the Battle of Antietam, Lee retreated into Virginia, and Union troops reoccupied Harpers Ferry. The Federal 12th Corps of the Army of the Potomac reoccupied Maryland Heights on September 20th, 1862. On the 22nd, the Second Division of the corps camped on Loudoun Heights. The fifth Ohio Infantry was the first Union troops to occupy Harpers Ferry (Frye and Frye 1989:65; Winter and Frye 1992:21).

> With the early arrivals came the 14th Connecticut, whose fine band struck up the new and popular air "John Brown's Body." The entire division took up the song as they crossed the river, and a few minutes later the ragged formation solemnly trudged by Brown's fort in hushed tones. (Hearn 1996:192)

Reoccupation was not a pleasant scene. Harpers Ferry was "sadly worn, almost washed away by the ebb and flow of war" (quoted in Hearn 1996:192). Miles Clayton Huyette of the 125th Pennsylvania Infantry remarked, "All about us was the wreckage of the fighting . . . and the unburied bodies of the dead of both armies." Gen. Alpheus Williams wrote that the "stench proved abundantly" (Frye and Frye 1989:65).

In October 1862, President Lincoln visited Harpers Ferry to congratulate General McClellan and his troops for their victory at Antietam and to urge McClellan to push on. The president visited the armory grounds and John Brown's fort (Hearn 1996:194). On Bolivar Heights, where Miles had surrendered a few weeks earlier, Union troops marched in review before McClellan and President Lincoln. Lincoln also reviewed the troops on Loudoun Heights where the proceedings were comparatively quiet since "there was no room for maneuvering troops at this camp" (quoted in

Winter and Frye 1992:23). Loudoun Heights remained occupied until October 28, 1862, when the second Division was moved to Bolivar Heights (Winter and Frye 1992:30–37).

One soldier from the fifth New York Heavy Artillery wrote:

> There is nothing here but desolation and magnificent scenery. Roofless houses and those that are occupied C- many bears the marks of cannon balls—the smells are not very agreeable as there are a number of dead horses still remaining unburied. (Letter, Fred Frederickson to his wife 7 May 1863)

Spring brought new hope to the region as Unionist counties in the western part of Virginia voted to rejoin the Union. Jefferson County, which contained Harpers Ferry, had many southern cultural ties. Even so, under Union occupation, citizens felt safe from marauding Confederate guerrilla bands. On May 28, the polls opened and Harpers Ferrians voted 196:1 to rejoin the Union. On June 20, West Virginia became a state in the Union.

In June 1863, after the Confederates routed Federal troops at the Second Battle of Winchester, the Federal garrison in Martinsburg and the retreating troops from Winchester fell back to Harpers Ferry. Rather than turning their attack on Harpers Ferry, the Confederates continued to march north into Pennsylvania. One soldier reported:

> The evidence of a heavy force in front of us and around continues to be visible. For several days past, we have seen trains of wagons of almost endless length, creeping along our front from left to right. (from Frye and Frye 1989:69)

Reports stated that on June 24, 1863, Confederate wagons stretched from Berryville, Virginia, to Sharpsburg, Maryland (USWD 1880 27(2):28). General Hooker, now commander of the Army of the Potomac, requested a withdrawal of troops from Harpers Ferry to join the other troops waiting to clash with the Confederates. "Here [at Harpers Ferry] they are of no earthly account. They cannot defend a ford of the river, and, as far as Harpers Ferry is concerned, there is nothing of it" (USWD 1880 27(1):60).

Lincoln replaced Hooker with General George Meade on June 27, 1863, and he placed Harpers Ferry under Meade's direct orders. Meade ordered the evacuation of Harpers Ferry on June 28, and had most of the equipment and artillery removed to Washington, D.C. via the Chesapeake and Ohio Canal. Federal troops marched to Gettysburg in preparation for what was to become one of the war's major confrontations. The Confederates occupied and held uncontested control of Harpers Ferry into the first few days of July. There they found large quantities of abandoned commissary, quartermaster, and ordnance supplies (Hearn 1996:222). After Lee's retreat from Gettysburg, the Federals reoccupied Harpers Ferry. They marched to the Maryland shore and reached it by July 6. On July 7, they drove off a weak Confederate force from Maryland Heights. Charles Moulton, described the Union's reentry onto Maryland Heights: "The mud was two feet deep in places, from which a most nauseous, putrefied scent arose, nearly smothering us and forcibly reminding one of the 'Valley of Death'" (Moulton in Drickamer and Drickamer 1987:120).

Sharpshooter fire delayed the repair of the railroad bridge for two days, allowing Lee enough time to escape from Shepherdstown into Virginia (Frye and Frye 1989:70). Federal troops made their way into town by July 13, 1863, and never again abandoned Harpers Ferry. One soldier described, "I wish you could have seen the people come out and welcome us. Some of the women fairly cried for joy and pulled us into the houses and gave us all we wanted to eat, but they are pretty destitute here, having been stripped of everything by the rebs" (Ward 1985:63). Moulton described the town as desolate and in ruins. "[W]ar has had its effect and laid every thing waste and barren . . . and the entire place is not worth $10" (Moulton in Drickamer and Drickamer 1987:124).

Martial law prevailed in the town. Guards were stationed at every corner of the street and no one could proceed without showing a pass. Children needed passes to go to school, andno one could roam the streets after dark without a pass. If they did not have one, they could be placed in the guardhouse overnight. Moulton noted that he saw the guardhouse filled every morning (Moulton in Drickamer and Drickamer 1987:166).

Lower Town Harpers Ferry became a major depot and supply center. Returning citizens and merchants flocked there to provide services to the occupying army. Boardinghouses developed along the main transportation corridors, catering to soldiers and other visitors, such as wartime correspondents (Snell 1959:60; Moulton in Drickamer and Drickamer 1987:130). A soldier, Joseph Ward, wrote in August: "You have never seen a place grow as this has since we came in. Now the streets about sunset are full of ladies, but when we came there was none to be seen" (Ward 1985:70).

Moulton described the native population as being mostly illiterate and vulgar. He was "surprised to find most of the people so ignorant as they really are. Some of them are very smart, pretty looking young ladies, dressed in fine style, but cannot write a word" (Moulton in Drickamer and Drickamer 1987:134, 139). Joseph Ward of the 34th regiment, Massachusetts volunteers, also noted the people do not know "anything about arithmetic or grammar" (Ward 1985:67).

While occupying the town, Union troops faced southern sentiment among some of the town's people. Skirmishes continued around the town. The Union forces continually captured Confederate soldiers on patrol, while other rebels willfully surrendered without a struggle. Tired of war, lacking clothing and food, Confederates deserted by the thousands every month starting in the spring of 1864 (Moulton in Drickamer and Drickamer 1987:172; Ward 1985:68ff). Moulton described these worn, battered men as "the dirtiest looking set of human beings I ever laid eyes on" (Moulton in Drickamer and Drickamer 1987:195).

Rules limited merchants' activities since the military regulated prices, weights, and measurements. If merchants did not obey, soldiers confiscated their goods (Moulton in Drickamer and Drickamer 1987:146). Consumer goods and food were scarce and people purchased whatever was available since quality products were far and few between. Moulton remarked, "If you purchase a piece of cheese at the Sutler's and it is full of grubs, big, fat, and enough for fish bait, and you choose to mumble about it, that kind of vendor will console you with the fact that maggots will not get into bad or poor cheese" (Moulton in Drickamer and Drickamer 1987:127).

During February 1964 a smallpox epidemic erupted in Harpers Ferry. The high influx of people, including prisoners, newly freed slaves, and Union troops, contributed to the spread. The military quickly set up hospitals and established a quarantine (Moulton in Drickamer and Drickamer 1987:166).

Any semblance of peace and tranquility for the townspeople under the Union occupation was short lived. One year after the Gettysburg campaign, Jubal Early marched on Harpers Ferry on his way to Maryland. On the morning of the July 4, 1864, the Confederates made their push toward Harpers Ferry. Union troops withdrew from the Lower Town area to Maryland Heights. By the evening Confederate troops controlled Bolivar Heights, Camp Hill and Lower Town Harpers Ferry. Positioned on Maryland Heights, Moulton wrote, "It was a grand and sublime sight to look over into the Ferry and see the flames shooting upwards from all parts and directions of the old town, we had to take our departure from, and listen to the deep booming of the shells over our heads all through the night" (Moulton in Drickamer and Drickamer 1987:193). The quartermaster's storehouse burned and the government bakery was destroyed.

A large Confederate force did not exist on the Harpers Ferry front. Still, on July 5, Confederate squads frequently moved in and out of the town. Considerable fire was reported the following days and the Confederates pilfered from all the houses (Snell 1960b:23–26).

By Friday morning, July 8, Confederate troops had withdrawn, and by that evening Federal troops controlled Harpers Ferry and Bolivar Heights. According to Moulton, the Confederates set fire to 20,000 bushels of oats and corn along with the other supplies and left these behind to smolder. The townspeople told Moulton that the rebels were so drunk when they were plundering the town that the Federal troops could have easily captured them (Moulton in Drickamer and Drickamer 1987:194). Joseph Barry took an inventory of the civilian casualties: A woman and child died; another woman was wounded by the Federal artillery fire from Maryland Heights. The Confederates had no casualties (Barry 1988 [1903]:130).

Mary Jane Coates Griffith, a Harpers Ferrian, described civilian life during Early's attack. She wrote to her sister:

> Linie, you may thank your lucky stars. You were not here for you would have died of fright. They shelled this place day and one night [and] threw some of them into several houses. Where ever they burst they destroy everything within reach. Sis' house, the brick part, is knocked all to pieces. She was obliged to fly to the cellar as that seemed to be the only place of safety. Several balls entered father's house. They fired two through the windows, one where I was sleeping and one in the sitting room. . . . Balls fell like hail through the yard. The last night of shelling we had to run in the cellar and stay all night and I have not been well since. We thought it would kill mother. . . . Every [Union soldier] that could get away went of[f] at double quick when they heard the Rebels were coming. I hope I may never witness such a time again. . . . The Rebels took everything they could put their hands on and what they could carry of[f]. Destroyed vinegar, coal, oil, molasses. They knocked out the spickets and let it run out. Some families are without a mouthful to eat and several without homes. I have seen plenty of cowardice here. The day of the battle it was another Miles affair. (Letter, Mary Jane Coates Griffith to her sister 20 July 1864)

On August 1, 1864, General Grant placed Major General Philip S. Sheridan in command of Harpers Ferry to stage his Shenandoah campaign. He used the abandoned armory paymaster's House on Camp Hill as his headquarters (Snell 1960b:35–36). Sheridan described it as "a small dilapidated hotel" (Hearn 1996:262). None of the citizens of Harpers Ferry had heard of Sheridan and they prepared themselves for another inept command (Hearn 1996:260).

REVITALIZATION OF OCCUPIED HARPERS FERRY

Sheridan immediately saw the need to fortify Harpers Ferry and to secure Bolivar Heights for his wagon trains (USWD 1880 43(1):745). The Baltimore & Ohio Railroad repaired the bridge and had it placed in running order by the end of July. Federals secured a pontoon bridge to assist the flow of troops, supplies, and equipment. Sheridan reroofed the burned musket factory buildings and the Quartermaster Corps developed a substantial supply depot there. The Ordnance Department established a place for the issuing and repairing of weapons and ammunition. The army also established a large medical depot (Snell 1960b:39–40).

By the middle of August merchants and citizens flocked back in town and it once again became a bustling center. Moulton described this new energy: "The street is blockaded from morning till night with army wagons" (Moulton in Drickamer and Drickamer 1987:204) (Figure 9). Many journalists came to Harpers Ferry to report on the Union's reoccupation of the town and the upcoming campaign. Boardinghouses sprang up through the town.

On August 28, 1864, Sheridan began his historic campaign down the Shenandoah Valley. General Grant ordered Sheridan to

> Do all the damage to railroads and crops you can. Carry off stock of all descriptions, and negroes, so as to prevent further planting. If the war is to last another year, we want the Shenandoah valley to remain a barren waste. (USWD 1880 43(1):202)

As many as 1000 wagons and railroad cars, escorted by thousands of Union soldiers, supplied Sheridan's efforts. The wagon trains and railroad cars returned, usually filled with wounded soldiers from both sides, and prisoners (Figure 10). In the late summer and early fall an average of 100

Figure 9. Railroad cars entering and leaving Harpers Ferry, Fall 1864. (Courtesy, Harpers Ferry National Historical Park, HF-1319)

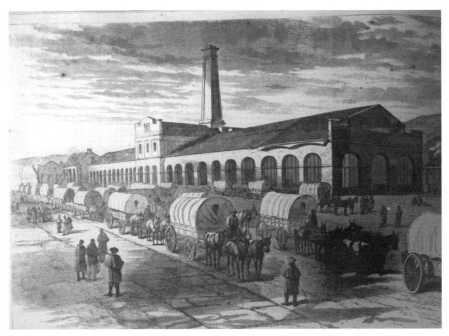

Figure 10. Wagon trains leaving the armory grounds to supply Sheridan's Shenandoah Campaign, Spring 1865. (*Harper's Weekly.* Courtesy, The Winterthur Library: Printed Books and Periodical Collection)

prisoners a day was processed through Harpers Ferry (Moulton in Drickamer and Drickamer 1987:206). Sheridan had soundly defeated Early at Winchester on September 19, and again three days later at Fisher's Hill. The Confederate hold on the Shenandoah Valley had been weakened severely. By the end of September the Baltimore & Ohio Railroad had repaired and opened the line to Martinsburg where they sent supplies. There, wagons could use a macadamized road that ran south to Staunton, Virginia. After his victorious campaign down the valley to Staunton, Sheridan withdrew to Martinsburg for the winter and the supply depot was shifted back to the Rifle Factory on Hall's Island in Harpers Ferry (Snell 1960b:47–49; Moulton in Drickamer and Drickamer 1987:218).

Goods and soldiers may have entered the town with relative ease, but this scenario was not true for people living in the surrounding countryside. Citizens living south of the Harpers Ferry command post could enter the town only twice a month. They had passes that limited them to six hours, and they could not acquire more than $50 dollar's worth of goods (Moulton in Drickamer and Drickamer 1987:218).

At the end of the war Harpers Ferry existed in a deteriorated state.

Union troops occupied the town for more than a year after Lee's surrender at Appomattox. Every day, residents endured "the ear-piercing notes of the fife and the boom of the drum heard on the streets" (Barry 1988 [1903]:140). Many Confederate sympathizers returned to Harpers Ferry only to find their dwellings either ransacked, rented by the United States government, or occupied by squatters. The squatters declared their loyalty to the Union and claimed these houses were the booty of war. The government took a passive role regarding the private ownership of buildings, but a new commanding officer, General Eagan, attempted to allow the Confederate sympathizers to reclaim their property. However, the army reassigned Eagan before he could complete this task (Barry 1988 [1903]:140–41).

"What a God forsaken place!", wrote Annie Marmion of the condition of Harpers Ferry. A New Englander visiting the town said this about the destruction and general decay:

> It is said to have been a pleasant and picturesque place formerly. The streets were well graded, and the hillside above were graced with terraces and trees. But war has changed all. Freshets tear down the centre of the streets, and the hill-sides present only ragged growths of weeds. The

Figure 11. United States Rifle Works at Harpers Ferry, 1865. (Courtesy, Harpers Ferry National Historical Park, HF-37)

town itself lies half in ruins... Of the bridge across the Shenandoah only
the ruined piers are left; still less remains of the old bridge over the
Potomac. And all about the town are rubbish, filth and stench. (from
Murfin 1989:23)

A Maryland resident remarked:

The ruins of the Government works . . . are a brickyard. Churches have
become hospitals; gardens and pleasure grounds, graveyards; private
residences, barracks and stables. Most of the inhabitants have fledOnly
nature is as calm and magnificent as ever. (from Murfin 1989:23)

From John Brown's raid in 1859 through the end of the Civil War, Harpers Ferry had experienced "six years of hell" (Hearn 1996:292) (Figure 11).

"A Village of Paupers" | 2

An Archaeology of Occupied Harpers Ferry

BEYOND GREAT MEN

As a counterpoint to the interpretation of the "great man" myth of the Civil War, the archaeology of the lives of soldiers, and working-class and middle-class people contributes significantly to creating a countermemory of the Civil War era. With a substantial effort from historians and archaeologists, this countermemory can become part of the official memory of the Civil War. Going beyond troop movements and "great men" histories can provide a deeper and richer and a more contextualized interpretation of Harpers Ferry's Civil War era.

CAMPGROUNDS ON THE HEIGHTS

The archaeological survey of Maryland and Loudoun Heights was done in the 1980s and was the first systematic effort to record the above-ground remains of Civil War campgrounds. The heights surround Harpers Ferry. Military occupation of these lands meant control of a key transportation hub and the northern part of the Shenandoah Valley.

The Maryland Heights archaeological survey (Frye and Frye 1989:376–377) identified seven fortifications and their ancillary structures and 13 campgrounds. The systematic mapping of the campgrounds is an important effort in presenting a Civil War history of the soldiers. Civil War archaeologists, for the most part, have focused on battlefields and campaigns and have directed little attention toward encampments. The 13 campground areas, totaling nearly 60 acres, contained 319 features that included stone foundations, leveled platforms (or depressions). Most of the campgrounds sit either on the crest or the plateau just below and west of the crest of Maryland Heights. The platforms and foundations are usually 6 feet × 8 feet (Figure 12) and supported shelter tents and wedge tents. The platforms and foundations kept water out of the tents, especially

Figure 12. Stone foundations for shelter on Maryland Heights.

those situated on slopes. The stone foundations supported log superstructures

These log structures were used as winter quarters or as guardhouses and cookhouses. One soldier described his winter quarter. "[T]he sides were built of logs and the chinks filled in with clay; the roof was laid with saplings covered with the earth which we dug while leveling the space" (quoted in Frye and Frye 1989:180). The cabins appear to have been inadequately constructed. One officer wrote: "[I]t rains right through, so that my bed, over which I have laid an india-rubber blanket, has a puddle of water in the centre three or four inches deep" (Irving 1878:88).

According to military regulations a campground site should (1) provide for the health and comfort of the troops; (2) facilitate good communications; (3) offer convenience of wood and water; and (4) provide adequate resources in provisions and food (*Revised United States Army Regulations of 1861* 1863:74). The regulations required an infantry campsite to measure approximately 1,200 feet (400 paces) × 1,293 feet (431 paces). The tents should be arranged by rank, with each company pitching their tents in two files, facing a street. The width of the street should not be fewer than five paces. Kitchens and sutlers sat behind the rear flank, and officers situated themselves behind them. Latrines sat 400 feet (135 paces) to the rear of the officers' tents, and infantry latrines were 450 feet (150 paces) at the opposite end of the camp (Frye and Frye 1989:171).

No plateau on the heights was wide enough to fit the placement of an official army regulation campsite for a regiment (400 feet × 450 feet). One would expect some type of improvisation of the grid pattern for the camp- sites. The archaeological survey shows that the campgrounds on the heights were not laid out in a grid arrangement as one might expect in a military campground. Perhaps commanders did not require a formal layout. Soldiers may have built their own platforms and huts within a prescribed boundary.

Slopes, rocks, and boulders in some areas prohibited a grid-like camp- ground. One soldier, who camped at Naval Battery on Maryland Heights, wrote: "We drove stakes in the ground and placed logs above them so that we would not slide down hill when sleeping. [We] would wake nights sitting against the uphill side of the logs with legs hanging over" (quoted in Frye and Frye 1989:179).

Since bedrock existed only several inches below the surface fresh water was unavailable. It had to be transported up the steep slopes, mak- ing the protection of Maryland Heights a labor-intensive activity. Shallow bedrock also made the construction of privies impossible; none were found in the archaeological survey. Proper hygiene became an important issue after the Union's reoccupation of the heights after the Antietam campaign (September, 1862). Third brigade commander Colonel Thomas H. Ruger instructed that "[S]inks (latrines) will be dug for each regiment and kept in proper order and daily inspected and covered and no other portion of the grounds will be resorted to by the men for necessary purposes" (quoted in Frye and Frye 1989:176). They could not have been very deep because the bedrock was no deeper than a few inches in all parts of the heights. Proper sanitation remained a concern throughout the war. Another officer later ordered "All officers and soldiers are requested at the calls of nature to make use of the sinks[.] [A]ny officer or soldier found at any time committing a nuisance about the sinks will be severely punished" (quoted in Frye and Frye 1989:176).

On Loudoun Heights the campgrounds are better preserved, although historical documentation and maps are limited, making it difficult to cor- relate the features with specific occupations (Winter and Frye 1992:130). The remains of three block houses and eight campgrounds are located near the crest. Federal troops occupied Loudoun Heights for only five weeks but inhabited Maryland Heights for almost three years. Surpris- ingly, Loudoun Heights had 435 visible campground features (mainly plat- forms and hut foundations) compared with the 319 features on Maryland Heights within 13 campgrounds.

A review of the archaeological surveys of the wartime campgrounds around Harpers Ferry provides some insight into the daily conditions of soldiers. Regimental guides may have dictated the size and dimensions of campgrounds, but they were not followed at Harpers Ferry on Maryland and Loudoun Heights. Steep slopes and few horizontal surfaces required deviations from the plan. Poor sanitary conditions, and uncomfortable living quarters prevailed. While public memory at Harpers Ferry celebrates Jackson's capture of the town, additional stories about life in the encampments are important elements that provide an additional history of the war.

MRS. STIPES' BOARDINGHOUSE: THE ARCHAEOLOGICAL RECORD

Their health and welfare suffered while the soldiers were encamped around Harpers Ferry, and many citizens also suffered the hardships of war. Artist James Taylor, sent by Frank Leslie to cover the Shenandoah campaign, observed the dire situation of one of Harpers Ferry's townspeople. Staying at Mrs. Stipes' boardinghouse in Lower Town, he explained, "Mrs. Stipes catered to sojourners at the Ferry to the extent of table board and lodging, not from choice but necessity caused by her husband's business reverses owing to the War, and his inability to catch on again, when it fell to the lot of Madam to entertain transients to keep the wolf from the door" (Taylor 1989:30).

Most of the Harpers Ferry's archaeological materials from the Civil War era date from the town's revitalization era (1864–1865), when Sheridan staged his Shenandoah campaign. One example comes from Mrs. Stipes' yard, behind the boardinghouse she operated starting in October 1862 (Report, Young to Craig).

Taylor does not mention specific foods served to him at Mrs. Stipes' boardinghouse, but he may have eaten foods similar to those found in other boardinghouses in Harpers Ferry. Charles Moulton, who lived in another Lower Town boardinghouse noted that his meals consisted of roasts or stews. He wrote "I always find my meals looking hot just from the pot or oven" (Moulton in Drickamer and Drickamer 1987:188).

There are some clues that Mrs. Stipes may not have exclusively relied on the local markets to supply her boarders' needs (Table 1). For instance, turtle shell is present in the backyard trash deposits. Turtles are common in the area along the riverine environment and their appearance in the archaeological record suggests that Mrs. Stipes used them for her boardinghouse soups (Burk 1993b:10:8). The presence of Eastern Cottontail

Table 1. Summary Table for Civil War Faunal Assemblage[a]

Taxon	N	Percent	MNI	Percent	Meat weight (lbx)	Total meat weight (lbs)	Percent	Weight (grams)	Percent	Biomass (kg)	Percent
Class Osteichthyes (bony fish)	19	1.1	0/0	0.0	0.0/0.0	0.0	0.0	3.2	0.0	0.02	0.1
cf. Terrapene carolina (box turtle)	1	0.1	1/0	4.2	0.0/0.0	0.0	0.0	0.3	0.0	0.01	0.0
Class Aves (bird)	218	12.1	0/0	0.0	0.0/0.0	0.0	0.0	109.9	1.5	0.38	1.7
Class Aves/mammalia III	3	0.2	0/0	0.0	0.0/0.0	0.0	0.0	1.4	0.0	0.01	0.0
Anser spp. (goose)	1	0.1	1/0	4.2	0.0/0.0	0.0	0.0	0.7	0.0	0.00	0.0
cf. Anser anser (dom. goose)	1	0.1	0/0	0.0	0.0/0.0	0.0	0.0	2.2	0.0	0.01	0.0
Family Phasianidae	2	0.1	0/0	0.0	0.0/0.0	0.0	0.0	1.3	0.0	0.01	0.0
Melegris gallopavo (turkey)	1	0.1	1/0	4.2	7.5/7.5	7.5	0.4	10.2	0.1	0.04	0.2
cf. Melegris gallopavo (turkey)	2	0.1	0/0	0.0	0.0/0.0	0.0	0.0	1.4	0.0	0.01	0.0
Gallus gallus (chicken)	85	4.7	3/1	16.7	2.5/1.0	8.5	0.5	89.7	1.2	0.32	1.4
cf. Gallus gallus (chicken)	8	0.4	0/0	0.0	0.0/0.0	0.0	0.0	12.6	0.2	0.05	0.2
Class Mammalia (mammal)	937	51.8	0/0	0.0	0.0/0.0	0.0	0.0	1426.7	19.6	4.22	18.8
Class Mammalia I (large mammal)	93	5.1	0/0	0.0	0.0/0.0	0.0	0.0	1340.6	18.4	3.99	17.8
cf. Class Mammalia I (large mammal)	3	0.2	0/0	0.0	0.0/0.0	0.0	0.0	4.6	0.1	0.02	0.1
Class Mammalia II (med. mammal)	136	7.5	0/0	0.0	0.0/0.0	0.0	0.0	484.7	6.6	1.60	7.1
Class Mammalia III (sm. mammal)	67	3.7	0/0	0.0	0.0/0.0	0.0	0.0	77.0	1.1	0.31	1.4
Sylvilagus floridanus (cottontail)	5	0.3	2/0	8.3	2.0/2.0	4.0	0.2	3.0	0.0	0.02	0.1
cf. Sylvilagus floridanus	1	0.1	0/0	0.0	0.0/0.0	0.0	0.0	0.3	0.0	0.00	0.0
Order Rodentia (rodent)	3	0.2	0/0	0.0	0.0/0.0	0.0	0.0	0.5	0.0	0.00	0.0
Rattus spp. (Old World rat)	23	1.3	5/0	20.8	0.0/0.0	0.0	0.0	6.5	0.1	0.03	0.1
Order Artiodactyla I	5	0.3	0/0	0.0	0.0/0.0	0.0	0.0	41.2	0.6	0.17	0.8
Order Artiodactyla II	6	0.3	0/0	0.0	0.0/0.0	0.0	0.0	50.8	0.7	0.21	0.9
Sus scrofa (dom. cow)	92	5.1	3/1	16.7	100.0/50.0	350.0	21.0	660.5	9.1	2.11	9.4
cf. Sus scrofa (dom. cow)	17	0.9	0/0	0.0	0.0/0.0	0.0	0.0	116.6	1.6	0.44	2.0
Bos taurus (dom. pig)	52	2.9	3/1	16.7	400.0/50.0	1250.0	74.9	2058.1	28.2	5.87	26.2
cf. Bos taurus (dom. pig)	15	0.8	0/0	0.0	0.0/0.0	0.0	0.0	687.1	9.4	2.19	9.7
Ovis aries/Capra hircus (sheep/goat)	11	0.6	1/1	8.3	35.0/15.0	50.0	3.0	89.1	1.2	0.35	1.6
cf. Ovis aries/Capra hircus	2	0.1	0/0	0.0	0.0/0.0	0.0	0.0	10.2	0.1	0.05	0.2

Columns: (N) number of bones identified to that taxon; (MNI) Minimum Number of Individuals. The number before the slash is the number of adults and the number of immature specimens follows the slash. (Meat Weight) meat weight of the entire animal; (adult/immature) (Total Meat Weight) derived by multiplying the MNI by the Meat Weight and then adding the two sides of the slash together; (Weight) weight of the actual archaeological bones; (Biomass) skeletal weight. [a]Burk (1993b:10.2) remains also suggests that she used other wild foods to supplement her family's or her tenant's diets (Burk 1993b:10.9).

A variety of domestic birds are part of the faunal assemblage and include goose, domestic goose, turkey, and chicken (Burk 1993b:10.9). Both the goose and the turkey assemblages are small. These foods are not average boardinghouse fare and may represent the remains of a holiday meal. Moulton wrote of a holiday dinner he consumed at a Harpers Ferry boardinghouse. The meal, considered a great treat, consisted of a turkey dinner "at the expense of our kind landlady" (Moulton in Drickamer and Drickamer 1987:152). There is a good likelihood that the Stipes purchased the goose and the turkey at the market, because the assemblages are small and incomplete. If the poultry had been raised in the backyard they would have been butchered there, and a larger and more complete assemblage would be present, like the chicken assemblage. The possibility also exists that Mrs. Stipes' husband hunted these birds to supplement meals and stretch the income from the boarders (Burk 1993b).

Chicken represents the largest assemblage of bird bones, and most parts of the chicken are present. Of the 93 chicken bones are present, two-thirds of these ($n = 61$) are from a nearly articulated chicken. Chickens are valuable for yielding a daily supply of eggs, and when they no longer produced they would have been butchered (Burk 1993b:10.9). The skull and mandible would have been discarded at the time of butchering, and the rest of the bird, served at dinner, would have been part of the dinner trash discarded in the yard.

Domesticated mammals, such as pig, cow, and sheep or goat make up most of the boardinghouse deposits, representing 49.1 percent of the biomass of the entire assemblage. Cow (35.9 percent) was far greater than the other mammals, and pig constitutes the second largest biomass percentage (11.4 percent). Sheep or goat biomass is small (1.8 percent) at this site (Burk 1993b:10.9–10.11). The presence of teeth and skull elements from pig, cow, and sheep suggests the possible consumption of calf's head soups. A search through contemporary cookbooks suggests that these meals were common (see for instance Hall 1855:66; Tyree 1879:77).

Twice as many pig bones (25.0 percent, $n = 27$) have cleaver and/or axe butchering marks than do the cow bones (13.8 percent, $n = 9$). This trend generally holds true for the large (7.1 percent) and medium (20.0 percent) mammals in the assemblage. The greater use of an ax or cleaver on the medium mammals points to home or local processing. This type of processing indicates the boardinghouse keeper's reliance on local markets, rather than solely on mass-butchered meats from eastern markets. The only documentation that exists—letters from soldiers and James Taylor—shows that townspeople did rely upon local markets for their food (Burk 1993b:10:14).

The Federals regulated a daily outdoor market in town on the banks of the Shenandoah River. Farmers and merchants were penned into a roped-off area surrounded by guards. Farmers could trade irrespectively of their political sentiment if they did not discuss their views. Villagers, such as Mrs. Stipes, conducted their transactions with the farmers over the rope barriers. The guards, with loaded weapons, were ordered to prevent, "at all hazards, surreptitious communications passing between the disloyal residents and secret emissaries of the Confederacy in the guise of hucksters, and to guard against spies slipping through the bound" (Taylor 1989:31). Food seemed plentiful for the towns people and the army mess caterers. Taylor noted that some of the market goods available to Mrs. Stipes included butter, head cheese, eggs, poultry, beef, bacon, lamb, ham, spare ribs, new potatoes, and blackberries (Taylor 1989:31). Horace Ball (n.d.: 125), of the 34th Massachusetts Regiment, also noted the sale of cake, bread, pies, and apples in the market.

While most of the historical documentation suggests that Mrs. Stipes acquired her meats at the market, it is surprising that the overwhelming majority of the archaeologically recovered cow bones (86.2 percent) have saw marks (Burk 1993b:10.14). Since the Civil War stimulated mass production and industrialization, animals, too, were mass butchered and processed to supply large armies. The mechanical saw facilitated mass butchering at a central processing point. The products were then transported to Harpers Ferry. The presence of sawed cuts of meat in the boardinghouse assemblage suggests that Mrs. Stipes bartered for these foods with the army's commissary, since townspeople typically relied on local markets at this time.

Trash found in backyard deposits associated with Mrs. Stipes' boardinghouse is also indicative of boarders' foodways. These materials include peanut shells, walnut shells, cherry pits, peach pits, pumpkin seeds, watermelon seeds, egg shells, clam shells, and a large abundance of oyster shells. Other foods identified through pollen analyses include: fig, tomatillo/ground cherry, and raspberry (Cummings 1993:7.25). Archaeobotanical samples from the yard contain weeds such as pigweed, goosefoot, nutgrass, carpetweed, purslane, chickweed, wiregrass, tomatillo/ground cherry, and buffalo bur (Cummings 1993:7.25, 1994; Rovner 1993:6.8, 1994). The backyards were strewn with litter and kitchen refuse, and health conditions were probably deplorable. Rodents infiltrated the area and gnawed at bones from the boardinghouse kitchen wastes. Unsanitary conditions prevailed during the military occupation.

The boardinghouse ceramic assemblage consists of a variety of wares and types. One of the largest assemblages includes American grey salt-glazed stoneware jars used for food storage. Tin cans and glass jars are also part of this food storage assemblage. The tin cans are additional evidence of the development of massive food processing and storage developed during the Civil War. Their presence demonstrates that the boardinghouse keeper obtained goods from larger regional markets, maybe from bartering with the commissary.

Food service china included a variety of platters. Matched place settings are almost nonexistent and the ceramic assemblage includes a mix of items that includes ironstones and edge-decorated whitewares, undecorated whitewares, and a large variety of transfer printed whiteware. The assemblage also includes one transfer-printed tea cup and an undecorated saucer (Shackel et al. 1993). This eclectic assemblage may have been a product of purchasing goods when needed, regardless of style, to have the necessary tableware to accommodate boarders. The large variety of dinner wares suggests Mrs. Stipes did not maintain the kind of high-style boardinghouse that many Washington correspondents preferred. After all, Taylor mockingly nicknamed the establishment "Hotel de Stipes."

Martial law forbade the sale and consumption of alcohol in town, and the provost marshal enforced "orders involving the sale of intoxicating liquors whether by tradesmen or sutlers" (Moore 1962:122–23). The military sometimes raided households thought to be bootlegging liquor. Those found with liquor in their houses, or caught selling liquor within the boundaries of Harpers Ferry, were forcefully removed to outside the military district (Moulton in Drickamer and Drickamer 1987:74–76; Lincoln 1879:135). Apparently, the provost marshal had limited control in Harpers Ferry. Materials from the archaeological record behind Mrs. Stipes' boardinghouse reveal an abundance of wine or champagne bottles even though her establishment was next to the provost marshal's headquarters. Alcohol abuse was sometimes reported in personal letters from soldiers stationed in Harpers Ferry. For instance, Robert Gould Shaw wrote that when he and his company were stationed on Maryland Heights they were occasionally assigned to guard the "ferry." However, it was an unruly situation and Shaw saw the need to bring some order to the Union troops. He (Shaw in Duncan 1992:124) remarked:

> While there, the Fifth Connecticut came in, and a great many of the men wandered off and got drunk. Some of their officers were really not ashamed to ask me to send their own men to their quarters, and to lock the unruly ones up in our guard-house! In fact, before long, the whole management of the regiment seemed to devolve upon us, and one of our sergeants broke his knuckles knocking men down . . .

Medicine bottles are also present in the boardinghouse assemblage. While patent medicines were sometimes consumed for their alcohol content (see for instance Bond 1989), it is also important to note that they were also consumed for their medicinal use (Larsen 1993). It is likely that the high incidence of disease and the pain and suffering induced by war contributed to the consumption of proprietary medicines and home remedies.

Sickness prevailed in occupied Harpers Ferry. For instance, Chaplain John H. Strickland of the 145th Pennsylvania described Harpers Ferry's water and food as being contaminated with "living creatures...pork alive with skippers" (quoted in Hearn 1996:196). Soldiers in the town were afflicted with diarrhea, dysentery, rheumatism, measles, and colds, and continually came to the chaplain looking for a discharge (Hearn 1996:196). Since medical facilities may not have been readily available to soldiers with minor maladies, soldiers depended upon themselves for self-medication.

While soldiers occupied the town, domestic activities of citizens went on around them. For instance, domestic artifacts found include doll parts, hair pins, and nonmilitary buttons. They were found next to military artifacts such as a knapsack buckle, a .22 caliber cartridge case, musket ball, percussion cap, and minie balls ranging from .42, .54, and .57 caliber. Also, included were more than 20 tobacco pipes (Figure 13).

There are items associated with clothing production present in the archaeological assemblage: 27 straight pins, one safety pin, and one brass thimble. These items are often considered a part of a domestic assemblage, but they may well have belonged to soldiers. Soldiers were issued a "house wife," a sewing kit for mending their garments. It became an especially important kit because issued clothing was sometimes of poor quality and needed constant repair (Wiley 1971:64; Stern 1961:53–54; Beverly 1992).

The presence of some domestic items, such as pins, nonmilitary buttons, porcelain doll fragments, and a hair pin, along with the various military related items, shows how closely domestic life and military life coexisted in this military occupied town. The boardinghouse keeper's household made significant contributions to the archaeological assemblage since civilians of all ages commingled in the same areas as soldiers.

HARPERS FERRY DURING SHERIDAN'S SHENANDOAH CAMPAIGN

Shanty Kitchens

Sheridan's 1864 campaign reenergized the town's commerce. An increasing number of entrepreneurs catered to the army, the townspeople, and a growing band of journalists. Some built a set of "shanty kitchens" that lined the Winchester and Potomac Railroad bed, behind Mrs. Stipes'

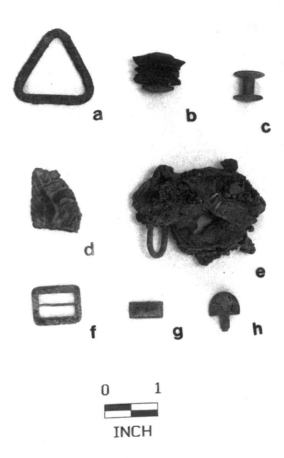

0   1

INCH

Figure 13. Civil War era artifacts from Mrs. Stipe's boardinghouse assemblage: (a) brass triangular ring; (b,c) knapsack fittings, (d) brass military hat insignia, (e) gun barrel band, (f) brass kepi buckle, (g) probable officer's insignia, and (h) rocking tab for shoulder scale. (Photography by Cari YoungRavehorst)

boardinghouse. The shanty kitchens' assemblage (Figure 14) contains evidence of open trade and access to larger regional markets. Local entrepreneurs took advantage of the poor quality of military foods by operating these facilities that catered to soldiers' tastes. Excavations at the shanty kitchens yielded many cut nails related to the structure. Bone shank buttons and white tobacco clay pipe fragments are also present in the assemblage, suggesting that the kitchens facilitated socialization, perhaps between townspeople, visitors, and soldiers (Shackel et al. 1993).

Most of the boardinghouse food remains include cow and pig bone

Figure 14. Shanty kitchens in Harpers Ferry, spring 1865. Five are located to the right of the two men standing to the far left. (*Harper's Weekly*. Courtesy, Harpers Ferry National Historical Park, HF-141)

and several peach pits. A small proportion of the faunal assemblage includes bird bones. A large amount of oyster and clam shells found in the archaeological record, transported from the Baltimore markets, is another indication of the types of foods Harpers Ferrians received from larger markets during the war as they attempted to diversify their foodways and to make a profit (Shackel et al. 1993).

Military Surgery on a Domestic Site

During Sheridan's Shenandoah campaign, the medical director of transportation was transferred to Harpers Ferry. The town garrison contained four hospital and two passenger railroad cars. For the rest of the war Harpers Ferry served as a strategic supply base and hospital center for Sheridan's army.

There is evidence that surgery related to the war occurred in Harpers Ferry's nonmilitary areas. In Lower Town, along Public Walk, stood Dr. Marmion's office. His domicile sat across from his house. Today, the remains of the doctor's office only exist underground. The foundations are buried under about one foot of topsoil, and the surrounding lands are incorporated into a terraced landscape (Figure 15). Previous archaeology was done in the area primarily to locate landscape features (Cotter 1959) and for stabilization needs (Inashima 1981). Recent archaeology (Parsons 1995) located the foundations of Marmion's office, and some work proceeded in the building's yard area. Archaeologists discovered a plethora of Civil War era artifacts including domestic and military objects. The latter includes buckles, a canteen, and uniform pieces. Most notable is the large quantity of Union uniform buttons found in and around the building. Archaeologists also found several bullets with teeth marks. One can imagine Dr. Marmion, or some military doctor, cutting a uniform open, sending buttons flying, and a soldier biting on a bullet during a surgery or amputation. This type of assemblage, with an unusually high amount of uniform buttons, has also been found at other Civil War medical sites such as the Hatcher-Cheatham site. Clarence Geier observes that after the Battle of Drewry's Bluff, the military seized a domestic site and converted it to an aid station. There Geier found a large amount of personal clothing parts, including clothing straps, shoe eyelets, suspender buckles, and buttons (Geier et al. 1989:124–125, 1994:204–208).

Figure 15. Excavation Units 6 and 7 located the foundations of Dr. Marmion's office—across the road from his residence in Building 1-B. (Drawn by John Ravenhorst)

LANDSCAPE AND CIVIL WAR RUINS

After the war, many of the Harpers Ferry's buildings stood in ruins. It took over a decade for the town's economy to recover. With no economic base remaining, Harpers Ferry was characterized as "Next to Dead" and a "Village of Paupers" (*VFP* 25 November 1869:2). In 1867 General Grant reported to the Secretary of War that the United States no longer required the Harpers Ferry grounds and recommended against rebuilding the armory. He proposed the lands be sold, if not leased (*VFP* 19 December 1867:1). In 1868, Congress passed an act to sell public lands, buildings, machinery, as well as the water power privileges to the Shenandoah and Potomac Rivers.

Today, Harpers Ferry lacks the multitudes of granite obelisks dedicated to recalling the heroism of a specific battle in the war, like those at Gettysburg and Vicksburg. From the end of the Civil War, the industrial ruins of the Civil War, such as the armory buildings and Herr's flour mill, became part of a memorializing landscape. The landscape commemorated the once economically prosperous regional manufacturing center and the home for the national armory. The ruins created a new commemorative landscape. Townspeople, industrialists, and the Baltimore & Ohio Railroad went to great lengths to preserve these ruins. As National Park Service historian Richard Sellars (1987:19) notes "Even without monuments, [preservation] is an act of memorializing. Preservation acknowledges that something so important happened that it must be remembered and at least some terrain set aside." Allowing ruins to stand in a decaying state is a form of preservation that memorializes past events.

Most of the townspeople redeveloped the commercial and residential sections while they allowed industrial ruins of private and government factories to stand in a decayed state. Harpers Ferry's armory and industrial ruins served to memorialize the war's industrial history. The Civil War was a sharp dividing line in the town's history and Harpers Ferrians, as well as outside interests, like the Baltimore & Ohio Railroad, helped to transform the area from a manufacturing town in to a symbol of industrial precedence. Industrial ruins functioned as a conduit to the past by creating monuments to the early industrial era and they placed the Civil War within an industrial context, the first major conflict of the industrial era. During the hostilities, both sides exploited new industrial technologies. Armies extensively used the railroads; new technologies developed fast-firing weapons; and people and machines mass-produced guns, uniforms, and other equipment. The commemoration of this new industrial phenomenon in Harpers Ferry and other areas throughout the country helped reinforce an industrial consciousness, and still serves as a reminder of the "immutable" traditions of industrialization (Shackel 1994).

After the Civil War, Harpers Ferry became a popular tourist spot along the Baltimore & Ohio Railroad and the Chesapeake and Ohio Canal. Visitors were either day travelers or those who owned or rented cottages in the community for the summer. Harpers Ferry also served as a major tourist destination for blacks from Washington, D.C. Tourist brochures described several important landmarks including the ruins of the United States Armory (Anonymous circa.1910; Anonymous n.d.; Taft 1898). A northern entrepreneur, interested in reexploiting the river's water power potential, purchased the United States Armory grounds along the Potomac River. He sold a right-of-way to the Baltimore & Ohio Railroad. After 1891, ten feet of railroad berm fill covered part of the original armory factory foundations. After 1893, the first thing tourists saw as they entered Harpers Ferry via the train was an obelisk monument erected by the railroad marking the fort's original location (Figure 16). Beside this monument were iron tablets placed by the federal government to commemorate the Confederates' 1862 siege of the town. They were mounted there for "the enlightenment of travelers concerning the fighting that took place in the capture of Harpers Ferry by the Confederate Army in September, 1862"

Figure 16. Obelisk marking the location of John Brown's Fort, and five tablets commemorating Stonewall Jackson's siege and capture of Harpers Ferry. (Courtesy, Harpers Ferry National Historical Park, HF-1142)

(Quoted in Gilbert et al. 1993:3.88) Also visible from the tracks were several remaining foundations of the former musket factory.

In 1916 the Baltimore & Ohio Railroad landscaped the grounds around the musket factory foundations, planting flower beds and trees. By 1923 a large garden filled the remains of the old armory grounds (*SoJ* 16 May 1896:2; Gilbert et al. 1993:3.95). The garden's design "incorporated the embankment, the matured trees and ornamental shrubs planted along the old river wall, and the rectangular outlines of old building foundations, creating a distinctive gateway of monuments, history, and ornamental landscape" (*SoJ* 16 May 1916:2; Gilbert et al. 1993:3.95–3.96; also see Shackel 1994:266) (Figure 17). The town celebrated many of the landscape changes made by the railroad as they incorporated them into an unofficial public square.

On the Shenandoah River portion of Harpers Ferry northern entrepreneurs eagerly invested in Virginius Island's industrial revitalization. They repaired the old cotton factory and converted it to a flour mill. Even though they renovated the worker's domestic dwellings and surrounding grounds, they allowed the substantial ruins of Herr's flour mill to stand

Figure 17. Outlined armory building foundations and landscaped grounds by the Baltimore and Ohio Railroad. Notice the ornamental shrubbery and the interpretive placards. (Courtesy, Harpers Ferry National Historical Park, HF-1039)

Figure 18. The former Herr flour mill ruins on Virginius Island, ca. 1898. By the end of the 19th century they were often misidentified as the United States armory ruins. (Taft Collection, Courtesy, Harpers Ferry National Historic Park)

and be incorporated into the vernacular landscape of the island (Figure 18). Herr's flour mill ruins continued to stand on Virginius Island into the middle of the 20th century, and tourists often mistook it as the "Rifle Factory ruins" of Hall's Island (Taft 1898). A 1941 guide book describes the island as containing Herr's mill and the rifle factory (Writer's Program 1941:234; Joseph et al. 1993). Virginius Island never contained the rifle factory, rather it stood to the north on Hall's Island.

The ruins created by the Civil War served as a symbol that has helped Americans reaffirm their connection with a particular heritage and to reinforce critical messages that create an American identity. Preservation, reconstruction, or stabilization of public symbols, and in this case the industrial ruins, provides an avenue to interpret past events in civic arenas. They help influence people's beliefs about historic legends and the current attitudes they serve. The Civil War generated a landscape of ruins that allowed industrialists to commemorate a prosperous past. Commemorating this history by preserving ruins is one method of creating and reinforcing this national ideology. Commemorating the industrial past is embedded in the National Park Service's interpretation of Harpers Ferry. Throughout many exhibits, waysides, plaques, and brochures, visitors are told about industrial advancements and how they contributed to our modern lifestyle (Shackel 1994).

Different groups in their preserving of ruins or saving graphic reminders of the past have met with varying degrees of success. Many working class members view the preservation of old buildings and ruins as an attempt to save a degrading phase of human history. Robert Vogel of the Smithsonian Institution notes "The dirt, noise, bad smell, hard labor and other forms of exploitation associated with these kinds of places make preservation [of industrial sites] ludicrous. 'Preserve a steel mill?' people say, 'It killed my father. Who wants to preserve that?'" (Quoted in Lowenthal 1985:403). By preserving ruins, we provide symbolic links to the past and a sense of continuity between past and present. Ruins show the impact of time and lend credibility to the long-term establishment of any particular institution that became that ruin or that occupied that site.

In Harpers Ferry, the Civil War destroyed many of the town's buildings and it created ruins of the armory and the flour mill. Postwar local entrepreneurs from the commercial district renovated their community with various construction materials, including those salvaged from industries found on the armory grounds and on Virginius Island. These actions dismembered many prominent standing industrial structures and symbolically dismantled the industrial ideals that the community resisted through the armory's occupation of the town (see Smith 1977; Shackel 1996). While local entrepreneurs dismantled the town's industries, northern capitalists purchased industrial sites and kept the armory and flour mill ruins intact and visible to the community and tourists. These northern entrepreneurs developed or redeveloped industries according to northern industrial ideals. Their enterprises stood next to the decaying ruins that served to show the long-term establishment of industrialization (Shackel 1994). David Lowenthal reminds us that "precedence legitimates action on the assumption, explicit or implicit, that what has been should continue to be or be again" (Lowenthal 1985:40).

Memory does serve a major function in any society, including industrial society. Some claim that preserving ruins may run counter to the spirit of modern enterprise (see Plumb in Lowenthal 1985:402–403), but this is not so in Harpers Ferry. While the Civil War left much of Harpers Ferry's industry in ruins, these remains served as a symbol of historical precedence to claim roots in an industrial past. The existence of decaying ruins amplifies the age of the industrial era and ground its symbolic meanings in a legitimate past. Decay secures antiquity. Ruins help to inspire reflections on institutions that had once been proud or strong. As Lowenthal (1985:197) again reminds us, "remembering the past is crucial for our sense of identity . . . to know what we were confirms that we are."

PUBLIC MEMORY

The Civil War created a landscape of ruins that became a useful tool for industrialists to claim a long tradition of industry. This tradition continues today with the National Park Service's interpretation of the town's history. Nevertheless, the Civil War memory of Harpers Ferry delivered by the National Park Service does not mention industry, nor does it focus on the citizens of the town. When people visit Harpers Ferry National Historical Park, they usually hear of Stonewall Jackson's siege and capture of Harpers Ferry. The national park has recently developed an exhibit that is dedicated to interpreting this event. It is portrayed as a spectacular feat, despite the fact that a military investigation of the surrender found that Miles' actions "amounting to almost imbecility" (quoted in Hearn 1996:190).

Why, then, at Harpers Ferry and many other historic sites, is the focus almost exclusively about interpreting the "great men" at the expense of the civilians? Why are stories about Mrs. Stipes' boardinghouse and Dr. Marmion's office absent from park interpretations? Apparently the creation of the myths of "great men" still plays an important role in our culture.

An examination of the public memory at Harpers Ferry is about how and why an institution, group, or formal organization selects and interprets a memory to serve their ends. People search for common memories to meet their needs (Thelen 1989:1123–1124). As historian David Blight (1989:1169) writes, " . . . historical memory is . . . a matter of choice, a question of will. As a culture, we choose which footprints from the past will best help us walk in the present." Archaeology plays a unique role in telling the story of people who have been traditionally excluded from history; it can transform the memory of the Civil War that is more inclusive.

"The Place Never Will Be Anything Again"

Lower Town Harpers Ferry and Victorian America

AN 1865 ETHNOGRAPHIC ACCOUNT OF HARPERS FERRY

After the Civil War, Harpers Ferry was a shell of its former self. Many former residents never returned. Many of the armorers had fled to the north or south to find employment in arms production. Others, who did not relish the task of rebuilding a war-torn town, abandoned their hopes and dreams of ever living in Harpers Ferry again. After the war, however, many Americans became intrigued with the social and economic conditions of the defeated south. Ironically, this phenomenon served as a catalyst to redeveloping many southern towns, including Harpers Ferry.

A new genre of literature developed after the war and included the travel accounts of northerners who reported on the social and economic conditions of the south. These anecdotes provide valuable ethnographic regional descriptions. One such account is J. T. Trowbridge's visit to Harpers Ferry during the summer of 1865. He wrote from the position of an abolitionist, although he claimed that all of his writings were nonbiased and faithful. His accounts are important because they present a new and different perspective of the town's postbellum condition that has been absent from the modern histories that document Harpers Ferry's postwar condition. The town was not completely desolate, but rather it began its struggle to recover, almost immediately after the war.

Trowbridge arrived in Harpers Ferry at dusk and went to the only existing town hotel. The Shenandoah House was a new, unpainted, four-storey wooden building that looked more like a barracks than a hotel. It lacked shutters and window blinds. "The main entrance from the street was through a bar where merry men were clicking glasses, and sucking dark-colored stuff through straws. And this was a 'first-class' hotel kept on the European plan" (Trowbridge 1866:62). The only thing that consoled him was that the hotel sat on the Potomac banks and had a view of Maryland Heights.

Trowbridge's rustic room lacked wallpaper and carpet and did not even have a peg or a nail to hang his hat. "The bed was furnished with sheets which came down just below a man's knees, and a mattress which had the appearance of being stuffed with shingles" (Trowbridge 1866:63). No servants came when he called for help, so he went on his own expedition to claim a chair, a dressing-table, and another bed.

Situated along the Potomac River, the hotel also stood next to the Baltimore & Ohio Railroad. Naturally, this proximity to the tracks meant a restless night for Trowbridge (1866:63).

> How often during the night the trains passed I cannot now compute; each approaching and departing with clatter and clang, and shouts of men and bell-ringing and sudden glares of light, and the voices of steam-whistle projecting its shrill shriek into the ear of the horrified night, and setting the giant mountains to tossing and retossing the echo like a ball.

The town, Trowbridge noted, stood in the midst of stupendous scenery, and he claimed that it could become a favorite resort area. After climbing Maryland Heights on the winding, military roads, he viewed the surrounding valleys and the town below. He observed that Harpers Ferry once had nicely graded streets and treed hillsides, but that five years of war created a town mostly destroyed, surrounded by rubbish, filth, and stench (Trowbridge 1866:66).

Trowbridge described Harpers Ferry as the folly of secession. The government works had employed hundreds of people, and Harpers Ferry had existed as a thriving industrial town. The attempt to overthrow the government failed, but the towns' own prosperity diminished. "The place never will be anything again" remarked one Harpers Ferry citizen to Trowbridge (Trowbridge 1966:68).

John Brown's "Engine House" had escaped destruction and still stood in the armory grounds. It had suffered some damage from battle, but " . . . no rebel hands were permitted to demolish [it]. It is now used as a storehouse for arms" (Trowbridge, 1866:67). While standing near John Brown's Fort, Trowbridge met a gentleman who came out of one of the government repair shops. Trowbridge retold the gentleman's story of John Brown.

> So they took the old man and hung him; and all the time the men that did it were plotting treason and murder by the wholesale. They did it in a hurry, because if they delayed, they wouldn't have been able to hang him at all. A strong current of public feeling was turning in his favor. Such a sacrifice of himself set many to thinking on the subject who never thought before; many who had to acknowledge in their hearts that slavery was wrong and that old John Brown was right. I speak what I

know, for I was here at the time. I have lived in Harpers Ferry for 15 years. I was born and bred in a Slave state, but I never let my love of the institution blind me to everything else. Slavery had been a curse of this country, and she is now beginning to bless the day she was delivered from it. (Trowbridge 1866:67)

The worker, reported Trowbridge, also said that public sentiment regarding slavery was slowly changing in Harpers Ferry.

The most of them are coming round to right views of Negro suffrage, too. That is the only justice for the blacks, and it is the only safety for us. The idea of allowing the loyal colored population to be represented by the whites, the most of whom were traitors—of letting a Rebel just out of the Confederate army vote, and telling a colored man just out of the Union army that he has no vote—the idea is so perfectly absurd that the Rebels themselves must acknowledge it. (Trowbridge 1866:67)

Harpers Ferry, "redeemed from slavery, and opened to Northern enterprise, should become a beautiful and busy town" (Trowbridge 1866:68).

Trowbridge traveled east to Charles Town to see the place of John Brown's martyrdom. He found a desolate landscape void of any crops in the field. When he came to a boardinghouse, a northerner greeted him and exclaimed that "they are all rebels here—all rebels" (in Trowbridge 1866:70). Southern sentiment was still very strong in the area. Food was very scarce; the boardinghouse mistress served salt fish and fried potatoes three times a day. Trowbridge's northern friend complained that at supper they will be served "treason, salt-fish, fried potatoes, and a little more treason" (Trowbridge 1866:71).

Trowbridge's acquaintance remarked that "the war-feeling here is like a burning bush with a wet blanket wrapped around it. Look at it from the outside, the fire seems quenched. But just peep under the blanket, and there it is, all alive, and eating, eating in. The wet blanket is the present government policy; and every act of conciliation shown the Rebels is just letting in so much air to feed the fire" (Trowbridge 1866:71).

Visiting the site of John Brown's trial, Trowbridge found the courthouse in ruins. The four white massive pillars in front of the building still stood and "supported a riddled roof, through which God's blue sky and gracious sunshine smiled" (Trowbridge 1866:71). Soldiers, he was told, had gone through the building and stripped it of most of its wood, probably souvenir hunting. As they destroyed the building, they sung the tune "John Brown's Body," reminding the citizens "that his soul was marching on" (Trowbridge 1866:71).

Trowbridge walked to the other side of town, looking for the place where John Brown was hanged. Nothing stood there but a weed-infested field. A girl told him "Nobody knows just where the gallows stood. There was a tree here, but that has been cut down and carried away, stump and roots and all, by folks that wanted something to remember John Brown by. Every soldier took a piece of it, if't was only a little chip" (Trowbridge 1866:73).

NATIONAL RECONSTRUCTION

Viewing Harpers Ferry's place in time within the context of America's Reconstruction and post-Reconstruction eras is important. President Andrew Johnson recognized the new state governments of the south only after they had met certain preconditions, including the renunciation of secession and the abolition of slavery. By December 1865, ten of the 11 southern states had accepted the stipulation. These states elected an all white government, without black representation. Former-Confederate politicians and military officials represented the New South. These legislators passed the Black Codes of 1865–1866 that restricted many blacks' rights and reestablished a new type of slavery. Most noticeably, blacks could be sold into forced labor to pay fines or for breach of contract (see Foner 1988).

Congress, under the leadership of the Radical Republicans, barred southerners from their seats in Congress. They placed more stringent conditions upon the southern states before they could be fully readmitted and allowed representation. This condition included their ratification of the 14th Amendment, which gave citizenship to former enslaved people.

President Johnson favored a more lenient policy, and in 1866 he campaigned for members of Congress who backed his program. Speaking through congressional elections, the American public appeared to rebuke his program: Two-thirds of the newly elected Congress consisted of anti-Johnson forces. Johnson reacted by encouraging southern states not to pass the 14th Amendment. All of the southern states, except Tennessee, rejected the amendment. In retaliation, an angry Congress imposed a military reconstruction on the South the following year. The United States Army provided oversight for the new southern governments and required them to pass both the 14th and 15th Amendments. The latter amendment gave black men the right to vote. In 1868, Congress attempted to impeach Johnson, but failed.

Military presence after the surrender of the Confederacy lasted an average of three years in each southern state, except in Louisiana and South Carolina, where it lasted until 1877. Generally, white and black Republicans outvoted the white Democrats during this reconstruction period, but the white Democrats eventually intimidated or destroyed the black vote. While economic reconstruction managed to get the cotton-based economy rolling again, social reconstruction had not been as successful.

Southern revisionists, such as W.A. Dunning (1907) of Columbia University, wrote in 1907 that the North fought admirably during the war, but they reconstructed the South dishonorably. He reasoned

> Nothing could come out of the Negro–carpetbagger–scalawag governments, the argument ran, and the conservative whites–the "redeemers"–finally felt justified in using the brutal methods of the Ku Klux Klan to rescue the South from misrule by their former bondsmen. (Bailey 1973:402)

Murders, large-scale riots, and battles were fought in the South, with hundreds dead and thousands wounded in the last quarter of the 19th century (Bailey 1973:404). Tranquility and racial harmony did not exist in the South, nor did it fare well in Harpers Ferry.

RACIAL TENSIONS AND BLACK ACTIVISM

With the backing of Northern Baptists, Reverend N.C. Brackett, helped establish schools in postbellum Shenandoah Valley for former enslaved people. In February 1867, John Storer a philanthropist in Sanford, Maine, donated $10,000 to Reverend Brackett to set up such a school in Harpers Ferry. On October 2, 1867, Storer College (originally named Storer Normal School) began classes with 19 students. Initially, the school was located in the armory paymaster's former house, which served as a dormitory, school, and church. One year later, the college asked James Garfield's permission to acquire the former homes of other armory officials on Camp Hill, along with several acres. The Freedman's Bureau donated money which enabled a dormitory, Lincoln Hall, to be built (Everhart 1952:122–124; Noffsinger 1958:49–50).

Throughout its existence, the college had its mission dictated by whites who controlled the administration and the governing board. The goal of the school was to provide technical skills and an education for former enslaved people so they could provide for themselves in a segregated society.

Storer College developed in an era when the country remained deeply divided racially. The *Spirit of Jefferson*, the local Harpers Ferry newspaper, often confronted abolitionist policies. Faculty and students of Storer College were not welcome in Harpers Ferry's commercial district. The Ku Klux Klan often threatened students and teachers. On one occasion, when a Storer College teacher went to the post office, she was "hooted at" by local residents because of her affiliation with the college. On another occasion, residents stoned her several times as she walked in the street. Armed militiamen started escorting Storer College women on their excursions into town (Anthony 1891:10-11).

During the summer months Storer College converted its dormitories to boardinghouses to accommodate tourists who visited Harpers Ferry (*The Bee* 2 August 1884:3; 1 August 1885:2). In *The Bee* a Washington, D.C., black-oriented newspaper, one person wrote: "The whites have seized with avidity upon every spot, and only one hall is reserved for the colored people" (*The Bee* 16 June 1888:1). Visiting John Brown's Fort in Lower Town became an objective for many black visitors. One author in *The Bee* wrote that it stood "where a heroic soul made a stand for liberty, not for himself primarily, but for his 'brother in black. . . . ' His fort still stands, a shrine for lovers of liberty" (*The Bee* 16 June 1888:1).

In a letter to *The Bee*, a woman named Louise, who visited Harpers Ferry during August 1885, remarked on the racial tensions in town.

> . . . there was a little disturbance at Fussell's Ice Cream Saloon one evening last week. . . . I hope it will not affect our people any, as Mr. Fussell is very accommodating and much of a gentleman towards our people who patronize his place of business. (*The Bee* 1 August 1885:2)

Tourists may have happily visited John Brown's Fort (Figures 19 and 20), but some local townspeople were not as excited about the prospect of having the structure nearby. Discontent already existed within the community over Storer College's existence.

As long as the abolitionist symbol—John Brown's Fort—stood in Harpers Ferry, there remained the threat of a possible influx of blacks to visit the fort. Therefore, townspeople expressed their enthusiasm for ridding the town of the fort. In 1888 a rumor claimed that John Brown's Fort would be moved to a New York park. The local newspaper's editor wrote in favor of this idea and exclaimed "& joy go with it" (*SoJ* 14 August 1888:1).

Racial tensions grew, often ignited by rumors: In 1890 a *Spirit of Jefferson* supplement (21 October 1890) ran an article titled, "To Africanize West Virginia." The story spread fear among working-class families since the subtitle claimed "To colonize the state with the blacks of the south. West Virginia working men to be turned out of the mines and the shops, to give place for the Negro of the south" (*SoJ* 21 October 1890).

The following year Thomas Savery, proprietor, sold John Brown's Fort to the John Brown Fort Company. The company consisted of a group founded by A.J. Holmes, a Congressman from Iowa, who wished to exhibit the structure at the 1893 Columbian Exposition in Chicago. The sale became necessary when the Baltimore & Ohio Railroad planned to move the railroad tracks 250' west from the banks of the Potomac River. John Brown's Fort stood within the railroad's new right of way (*SoJ* 17 Septem-

Figure 19. John Brown's Fort, circa 1870s. (Courtesy, Harpers Ferry National Historical Park, HF-34)

ber 1889:3). In Chicago, the fort drew only 11 paid admissions at 50 cents a piece. The John Brown Fort Company had paid $60,000 to move the structure (Shackel 1995).

By 1895, Mary Katherine Keemle Field, a Washington, D.C. newspaper reporter, came to the fort's rescue. She was actively involved with social reform issues and concerned herself with the circumstances of post-Civil War blacks. For instance, Field had used her column in the late 1860s to make people aware that John Brown's farm and grave at North Elba, New York, was close to ruin and decay. She gained public support and funds to save the farmstead.

The railroad offered to move the fort to an area near the original site that would have encouraged tourism on the railroad line (Gee 1958:97). Rumors developed that John Brown's remains would be reburied at Harpers Ferry. A *Spirit of Jefferson* editorial spoke out against disinterring John Brown's remains and erecting a monument, although the paper favored the return of the fort "where Robert E. Lee captured the old villain" (*SoJ* 1 October 1895:2). Harpers Ferrians were also displeased about the idea of moving the raiders' bodies from their common grave on

Figure 20. Tourists in front of John Brown's Fort. (Courtesy, Harpers Ferry National Historical Park, HF-57)

the Shenandoah shores across from Harpers Ferry to reinter them with a marker at the restored fort (*SoJ* 8 October 1895:2).

Fields contacted Alexander Murphy, a local farmer and businessman, who agreed to deed five acres of his farm, Buena Vista, for the placement of the fort. With Field's efforts the fort was moved in 1895, several miles from its original location and from the railroad line. But this tactic did not prevent black groups from using the fort as a symbol of their fight against oppression during the Jim Crow era.

Former enslaved people had perceived John Brown's Fort as a symbol of their abolitionist struggle, but the structure became an overt symbol among blacks after the mid-1890s. After the Supreme Court upheld the legal segregation in *Plessy* v. *Ferguson,* John Brown's Fort became a prominent symbol in the struggle for racial equality. In July 1896, the first national convention of the National League of Colored Women met in Washington, D.C., and took a day trip to John Brown's Fort at the Murphy Farm (Shackel in press) (Figure 21).

One of the most momentous occasions in early 20th century activism took place on the Murphy farm a decade later. In August 1906, the Second Niagara Convention, led by W.E.B. Du Bois, was held in Harpers Ferry.

Figure 21. John Brown's Fort on the Murphy Farm with members of the National League of Colored Women, 1896. (Courtesy, Harpers Ferry National Historical Park, HF-599)

Many blacks saw Harpers Ferry as the symbolic starting point of the American Civil War, ignited by John Brown's Raid. The organization was founded in Buffalo, New York, in 1905 by 54 members from 18 states. They were forced to meet in Erie, Canada, July 11–13, because Buffalo hotels would not accommodate blacks. The principle guidelines (from Foner 1970:144-149) for establishing the movement include:

- Freedom of speech and criticism
- An unfettered and unsubsidized press
- Manhood suffrage
- The abolition of all caste distinctions based simply on race and color
- The recognition of the principle of human brotherhood as a practical present creed
- The recognition of the highest and best training as the monopoly of no class or race
- A belief in the dignity of labor
- United effort to realize these ideals under wise and courageous leadership

In 1906, nearly 100 visitors came to Storer College for the second meeting of the Niagara Movement. While in there celebrated John Brown's Day and came to the fort on August 17, 1906, to commemorate John Brown's 100th birthday and the 50th anniversary of the Battle of Osawatomie. At 6:00 A.M. the conference participants left college, and began their journey to the engine house, about a mile away. As they approached the fort, they formed a single file procession, removed their "shoes and socks, and walked barefoot as if treading on holy ground" (Quarles 1974:4).

The participants listened to a prayer led by Richard T. Greener. He relayed his personal recollections of John Brown and told the crowd that when he served as consul at Vladivostok, he heard Russian troops burst into song, singing "John Brown's body lies a-mouldering in the grave" (Quarles 1974:4). Later that day Du Bois read the Niagara address to the delegation, and his tone caused his detractors to label him as a militant and agitator. He told the congregation of their increasing loss of political and social rights: "We claim for ourselves every single right that belongs to a freeborn American, political, civil, and social; and until we get these rights we will never cease to protest and assail the ears of America" (Du Bois quoted in Fonner 1970:170–171). He continued:

> The battle we wage is not for ourselves alone but for all true Americans. It is a fight for ideals, lest this, our common fatherland, false in founding, become in truth the land of the thief and the home of the slave—a byword and a hissing among the nations for its sounding pretensions and pitiful accomplishments." (Du Bois quoted in Fonner 1970:170–171)

He claimed that he did not believe in obtaining equal rights through violence, but,

> we do believe in John Brown, in that incarnate spirit of justice, that hatred of a lie, the willingness to sacrifice money, reputation, and life itself on the altar of right. And here on the scene of John Brown's martyrdom we reconsecrate ourselves, our honor, our property to final emancipation of the race which John Brown died to make free. . . . Thank God for John Brown! Thank God for Garrison and Douglas! Sumner and Philips, Nat Turner and Robert Gould Shaw. . . . (Du Bois quoted in Fonner 1970:172–173)

The events of the Niagara Movement went virtually unnoticed by the local and national newspapers.

It is unclear from the historical documents just how many other visitors actually came to the fort while it was situated on the Murphy farm. It does appear that the structure was accessible to the black community and that it served as a place of homage for people who revered John Brown and the ideas of social reform.

In 1909 the Storer College college trustees voted to buy John Brown's Fort. Members of Storer College began negotiating Murphy shortly after his 1903 purchase, and in 1909 the college agreed to pay $900, which cleared Murphy's purchase price and court costs. Dismantled in 1910, the fort fell prey to souvenir hunters. The structure was rebuilt that same year near Lincoln Hall on campus grounds (Figure 22).

At the peak of the Jim Crow era, and while the southern revisionist movement was in full force, blacks continued to use the fort as a symbol of their cause for social justice (Fairbairn 1961:14). In 1909, W.E.B. Du Bois wrote a major biography of John Brown that recaptured and reinforced sympathy for the abolitionist. Calling John Brown a prophet, Du Bois justified Brown's militant actions at Harpers Ferry (Du Bois 1962 [1909]:339). His work countered the southern revisionist movement, which denigrated the methods and cause of the abolitionist movement. Du Bois, along with many others, encouraged the legacy of John Brown and the abolitionist movement to be remembered and the John Brown Fort served as a rallying point for these ideas.

Figure 22. A Storer College class in front of John Brown's Fort on the Storer College campus. (Courtesy, Harpers Ferry National Historical Park, HF-1098)

HARPERS FERRY'S REDEVELOPMENT

During the early years of Reconstruction, Harpers Ferry's physical complexion changed dramatically. Many remaining government-owned buildings stood in either fair or poor condition (Letter, Ramsey to Dyer 27 July 1865). The government decided to sell their interest in Harpers Ferry at an auction. Proceeds were to fund the construction of armories in the West.

In 1869, four years after Trowbridge's visit, the first postbellum government auction of buildings and lands took place in Harpers Ferry. The sale included timber rights on Loudoun and Maryland Heights, and water rights to the Potomac and Shenandoah Rivers. The government sold the land with easy terms—no money down—although deeds were not transferred until the government received the final payment. Citizens purchased 245 lots along with 22 dwellings. Most of the buyers were Harpers Ferrians who paid inflated prices only because they felt confident that prosperity existed around the corner. One reason townspeople overbid for their properties was based on the rumors that entrepreneur F.C. Adams, who purchased most of the government's holding on the rivers (including the old armory grounds), intended to reindustrialize the town.

Local Democratic Conservatives, who controlled the business community, also believed that the region needed to develop its mineral resources and industrialize. They developed many committees to attract industry since it had once prospered along the Shenandoah and Potomac River shores. Much like the rest of the country, Harpers Ferry was caught in an era where industry was equated with progress and potential growth seemed limitless; many business men were interested in rejuvenating the town (Fenicle 1993).

While the older leading families had lost considerable economic control of the town, new middle-class businessmen, merchants, and their families invested in the town's development. Inspired by Adam's promise to industrialize, families such as the Quinns, Decaulnes, Ames, Conways, Walshs, and McGraws, either constructed or rehabilitated war-torn structures (Gilbert et al. 1993:3.74–3.75).

The Bollman bridge was completed in 1870, bringing passengers and goods to town (Gilbert et al. 1993:3.77). Harpers Ferry became an important depot when the Baltimore & Ohio Railroad expanded to Wheeling, Pittsburgh, and other western cities in the 1870s and 1880s. The Chesapeake and Ohio Canal resumed operations, and entrepreneurs shipped coal, wheat, flour, lumber, and corn through Harpers Ferry to the port of Georgetown. The canal reached its commercial peak during the mid-1870s (Gilbert et al. 1993:3.78–3.80).

Water power had been the catalyst for much of the industrial growth before the Civil War. Steam power gained importance in the 1870s and 1880s because it was cheaper to use and water power was perceived as inadequate and more expensive. As a result, Harpers Ferry never regained the economic prominence it had during the 1840s and 1850s, although in the 1870s, some entrepreneurs attempted to reexploit the Shenandoah and the Potomac's water power. In the late 1860s, Child and McCreight converted an old textile mill and began operating a water-powered flour mill on the Shenandoah River. The mill persisted through the 1880s.

As the water-powered industry slowly recovered, many townspeople struggled to rejuvenate Harpers Ferry's commercial district. Disastrous floods in 1870 and 1877 had accelerated the deterioration of Lower Town Harpers Ferry. These floods were more devastating than those in the past. Timber along the Shenandoah Valley had been harvested or burned during the war, so there was little vegetation left to prevent or reduce the rate of soil erosion. The high waters carried topsoil down river, leaving deep layers of mud throughout Harpers Ferry.

Joseph Barry (1988 [1903]:164) commented on the 1870 flood:

> The very streets in many places ploughed up, as it were, and chasms many feet in depth were made in the road bed. Every house on the south side of the street, from the market house to the Island of Virginius was either entirely destroyed or badly injured. . . . Some 70 houses in all were either entirely demolished or rendered uninhabitable . . . in many instances, the very foundations obliterated.

The 1877 flood damaged the Chesapeake and Ohio Canal, and it never again regained the full commercial potential it had achieved earlier that decade (Gilbert et al. 1993:3.81).

A 1870s description of the town noted that it was (Bryant 1872):

> still more sleepy and dilapidated than its normal condition. The recent war stunned it, then came the disastrous flood of 1870. . . . Pass where you will, there are evidences of the desolation left behind by these two occurrences. And the people of Harpers Ferry have very naturally lost heart.

During the 1870s, townspeople realized Adam's promise to reindustrialize the area amounted to nothing more than a scheme since he appeared to only want to challenge the Baltimore & Ohio Railroad over legal rights to an already established rail line right-of-way. Adams had never intended to redevelop the armory grounds. By 1876, Adams' attempt for a settlement with the Baltimore & Ohio Railroad had failed in federal courts, and the land's ownership reverted to the United States. Adams did not lose any money because he never had to make a downpayment on his property.

Many of the armory buildings, claimed earlier by Adams, stood in a ruined state and the machinery, once salvageable, continued to decay. On June 14, 1878, an act of Congress allowed purchasers of lots to apply for abatement. Many of the buyers who purchased lands at the 1869 auction filed applications for abatement, claiming they had paid inflated prices and that their new, flood-damaged property had lost considerable value. They had based their bids on the promises that Adams would reindustrialize the town. Other government sales in the 1880s disposed of the remaining government lands in Harpers Ferry. This time money and deeds were transferred and a new sense of optimism arose in Harpers Ferry (Snell 1979).

By the 1880s citizens in Lower Town had developed and rebuilt the main business district on Shenandoah Street. New enterprises flourished and several substantial homes and businesses were added to the community. James McGraw, Murtha Walsh, Thomas Beale, and Edward Tearney constructed or expanded their establishments in Lower Town. A two-block corridor was filled with commercial establishments, giving the town an air of a bustling and profitable commercial district. Economic expansion and optimism were fueled by Thomas Savery purchasing both the armory grounds and the rifle factory site in an 1884 government auction. Adams had originally purchased these lands in 1869, but they had reverted to the federal government. Savery constructed a pulp mill on the rifle factory site and a paper mill in the armory grounds. He tended to be an absentee landlord.

James Garland Hurst purchased the new master armorer's house at the 1884 auction. Hurst already owned several properties throughout Harpers Ferry, although he concentrated his efforts on improving his Lower Town properties. He had the "best and most elaborately finished and furnished houses in Harpers Ferry" (*SoJ* 4 June 1889). He also had a "beautiful lawn, like green velvet" (*SoJ* 7 December 1897). Hurst, along with other downtown merchants, promoted a hygienic, beautiful town to attract manufacturers and tourists (*SoJ* 17 November 1896:3).

HEALTH, SANITATION, AND TOURISM IN HARPERS FERRY

In the late 19th century, health and hygiene had become correlated with material success.

> Health is wealth. Almost all of the fevers, cholera, and other plagues result from poisoning air coming from bad drains, unclean streets, and badly kept backyards. House slops and remnants from the table, or

decaying vegetables, should never be allowed to be thrown in the back
yard. Good drains, clean cellars, and general cleanliness about the house,
are the only safeguard of health. (Jeffries 1902:19)

Some Harpers Ferry traditions were difficult to stop. For instance, hogs
ran unattended through town streets. They would scavenge and, in effect,
provide a form of street sanitation. In 1873, "by a vote of 42:1, hogs are
permitted to run at large" (SoJ 17 January 1873:3). In 1891, the city
council permitted hogs within the boundaries of Harpers Ferry (SoJ 6
January 1891:2).

While most states had boards of health by the 1870s, West Virginia
had few substantial sanitary measures. The responsibility fell upon the
shoulders of local and municipal organizations (Ford 1993:12.17; 1994).
The Jefferson County Board of Health was established by 1885. The board
issued a notice that requested the local authorities to enforce basic sanitary measures during the upcoming summer months:

> Citizens of the county are hereby earnestly requested to adopt such
> measures of sanitation in their homes as will insure the greatest protection
> against the origin and spread of disease. The public authorities of
> Charlestown, Shepherdstown, Smithfield, Harpers Ferry and Bolivar are
> especially urged to give immediate attention to this important subject,
> and to move in the matter before the hot months are upon us.
>
> Before the first of June all streets and alleys should be thoroughly
> cleaned. All pig pens, cesspools, privy-vaults, all receptacles for filth of
> whatever description should be thoroughly cleaned and disinfected so as
> to afford the largest immunity from the disease which are fostered and
> propagated and often have their origin in such sources.
>
> On application to the undersigned, individuals or town authorities
> will be furnished with a list of disinfectants and directions on how to use
> them.
>
> Physicians of the county are reminded that it is their duty under
> the law to report promptly to this board all cases of 'endemic, infectious
> and contagious diseases' under their treatment.
>
> On the first of June the local board of health will, by authority of
> law, institute a house to house inspection, and whenever sanitary
> regulations have been neglected, the same will be enforced at the expense
> of the persons so offending.
>
> A M Evans, Sec. Local Board of Health, Jefferson County 5/12/85 (SoJ
> 12 May 1885:2)

In 1884, businessmen founded the Harpers Ferry Rural Improvement Company. This company "encouraged manufacturing, community
hygiene and beautification, and the promotion of Harpers Ferry as a
permanent place of residence and summer resort" (Chickering and Jenkins
1994:62–63; Ford 1993:12.18–12.19). The Spirit of Jefferson expressed the
growing mood for the cleaner and more sanitized town:

> The lines of the poet are apropos to the scenery of Harpers Ferry at this
> time of the year. It is truly a panorama of nature. Our homes have a
> healthy look and the streets somewhat improved, but if we would whip
> Cholera, Malaria and Typhoid, use lime artillery. Our streets and alleys,
> to elicit praise from strangers visiting us, must be swept. Paris, the most
> beautiful city in the world, has its streets swept every night, and every
> atom utilized even to the worms, which are used as fish baits. It shows
> economy as well as good taste on the part of the French, whose love for
> home is proverbial. They emigrate less than other nations. (*Spirit of
> Jefferson* 26 May 1875:2)

The group did not promote health reform, and any effort toward
sanitation reform was left up to the individual. James McGraw included a
privy and cistern in the boardinghouse he constructed in Lower Town in
1892. In 1895, he began to pipe in the "finest and purest" spring water
from Loudoun Heights for his brewery operations in 1895 (*SoJ* 16 April
1895:1). Within the next decade the water was being supplied to many
Lower Town residents (Jefferson County Deed Book [JCDB] 98, 27 October 1906:21; Ford 1993:12.19, 1994).

TOURISM IN HARPERS FERRY

Tourists continued to come to Harpers Ferry to visit many of its Civil
War sites and those of the surrounding areas. One newspaper account
claimed that "as a summer resort Harper's Ferry is becoming very popular, and destined to rival the most popular resorts in the country. . . . Crowds
pour in during the summer from the cities, where they find ample accommodations in the Ferry and on Camp Hill" (*The Bee* 30 June 1888:1). The
largest resort hotel, the Hill Top House, was built on the bluffs northeast
of town overlooking the Potomac River. This structure, along with many
other boardinghouses on Camp Hill, attracted tourists from Washington
and Baltimore and provided an escape from the city's heat, dirt, and noise.
There was much to do, including "beautiful drives, croqueting, boating,
fishing, hunting, pleasant walks to John Brown's cave, Rattling Springs,
Lovers Leap, Magazine Hill, and Island Park, where, during July and
August, large excursions come almost daily" (*The Bee* 30 June 1888:1).

The Baltimore & Ohio Railroad built Island Park, a 20-acre amusement park located on Byrne Island in the Potomac River in 1880 (*SoJ* 6
July 1880; Gilbert et al. 1993:3.90–3.91). Gilbert E. Perry a former mayor
of Harpers Ferry, mentioned the park when he described the atmosphere
of the town:

> "That was Island Park," he said. "You wouldn't believe it, but when I was
> a boy, it was every bit as gay as Coney Island."

"Downtown on Saturday nights," the mayor said, "you couldn't find a post to hitch your horse anywhere on Shenandoah Street. It wasn't a savory street then. saloons flourished; swinging doors, gambling, tin-pan music, and cancan dancers—we had 'em all in the gay Nineties."

"But we weren't all wild," Mayor Perry hastened to add. "We had out straight-laced side, too, in those horse-and-buggy days."

"Society people came from the city for the whole summer, or for a week or two during the racing season over at Charles Town. They lived in boarding houses here on the hill." (Wentzell 1957:402–408)

Tourism helped rejuvenate the town:

The town became a fashionable gathering place for those attracted by the beauty of the setting and for the curious who wished to visit the scene of John Brown's raid. For a time the Y-bridge across the Potomac was a favorite place for eloping couples to get married, for the tollgate keeper on the bridge was a retired parson, the honeymooners swelled the tide of visitors. (Writer's Group 1941:231) (Figure 23)

Others also felt optimistic about the town's growing economic success. James McGraw established the Harpers Ferry Brewery Company on the north bank of the Shenandoah River alongside Thomas Savery's paper mill and pulp mill. In 1898 McGraw sold the enterprise to the Belvedere Brewing Company, and it continued to operate under several other ownerships into the twentieth century.

Figure 23. Turn of the century image of Harpers Ferry, taken from Maryland Heights, circa 1900. (Courtesy, Harpers Ferry National Historical Park, HF-96)

The Wager family may have monopolized lands before the war, but a group of Irish and German families dominated the postbellum era. Generally, the Lower Town community was made up of both Irish and German people, many being descendants of the 1840s immigrants. And for the most part business leaders formed financial and political ties that transcended religious and ethnic differences.

THE EVENTUAL DEMISE OF HARPERS FERRY

Temperance organizations existed in Harpers Ferry during the 1830s, but by 1912, they had aggressively tried to close local saloons and liquor stores (*VFP* 1 September 1831:3; *VFP* 19 December 1912:5). Prohibition became part of the town politics and local election campaigns were fought by "wet" and "dry" candidates. In Harpers Ferry the "wet" candidates won. In 1911 all of Jefferson County became dry except for Harpers Ferry and Charles Town (*VFP* 13 April 1911:3; Fenicle 1993). Prohibition was forced on the two communities when the county court refused to issue any liquor licenses from July 1911 to January 1913. A new county commissioner changed the policy and issued the licenses (*VFP* 9 October 1913:2). Bars in the town did not stay open for long, however, because the entire state of West Virginia went dry in 1914, and National Prohibition went into effect in 1920 (Fenicle 1993). The owner converted his brewery into a soft drink bottling plant. By 1920 Harpers Ferry became a small town that catered to local and regional needs. Island Park fell into disrepair. The number of visitors decreased tremendously, although boardinghouses and hotels were still filled to capacity during the summer months.

The town contained

> a bank, three livery stables, two barber shops, a millinery store, two feed and hardware stores, a cleaning and pressing business, two department stores, a dry goods store, the Conner Hotel, three lunch rooms and a creamery, a bakery, a confectionery, two butcher shops, two blacksmiths, a shoe repair shop, a drug store, two doctors, two funeral parlors, three coal yards, the pulp mill, bottling works for soft drinks, and a volunteer fire department. (Gilbert et al. 1993:3.109)

It also appears that many of the residents found employment across the river in Brunswick in the Baltimore & Ohio Railroad yards (Writer's Program 1941).

As the automobile became an increasingly popular mode of transportation, railroad excursions decreased. By the 1920s Island Park ceased to be profitable for the Baltimore & Ohio Railroad (Gilbert et al. 1993:3.111).

Floods continued to hamper the town's growth. One person recollected:

> Then came the floods of 1924, washing away the Island Park bridge.
> Then in [1936] floods washed away the toll bridge. Another flood followed
> in [1942]. One by one businesses were ruined and closed out. Shirley
> Nichols moved his pharmacy to Charles Town and the A&P Store moved
> to Shepherdstown. (SoJ 11 June 1981)

The paper and pulp mills continued to operate into the 1920s. Harpers Ferry remained a small industrial town supported by mercantile businesses. The Interwoven Knitting Mills operated in Lower Town for several years. In 1925 a fire destroyed the paper mill. In 1935, the pulp mill ceased functioning. The bottling works discontinued operations in Harpers Ferry after the 1942 flood.

The 1936 flood destroyed the bridges that entered Harpers Ferry. When the highway department finally constructed river crossings in 1947 and 1949, they redirected the major automobile artery, Route 340, away from Lower Town Harpers Ferry. Highway traffic could now avoid the narrow streets and hills of Harpers Ferry, making transportation to points west of the town easier and quicker.

A 1941 history of Harpers Ferry noted "Today the town is wholly a residential and resort town. The water power once used to turn the wheels of the arsenal is utilized by a power company that generates electricity for use in Bolivar and Harpers Ferry and feeds its surplus current to Brunswick, Maryland" (Writer's Group 1941:231). By the 1940s the town had lost about 15 percent of its population to the neighboring community of Bolivar, which stood on higher grounds. A 1945 description of the town explained:

> Thus it had suffered so grievously from a succession of floods that the
> lower part of the town looks like an Italian hill village after the Nazis
> left, almost bereft of residents and trade alike. The little town is one of
> steep, narrow paths, rough winding stone steps, and tall narrow gabled
> houses, almost stately in their old time simplicity of line, even though
> half in ruin on their hillside perches. (Atwood 1945:49)

In 1943, Senator Jennings Randolph of West Virginia introduced legislation to create a national park at Harpers Ferry. The *Baltimore Sun* reported that Senator Randolph proposed to commemorate "the Harpers Ferry campaigns of the War Between the States and the great cause of human freedom." Matthew Page Andrews, member of the Sons of the Confederacy, protested the legislation. He wrote to the senator because he perceived this action as a "backdoor entrance into the original plan to honor John Brown and his ersatz brand of freedom" (Letter, Andrews to Randolph 1943:1). Andrews continued:

Such is the well-high universal ignorance of the true nature of this shrewdly
stupid hypocrite that few realize he was a small-scale edition of a Trotsky
or perhaps an awkward prototype of Schicklgruber, without either's gift
for rabble-rousing. . . . Brown engaged in secretly sowing sedition in the
U.S. Army and for a time seized a U.S. arsenal while proclaiming a
"provisional government" with himself as president or fuhrer. . . .
      Public opinion sometimes condones murder on a grand scale, but it
should at least be impossible to make a hero out of a masquerader guilty
of forgery and other felonies, just because he alleged he had in mind a
noble purpose. (Letter, Andrews to Randolph 1943:1)

Andrews then evoked the rhetoric of the Lost Cause, a southern ideology
that justified the South's secession from the Union. Andrews claimed a
depoliticized monument that conjures the feeling of heroism would be
more suitable at Harpers Ferry.

. . . that phrase about "human freedom" will be interpreted in its context
as pointing to a war waged by one side with such a purpose in view and
by the other in opposition thereto. . . . Such a "Monument" could well be
set apart in memory of heroism on either side; or, as it should be,
heroism on both sides. If this should be announced purport of the bill,
the monument would rest on a solid foundation rather than the sands of
variant opinions. (Letter, Andrews to Randolph 1943:1)

The United Daughters of the Confederacy (U.D.C.) simultaneously protested the legislation to create a monument at Harpers Ferry. An earlier
attempt by Randolph to establish "The John Brown Park" was met with a
storm of protests. In 1943 the president of the U.D.C. wrote "Now, by a
different wording 'The Harpers Ferry National Monument,' you are again
trying to accomplish the same thing in a new covering, but underneath is
the same old skeleton" (Letter, Powell to Randolph 1943:1)

      The creation of a national monument falls under the jurisdiction of
the 1906 Antiquities Act, which allows the president to create national
monuments without congressional approval. President Roosevelt signed
legislation in 1944 to create Harpers Ferry National Monument. Next, the
states of Maryland and West Virginia acquired 1,500 acres in Lower Town,
Maryland Heights, Loudoun Heights, and other areas to commemorate
"historic events at or near Harpers Ferry" (Murfin 1989:29). In 1954 West
Virginia donated lands for the creation of the monument. In 1963 Maryland made additional land donations and the area became Harpers Ferry
National Historical Park.

      The tourist industry thrives once again in Harpers Ferry. Each year,
close to a half-million people visit. They enjoy the scenery and learn about
the towns nationally significant past. People visit exhibits, Civil War fortifications, industrial ruins, and John Brown's Fort. John Brown's Fort

stands as a national icon that contributes to the town's significance and is a major site that all visitors come to see.

The park has struggled with interpreting the town's Victorian history because there are no histories of "great men" from this era. Rather, many working-class individuals who worked, struggled, and survived in a small industrial and tourist town played an important role in the story of Harpers Ferry. Nationally significant events occurred at Harpers Ferry during this Victorian era, such as the 1906 Niagara Movement, and the park has recently begun to celebrate this historic event. It is equally important for a working-class history to be told. Archaeology plays a role in discovering and presenting these histories as part of our national story. Through discovering, identifying, and interpreting artifacts from domestic sites, such as the Boardinghouses of Mrs. Stipes and James McGraw's Boardinghouses, archaeology can help reveal histories that have been lost, ignored, or subverted.

"The Handsomest House in Two Towns"

4

Urban Development of an Elite Household in Harpers Ferry

BACKGROUND

After the Civil War, a new industrial elite emerged across America and in Harpers Ferry as well. New town leaders and entrepreneurs replaced the entrenched hierarchy. The tension that developed between the old elite and the new entrepreneurs is often overlooked whenever Harpers Ferry's postbellum history is discussed today. Conflict and change issues are often averted for histories that discuss stability and prosperity.

In particular, I examine the Hurst household and their use of one of the more prominent structures in the town's business district, the new master armorer's house. Their tenure in Lower Town Harpers Ferry is characterized by their prosperity, entrepreneurialship, and eventual demise. James Garland Hurst and his wife Elizabeth Tearney Hurst occupied the new master armorer's house from the 1880s through 1920. Living on Shenandoah Street, in the center of the commercial district, they represented a new entrepreneurial commitment to the town's redevelopment. James was part of the new local Democratic Conservatives who believed in the industrialization and the exploitation of the county's mineral resources to redevelop the area's economy after the war. Both James and Elizabeth participated in community activities and worked vigorously for the town's revitalization. They thought improvement and beautification projects would help reindustrialize the town and people would see that Harpers Ferry was a suitable place to live, work, and vacation.

The historical documentation and archaeological remains of the Hurst family provide insight into this upper class household and show how a memory of one of Harpers Ferry's elite developed (Figure 24). A close examination of the archaeological materials allows us to challenge this public memory and break down preconceived notions about people, groups, and class stereotypes.

75

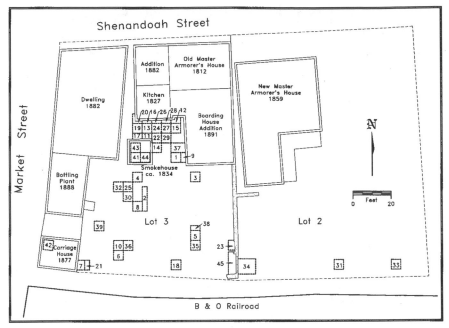

Figure 24. Excavations behind two urban lots in Lower Town Harpers Ferry. The Hursts occupied the New Master Armorer's House built in 1859. (Drawn by John Ravenhorst)

EARLY POSTBELLUM USE OF AN URBAN LOT

In 1859, the completion of the new master armorer's quarters, which the Hursts eventually inhabited in the 1880s, followed the general rehabilitation of the armory grounds in Lower Town. Renovations included the replacement of derelict fences and the filling and grading of the yards. Superintendent Barbour reported in June 1860 that "the quarters of the Master Armorer, Paymaster, and Clerks have received many additions to them, to render them comfortable, and the grounds, which were very rough, have been graded and improved" (quoted in Fisher 1989:42).

While the new master armorer's dwelling only served to house an armory official for less than a year, it later served municipal and private functions after the Civil War (for more than 99 percent of its existence). The National Park Service, until recently, interpreted the building as the master armorer's house, and an additional exhibit in the building told the story about the armory's history. No attention was devoted to either the building's use or the social conditions of the town after the Civil War. Historical archaeology allows us to collect additional information that helps create a more inclusive history of the building, the people, and the town.

After the Civil War, the government leased the new master armorer's house to several families, and the Department of War removed the property from the 1869 auction. In 1872, the Corporation of Harpers Ferry petitioned the Secretary of War to allow the town to use the new master armorer's house for public benefit since the town needed a townhouse, schoolhouse, jail, and a stationhouse. The new master armorer's house simultaneously served all of these functions. In 1880, the structure contained a post office, school, mayor's office, council room, and jail. Mrs. Trail, her two children, daughter-in-law, and two grandchildren rented the balance of the house, and often took in boarders to subsidize their income. While the property was being leased, John Koonce became its custodian for the United States government. As did many of his contemporaries in town and as part of following a growing trend in the United States, he paid some attention to health and hygiene concerns. In 1883 he had the "water closets" cleaned for the new master armorer's house. The term "water closet" was a euphemism for the outdoor household privy. While water closets became fashionable among the elite during this era, and historical and archaeological documentation shows that only a privy existed on the lot. Koonce moved it to the southwest corner of the property where it existed until the beginning of the 20th century.

HURST OCCUPATION: 1884–1920

The Hurst Household

The federal government auctioned the new master armorer's house in 1884 along with other Harpers Ferry government properties and water rights. Colonel James Garland Hurst, a prominent community member, purchased the house and lived there with his wife Elizabeth Tearney, the daughter of Edward Tearney, a prominent Harpers Ferry resident and one of James' major business partners. They did not have any children, but the household included a 23-year-old mulatto servant, John Baltimore. Servants remained part of the Hurst household for a good portion of their occupation at this home on Shenandoah Street.

Contemporary Victorian reformers wrote books and articles in popular magazines such as *The Ladies Home Journal*, about the abolishment of domestic servants. Since *The Ladies Home Journal* had wide appeal, it probably reached the literate wealthy class of Harpers Ferrians. The reformers claimed that servants should not exist in a democratic America.

Others argued that the household woman should be proficient in house-work, and domestic servants did not allow a housewife to do her duty (Hale 1844:127–128; Beecher and Stowe 1994 [1869]). Despite their ef-forts, these reformers failed to eliminate domestic servants in the United States, and the Hursts also continued to employ at least one throughout their lives.

The middle and upper classes did not believe servants knew proper and efficient housework techniques, although they did see them as "a necessary evil." *The Laws of Etiquette* (1836:185) noted that "all you can do is to take the most decent creature who applies, trust in providence, and lock everything up." The middle-class family felt obliged to teach the ser-vant middle-class etiquette. One author wrote:

> Some attention is absolutely necessary, in this country, to the training of servants, as they come here from the lowest ranks of English and Irish peasantry, with as much idea of politeness as the pig domesticated in the cabin of the latter. (Hartley 1860:242–243)

Household Work; or, Duties of a Female Servant (1863) provided actual guidelines for a maid-of-all-work, a house and parlor maid, and laundry maid. The manual provides guidelines for which household tasks should be done by the maid. These include completing morning duties, such as preparing breakfast; cleaning bedrooms, making beds, and chang-ing bedding; cleaning stone hearths, floors, doorsteps, the passage, halls, etc.; cleaning the stove and fire irons; cleaning the parlor and drawing room; cleaning the library or study; making the dinner, tea, and supper; washing plates, dishes, etc.; the cleaning of plate and silver; and washing laundry.

In 1890, *Good Housekeeping* said, "In spite of the fact that the larger portion of domestic servants are of low order of intelligence and abso-lutely unfamiliar with any of the refinements or necessities of modern life, they are excellent servants" (Campbell 1890c:279). Another article in *Good Housekeeping* suggested that servants were "stupid, awkward, and unintel-ligent" (House Service 1889:180). Nevertheless, domestic servants assisted the Hurst household. They also created an image of status for the Hursts within the Harpers Ferry community.

Interaction Within the Harpers Ferry Community

James Hurst served as deputy sheriff from 1874 and was appointed sheriff in 1883 after the death of the incumbent. The *Spirit of Jefferson* (27 March 1883:3) asserted "Mr. Hurst is well known to our people, and it is sufficient to say that a more popular or satisfactory appointment could not have been made." The following year, Hurst and a close business associate, Charles Trail, were elected sheriff and assessor of Harpers Ferry, respectively. Trail led a successful business career despite losing his arm in the Child–McCreight flour mill on Virginius Island in 1871 (Chickering and Jenkins 1994:62). At the time of his appointment to sheriff, Hurst was 36 years old and had been living in town since 1877. Harpers Ferrians reelected him sheriff in 1893, but he resigned in May 1895 (*FA* 2 May 1900:3; *SoJ* 7 May 1895:3).

His resignation came just before the scheduled execution of a convicted murderer, an black man named Andrew Scott. During this period, sheriffs acted as executioners. One person wrote in the *Farmers Advocate* (12 May 1900:2) that Hurst's resignation allowed him to avoid responsibility for the hanging. The newspaper also accused Hurst of courting Republican voters (*FA* 12 May 1900:2).

The next year, Harpers Ferrians elected him to the West Virginia State Legislature. Together, Hurst and Trail acquired a substantial portion of the town and greatly profited from their ventures. Hurst, his father-in-law Edward Tearney, and Trail incorporated the Harpers Ferry General Improvement Company in 1884 to "encourage manufacturing, community hygiene and beautification, and promote Harpers Ferry as a permanent place of residence and summer resort" (Chickering and Jenkins 1994:62–63). Newspaper accounts from 1887 say Hurst, also encouraged by the rejuvenation of Harpers Ferry, repaired his front sidewalk and improved Fillmore Street in the Camp Hill area (*SoJ* 15 November 1887:3). Hurst's domicile, considered the most "elaborately finished and furnished house in Harpers Ferry," was ruined in the 1889 flood (*SoJ* 4 June 1889:2). Rehabilitated by 1897, Hurst's home had the "most beautiful lawns of any house in two towns [Harpers Ferry and neighboring Bolivar]" (*SoJ* 7 December 1897:3).

In 1890, Trail, Hurst, and Tearney founded both the Harpers Ferry and Loudoun Bridge Company and the Harpers Ferry branch of the Southern Building and Loan Association. That same year, Hurst and Trail joined Will and Charles Rau of Bolivar to establish the Rau Mining and Manufacturing Company. In 1895, Hurst and Trail built a flour mill near Harpers Ferry. Hurst soon after became president of the Mutual German Savings and Loan Association in Wheeling, while Trail speculated for oil near Martinsburg. By 1898, both Trail and Hurst were influential members of the board of directors for the Harpers Ferry Light and Power Company. They helped negotiate a contract with the Harpers Ferry Paper Company to supply power for the town's first electric street lighting (Chickering and Jenkins 1994). Hurst became so popular that in 1896, a Charles Town band serenaded him (*VFP* 26 August 1896:3).

The national economic downturn of 1890s affected the Hurst family.

In financial trouble, Hurst sold his house in 1896 for $6,000 and his farm near Duffields (outside of Harpers Ferry) for $8,000 to his father-in-law. Hurst's farm consisted of 157 acres and produced corn and possibly potatoes. When he sold it, the farm had "6 mules, 4 horses and colts, 14 cows and cattle, 28 sheep, 1 buck, 24 hogs, 2 sows and pigs, and 1 boar" (*SoJ* 25 November 1902:2).

Tearney allowed the Hursts to remain in their home. Tearney either gave or sold Hurst's property to his wife Elizabeth. Though Hurst was in financial straights, people still considered him "one of, if not the most, personally popular man [sic] in the county . . ."(*FA* 5 May 1900:3).

In 1902, J. Garland Hurst declared bankruptcy. Tearney died the same year. After Tearney's death in 1902, the property was conveyed to Elizabeth Hurst. Elizabeth purchased the property in 1908 from special commissioners in a chancery suit (Chickering et al. 1994).

Hurst's liabilities amounted to about $75,000. By 1915, his health began to fail. In that year Harpers Ferrians elected him to the city council even though he was ill. From 1915 until 1920 Hurst was bedridden for extended periods. His health declined steadily, and both he and his wife Elizabeth died within a few months of each other in 1920. Elizabeth Hurst's estate at the time of her death in 1920 included $5,504.16 in real estate, $10,346.12 in bank bonds, and stocks, and personal property totaling $26,717.15. J. Garland had three life insurance policies worth less than $3,000 (*Accounts of Fiduciary* 1921 P.6).

AN ARCHAEOLOGY OF THE HURST FAMILY

Much of the archaeological information for the Hurst family comes from a privy that dates back to the 1890s. It is likely that Hurst constructed this latrine after 1884. He must have cleaned it out at least once because it did not contain any diagnostic materials that dated to earlier than 1891. The latrine seems to have fallen out of use in the early 20th century when the Hursts introduced indoor plumbing to their home. During that period, Hurst filled the privy with various types of material, including clay, brick, rubble, and sand.

Health Conditions among the Hurst Family

The Hursts's role in the general health and development of the town is often understood as an important part of Harpers Ferry's postbellum history. Surprisingly, the story is more of a myth that tries to reinforce our expectations of "good old days." For instance, the Hurst privy consisted of a brick superstructure set on top of a mortar-laid shale foundation nearly 14 feet deep. The superstructure was dismantled by the National Park Service in the 1950s. The vault's dimensions are 3.5 feet × 5.5 feet. All four walls are pargetted on the top visible portions. However, there was no pargetting on the southern half of the west wall, facing the boardinghouse privy. Privy matter therefore could leach from the latrine away from the domestic structure (Ford 1993).

Karl Reinhard (1993, 1994) tested the soil from the Hurst privy for parasite remains. His analysis provides important information about the general health of one of Harpers Ferry's leading families. His tests reveal that both intestinal roundworm and whipworm existed in high frequencies (Table 2). The concentration and amount of parasite eggs found in the Hurst latrine were greater than those found in the boardinghouse privy, a contemporaneous deposit found next door (see Chapter 6) (Reinhard 1994). This higher proportion of parasites is surprising, especially since the Hursts were proponents for general health reforms in town. A look at some national trends may be useful in understanding this anomaly.

In the late 19th century, many people proposed the use of human waste to fertilize gardens, following similar practices in many other areas of the world. Catherine Beecher and Harriet Beecher Stowe (1994 [1869]:403–404) promoted earthen closets as being more economical than a water system for removing human fecal waste. First, it was cheaper and more efficient than plumbing, especially in the early days of plumbing. Second, they claimed human waste could be used as a valuable product for fertilization.

> It is only of late years that attention has been turned to the employment of sewage as a manure—in this country, at least, for in many others its value has long been recognized. . . . The earth of the garden, if dried and powdered clay—will suck up the liquid part of the privy-soil; and, if applied at once and carefully mixed, will destroy all bad smell and all nasty appearance in the solid part, and will keep all of the value of the

Table 2. Concentration Values for Parasite Eggs per Milliliter of Soil in the Hurst Privy.[a]

Layer	T. Trichiura	A. Lumbricoides	N
G	None	141	1
G2	570	5,650	11
G3	1,130	21,470	40
H2	None	2,260	4
I			None present

(N) number of eggs counted
[a]Reinhard (1993:13.2)

> manure. . . . The proper way to apply it to your garden is either to powder
> or sift it, and scatter it in small quantities over your seed beds of cabbage,
> turnips, onions, or lettuce. Or if putting in peas or beans, then mix with
> water. . . . (Cassell's 1875:247)

They recommended that cleaning of the privy vault should occur about
twice a year "which is always worth the cost of removal as manure"
(Goodholme 1877:166).

During the same time period, *Cassell's Household Management*
(1875:302), a late 19th-century household management guide, noted that
worms existed as a common health problem, although the causes were
still unknown and were not associated with the use of human waste as
fertilizer.

> Worms are not so common in human beings, even in children, as is
> generally supposed. They are very rarely met within young children under
> a year. They are more frequently met within the children of the poor,
> which is probably due to the fact of their being ill-fed, and to their
> houses being badly ventilated and unhealthy. (Cassell's 1875:302)

The manual identified three principal worms: small threadworm, roundworm, and tapeworm. Thoroughly cooked food help to prevent the disease.
Some health reformers thought too much fruit, too much sugar, and
underdone meat helped to stimulate the diseases. They recognized tape
worms as a product from undercooked pork. Manuals prescribed various
household remedies (Cassell's 1875:302).

Treatment for the small threadworm was performed with an enema.
The remedy included tincture of perchloride of iron (1/2 drachm) infusion
of quassia (eight ounces). The manual prescribed that injection of one-
sixth of the formula into the bowel every other night until the symptoms
cleared. Treatment for the roundworm included drinking two or three
grains of satonine for one or two nights, followed by a dose of castor oil
the next morning. Treatment for tapeworm included the oil of a male fern
(1/2–1 drachm), mucilage of an acacia (one ounce), and peppermint water
(one ounce) (Cassell's 1875:302).

Only parasitic worms are noticeable in the Hurst privy, but there is a
strong likelihood that other fecal-borne protozoa and bacteria, which have
life cycles similar to the worms, existed. Like the parasites found in the
boardinghouse privy, protozoa species *Giardia lambia* and *Entamoeba
hystolitica* and bacteria genera such as *Salmonella* and *Shigella* are present
in the Hurst privy. The Hurst household suffered from pathogen-induced
diarrhea (Reinhard 1993). The presence of heal-all seeds in the latrine also
confirms the household's poor medical condition. People usually used heal-
all as a traditional treatment for fevers and diarrhea (Cummings 1993:7.10).

Generally, children were more often infected with intestinal parasites than adults. The mortality rate was high throughout the nineteenth century and the infant mortality rate stood even higher. Currently in the United States the infant mortality rate is between 11 and 12 per 1,000 live births (*Information Please Almanac* 1986). Infant mortality in late 19th-century Harpers Ferry ran at 127.5 per 1,000 live births (determined from Jefferson County Birth and Death Records 1870–1879), or at a rate ten times greater than today. People often attributed infant deaths to "brain fever, cholera infantum, inflammation of bowels," and many "unknowns" (Jefferson County Birth and Death Records 1868–1872; Larsen 1993:11.3, 1994:71).

Since the Hursts did not have children living in their household there must be some other explanation for their high infestation of parasites. One clue may exist in a local newspaper. The *Spirit of Jefferson* described their lawn as the handsomest in two towns, surrounding the house "like green velvet" (*SoJ* 12 July 1898: 1). The Hursts may have fertilized their garden and lawn with organic materials from their own privy. Diseases related to parasites infestation would have been transported to the rest of the family if they did not thoroughly wash their vegetables. The decline in James Garland Hurst's health, starting around 1915, may well be related, at least in part, to these parasitic diseases. The strong likelihood that pathogen-induced diarrhea existed, indicated by the presence of heal-all in the privy, provides other clues suggest reasons for Hurst's health problems.

The Hursts' general health condition can be further explained in the general context of Americans' changing attitudes toward medication. In the late 19th century a conflict between self-medication and professional medicines raged. *Cassell's Household Guide* (1875:41) and other late 19th-century household management guides (see for instance Allen 1878; Austin 1885) noted the appropriateness of self medication. The manual gave a few symptoms that should always be seen as grave enough to justify seeing a doctor. The first symptom was *rigor*, or stiff coldness. Most fevers were thought to begin with this condition. The second symptom was unusually high temperature. Diseases, such as scarlet fever, whooping cough, caused high fevers (Cassell's 1875:186, 226).

George Austin (1885:186), a proponent of self cures, suggested "many diseases of early life may be arrested by very simple remedies, if properly applied. Drugs are sometimes unnecessary, where articles of diet can be made to serve as medicines."

An analysis of glass containers recovered during the archaeological excavations provides information on medicinal use and general health conditions of the Hurst household. Identifiable bottles fit into six broad categories: medicine, alcohol, chemical, food, ink, and personal (Table 3). Of these glass vessels, 25 percent are medicine-related, but alcohol bottles make up the largest category (*n* = 55, 45.1 percent) (Larsen 1993).

Table 3. Glass Vessels Present in the the Hurst Privy

Container type	N	Percent
Medicine	30	24.6
Alcohol	55	45.1
Chemical	18	14.8
Food	0	0.0
Ink	3	2.5
Personal	2	1.6
Other	14	11.5
Total	**122**	**100.0**

(N) total number of containers; (Percent) percentage of identifiable bottles.
[a]from Larsen 1993:11.36.

Some archaeologists speculate there was a high consumption of medicine in the 19th century, particularly because of the often high alcohol and narcotic content of medicines (Bond 1989). I believe that the general health conditions of the era also need to be considered (also see Larsen 1993). Thirty medicinal bottles are identified from the Hurst privy, although only nine had embossed markings on them (Table 4). Labels from the other 21 bottles did not survive. One bottle, a digestive remedy, is a Buffalo Lithia Springs Water bottle, advertised as "useful in eliminating Kidney Stones, [and] Uric Acid" (Fike 1987:242).

Also present are two local prescription medicine bottles, "a sign of professional care through either a physician's prescription or a pharmacist's recommendation" (Larsen 1993:11.36). The bottles include MisKimon, a Harpers Ferry pharmacist, and C. Frank Jones, Ph.G., from Charlestown,

Table 4. Identifiable Medicine Bottles Found in the Hurst Privy

Container type	N	Percent
Digestive remedies	1	11.11
Pain killers	0	0.0
Tooth care	0	0.0
Child care	0	0.0
National Cures	3	33.33
Prescriptions	2	22.22
Other	3	33.33
Total	**9**	**100.0**

(N) total number of bottles; (Percent) percentage of identifiable bottles.
[a]from Larsen 1993:11.36.

West Virginia. Other identifiable bottles include a Fellows Syrup of Hypophosphites bottle, and a bottle of Acker's English Remedy. Three dioxygen bottles that held hydrogen peroxide were also present.

There were no bottles corresponding to pain killers, dental care, or pediatric care. The lack of pediatric medicines further supports the historical records there were no children to contribute to the high parasitic rate found in the Hurst privy. Proprietary medicines include a single Jos. R. Stonebraker & Co. bottle. Generally, the amount of medicine bottles associated with the Hurst occupation is dramatically smaller than the contemporaneous boardinghouse occupation next door (see Chapter 6).

Ritualized Dining among the Hurst Family

Household goods, such as ceramics, are a good indication of a family's general wealth and can serve as evidence of the Victorian guidelines that may have structured the Hursts' daily lives. Some published etiquette manuals show the various contemporary rituals associated with dining, and these manuals help provide a context for the ceramic assemblage found associated with the Hurst household.

For instance, *Cassell's Household Guide* (1875:371) notes three forms of setting the dinner table: Old English, French, and Russian (also see Lucas 1994 for an excellent analysis).

The Russian service is the most formal. At the initial seating no food is on the table except bowls of candy and nuts. All of the serving is done from the pantry or a serving table. The food is in serving dishes. Each person helps himself or herself, or portions are arranged upon everyone's plate and placed at their setting (Adams 1917:49). The courses are passed from the hosts' left side. A la Russe has been described as the simplest and most elegant manner of dining (Schuyler 1893:26).

The old English service is more informal. The food is placed on the table and served by the head of the table. If a maid is present, she passes the served food to each person; if a maid is not present, then this is done by those who are seated at the table (Adams 1917:49). By the 1870s the old English style fell out of favor, especially since social reformers called for the abolition of servants and maids.

The French style required the dishes, elaborately garnished, be placed before the host and hostess to give the guests an opportunity to admire the array of food. The dishes then would be removed. The meat would be carved and the meal would be served. By the 1890s the French custom in serving was out of style, even among the French (Schuyler 1893:26).

The mixed service is a combination of the Russian and English styles. Some courses are served "from the side" (Russian), and some "from the table" (English). The meats should be served from the table (English), and the vegetables served from the side (Russian).

Progressive dinner parties were in fashion during the mid-1890s. At these dinners, the men would have remained in their seats while the women changed seats and dinner companion with each course. That means that the hostess must have as many courses as there were couples present at the table. The host had a small bell that he would ring at the end of each course. Quotations for the women's guest cards state at the end of each course: "Westward the course of the empire takes its way," thus showing the direction of rotation. The other cards may read, "Press bravely on-ward," "Let us be then up and doing," "Onward, onward may we press," "A lovely apparition sent to be a moment's ornament." The men's cards would state "How happy could I be with either, were t'other dear charmer away," "Welcome the coming, speed the going guest," "We must endure their going hence, even as their coming hither," "variety's the very spice of life" (Langigan 1896:21).

The Hursts may have followed one of these ritual dinner services since they had the domestic service to help with any formalities. Michael Lucas (1993) performed the vessel analysis for tableware associated with the Hurst family. His analysis provides some clues about their dining rituals.

Tableware is the largest ceramic functional group (Table 5). The Hursts had a variety of individual tableware forms such as butter pats, bowls, and sauce dishes. They also had a large selection of various plate sizes. The tableware assemblage is relatively expensive and includes items such as French porcelain and transfer-printed ware. More than a fourth of the vessel forms is used for drinking tea and coffee. Many of these items are porcelains. Demitasse cups are also present, which "suggest that there was a greater amount of separation and formality practiced" at the Hurst household (Lucas 1993:14.9).

The dinner and tea sets in the Hurst assemblage are similar to the ones advertised in *The Ladies' Home Journal* (1889 October VI(II):23) (Figure 25). The advertisement explained:

> In all homes of culture and refinement, fine table ware is considered a necessity. Especially for entertaining company, a neat and attractive table should be considered indispensable. Ladies of refinement and taste, appreciate dainty china, and where the cost has hitherto proven a barrier to its acquisition, a set can not be secured fully equal to that of your wealthy neighbor, without the expenditure of any money.

The advertisement tells women that they could acquire dinner and tea sets at reduced prices by convincing their friends and neighbors to subscribe to *The Ladies' Home Journal*. The Venice hand-decorated tea set could be acquired for 30 subscriptions at $1.00 per year, or for 20 subscriptions

Table 5. Ceramic Vessel Forms Present in the Hurst Privy[a]

Functional category	Form	Context A (1890s)		
		N	Percent T	Percent F
Tableware	Plate 9 in.	0	0	0
	Plate 8.5 in.	1	6	3
	Plate 8 in.	2	12	6
	Plate 7.5 in.	3	18	10
	Plate 7 in	1	6	3
	Plate diameter	1	6	6
	Platter	2	12	6
	Butter pat	5	29	16
	Bowl	1	6	3
	Sauce dish	1	6	3
	Pitcher	0	0	0
	Baker	0	0	0
	Creamer	0	0	0
	Other	0	0	0
Subtotal		**17**	**100**	**55**
Tea and coffee ware	Cup	5	63	16
	Saucer	3	38	10
	Tea pot	0	0	0
Subtotal		**8**	**10**	**26**
Preparation storage	Crock/jar	2	100	6
	Pie plates	0	0	0
	Unidentifiable	0	0	0
Subtotal		**2**	**100**	**6**
Personal	Chamber pot	1	100	3
	Ewer	0	0	0
	Basin	0	0	0
	Slop jar	0	0	0
	Toothbrush holder	0	0	0
	Soap dish	0	0	0
	Chamber lids	0	0	0
Subtotal		**1**	**100**	**3**
Other vessels	Flowerpot	1	33	3
	Flowerpot saucer	1	33	3
	Other/unidentifiable	1	33	3
Total		**31**	**NA**	**100**

(N) total number of vessel forms found; (Percentage F) percentage of functional group; (Percentage T) percentage of total assemblage.
[a]from Lucas 1993:14.8

plus $2.50, or 10 subscriptions and $5.00 extra. The set sold for $9.00.

The Pearl Lace pattern dinnerware, which retailed for $14, could also be acquired for 35 subscriptions. The fewer the subscriptions, the higher the cost to the purchaser. The dinnerware was advertised as an

VENICE HAND-DECORATED TEA SET.
FULL SIZE 53 PIECES.

Given for 30 subscribers at $1.00 per year; or, for only 20 subscribers and $2.50 extra; or, for 10 subscribers and $5.00 extra.   Sent by Freight or Express, charges to be paid by the receiver.

Figure 25. Venice hand-decorated tea set advertised in the *Ladies' Home Journal*, 1889. The Hurst assemblage contained similar decorative patterns. (Courtesy, The Winterthur Library: Printed Books and Periodical Collection)

English underglaze pattern "by one of the oldest and most reliable potteries there, each piece bearing their imprint, and they cannot be excelled for quality and durability" (*The Ladies' Home Journal* 1889 October VI(II):23) (Figure 26). The decoration in the border has a soft pearl color,

> of a delicate spray of flowers, gracefully interwoven, producing a most pleasing effect. The design is first printed on the body of the goods, and afterwards covered by the glaze of the ware itself. The design then becomes part and parcel of the goods, rendering it impossible to remove it. This is an especially desirable feature, and one that cannot be attained in the over-glaze decoration. (*The Ladies' Home Journal* 1889 October VI(II):23)

The national appeal of *The Ladies' Home Journal*, and the strong marketing appeal of articles and advertisements in this journal and other similar ladies' journals, made it possible that Elizabeth Hurst may have been influenced by this national media.

Other matched sets that belonged to the Hursts have elaborate decoration and include a greater variety and number of vessel forms per set. The largest set is the "Indus" transfer-printed pattern, registered on June 15, 1877, by Ridgway, Sparks, and Ridgway (Kamm 1951:75). The set contains two butter pats, one platter, one plate, one demitasse cup, and

OUR NEW 75-PIECE DINNER SET.
"Gem" Shape. "Lace" Pattern.
Given as a premium for a club of 35 yearly subscribers at $1.00 each;
or, for 30 subscribers and $1.25; or, 25 subscribers and $2.50;
or, 20 subscribers and $3.75 additional. Sent carefully packed, by
freight or express, charges to be paid by the receiver.

Figure 26. Lace pattern dinner set advertised in the Ladies' Home Journal, 1889. The
Hurst assemblage contained similar decorative patterns. (Courtesy, The Winterthur Library:
Printed Books and Periodical Collection)

one tea cup (Figure 27). The second largest matched set, containing two
plates and two butter pats, is an undecorated French porcelain set made
by R. Delinieres and Company, Limoges, France (Kovel and Kovel 1986:170;
Lucas 1993:14.11).

Twenty-one glass vessels are present and they relate to the Hursts'
dining practices. Most of these vessels (50 percent, n = 11) are unmatched
tumblers, although three matching stemware vessels are present. Also
included are berry dishes, which may have been acquired through mail
order catalogs and used as part of a centerpiece (Sears, Roebuck & Co.
1970; The American Potter & Illuminator 1886; Lucas 1993:14.12–14.13).

The Hurst's tableware assemblage, which consists of relatively costly
items and large matched sets, indicates their household observed formal
dining practices. Since the Hursts were leading social and political family
figures, they likely held many formal dinners at their house. At least one
newspaper account documented their hosting a formal dinner (SoJ 7 No-

Figure 27. Indus pattern set from the Hurst assemblage. (Photograph by Cari Young Ravenhorst).

vember 1892:2) while other newspaper accounts reported that Elizabeth organized many private and public dinners (*SoJ* 1884:3, 1897:3, 1900a:3, 1900b:2, 1900c:3, 1902:2, 1903:3; *Harpers Ferry Times* 14 September 1906:5, 4 January 1907:5; also, see Lucas 1994:85).

The Hurst tableware assemblage contains an impressive collection of glassware and ceramics. Tumblers, berry glasses, and stemmed wine glasses graced their table. Complete sets of ceramics with a variety of forms are also present. With this formal service and Elizabeth's reputation for catering elaborate dinners, the Hursts carried out one of the more formal serving practices in their home.

Of particular interest is the elegant French porcelain set, with eight-inch plates. The smaller dinner plates would allow for a centerpiece, and less food would be placed on a smaller plate than a larger one, facilitating the service of multiple courses. The aid of a servant would have enabled the Hursts to carry out formal dining practices at home. This assemblage would have let Elizabeth and James to live up to their "social reputation, supporting and creating the family's influence" (Lucas 1994:89).

A wide range of fruits and vegetables are present in the Hurst assemblage (Cummings 1993, 1994) (Table 6). Fig is the only exotic fruit found. Locally grown fruits consumed by the Hursts include strawberry, rasp-

Table 6. Macrofloral Remains Recovered from the Hurst Privy[a]

Identification	Part	Char whole	Char frag	Unch whole	Unch frag
1890s: Layer G					
Compositae cf. Solidago	Seed			1	
Ficus (fig)	Seed		21*		
Ficus/Fragaria	Seed				14*
Fragaria (strawberry)	Seed		46*		
Gaylussacia (huckleberry)	Seed		10		
Lycopersicon (tomato)	Seed		362*	140*	
cf. Physalia sp.	Seed			1	
Rubus (raspberry)	Seed		876*	36*	
Vaccinium (blueberry)	Seed		2		
Vitis (grape)	Seed		28	153*	
Unidentifiable	Seed		2		
1890s: Layer G-2					
Apium graveolens (celery)	Seed		14		
Cheno-am	Seed		1		
cf. Cruciferae	Seed		2		
Cucumis sp.	Seed			3	
Ficus (fig)	Seed		15*		
Ficus/Fragaria	Seed			23*	
Fragaria (strawberry)	Seed		73*		
Gaylussacia (huckleberry)	Seed		26*		
Lycopersicon (tomato)	Seed		400*	272*	
Physalis (tomatillo)	Seed		1		
cf. Prunus sp. (Cheery)	Seed			1	
Rubus (raspberry)	Seed			51*	
Vaccinium (blueberry)	Seed		20	5	
Vitis (grape)	Seed		67*	14*	
Unidentifiable	cf. Berry	2			
Unidentifiable	Seed			1	
1890s: Layer H					
cf. Apium (celery)	Seed		12	1	
Citrullus (watermelon)	Seed			1	
Cucimis sp.	Seed				1
Ficus	Seed		15*		
Ficus/Fragaria	Seed			2*	
Fragaria (strawberry)	Seed		5*		
Gaylussacia (huckleberry)	Seed		126*	2*	
Solanaceae cf. Capsicum (hot pepper)	Seed		1		
Lycopersicon (tomato)	Seed		544*	72*	
Physalia (tomatillo)	Seed		1		
Rubus (raspberry)	Seed		543*	18*	
Vaccinium (blueberry)	Seed		6		
Vitis (grape)	Seed		35*	6*	

Continued

Table 6. Continued

Identification	Part	Char whole	Char frag	Unch whole	Unch frag
1890s: Layer G-3					
Apium (celery)	Seed		5		
Brassica sp.	Seed		4		
Bromus cf. marginatus	Seed		1		
Citrullus sp. (Watermelon)	Seed		3	1	
Coriandrum (coriander)	Seed		1		
Cucimis sp.	Seed			5	
Ficus (fig)	Seed		168*		
Ficus/Fragaria	Seed			11*	
Fragaria (strawberry)	Seed		163*		
Gaylussacia (huckleberry)	Seed		87*	2*	
Labiatae	Seed		1		
Lycopersicon (tomato)	Seed		1839*	304*	
Malus sp. (apple)	Seed		1		
Physalis (tomatillo)	Seed		16*		
Portulaca	Seed		1		
Prunus sp. (cherry)	Seed		6		
Rubus (raspberry)	Seed		3272*	117*	
Vaccinium (blueberry)	Seed		10*		
Vitis (grape)	Seed		279*	16*	
1890s: Layer H-2					
Amaranthus sp. (pigweed)	Seed		1		
Apium graveolens (celery)	Seed		3	14*	
Brassica juncea (mustard)	Seed		2		
cf. Brassicaceae	Seed		2	2	
Citrullus (watermelon)	Seed			1	
Coriandrum (coriander)	Seed		3	1	
Cucimis sp. (cantaloupe & cucumber)	Seed		5	4	
Cyprus cf. rotundus	Seed		1		
Ficus (fig)	Seed		25*		
Ficus/Fragaria	Seed			2*	
Fragaria (strawberry)	Seed		129*		
Gaylussacia (huckleberry)	Seed		222*	68*	
Lycopersicon (tomato)	Seed		763*	77*	
cf. Lycopersicon	Seed		1		
Malus (apple)	Seed		1	1	
Prunus sp. (cherry)	Seed		1		
Rubus (raspberry)	Seed		1825*	67*	
Vaccinium (blueberry)	Seed		2		
Vitis (grape)	Seed		116*	13*	
Unknown J	Seed		1		
Unidentified	Seed			1	
Unidentifiable	Seed			4	
Unidentifiable	Seed			18	

Continued

Table 6. Continued

Identification	Part	Char whole	Char frag	Unch whole	Unch frag
1890s: Layer I					
Amaranthus sp.	Seed		4		
Brassica sp.	Seed			1	
Cucumis sp.	Seed			1	
Cyprus sp.	Seed		2		
Digitaria sanguinalis (crabgrass)	Seed		2		
Eleucine cf. indica	Seed		1		
Ficus (fig)	Seed		178*		
Ficus/Fragaria	Seed			16*	
Fragaria (strawberry)	Seed		357*		
Gaylassacia (huckleberry)	Seed		22	3	
Lycopersicon (tomatoe)	Seed		36	4	
Oxalis cf. stricta	Seed		1		
Portulaca (purslane/moss rose)	Seed		10	1	
Prunus sp. (cherry)	Seed		1		
Rubus (raspberry)	Seed		120*		
Vitis (grape)	Seed		1	15	1
Unidentified tissue	Docit			1	
Unidentified tissue	Monocot		2		

*indicates an estimated seed or seed fragment frequency based on a sorted portion of the total volume floated.
[a]from Cummings 1993:7.30

berry, black huckleberry, grape, cherry, apple, celery, huckleberry, blueberry, and watermelon (Cummings 1993:7.21–7.40). Vegetables are present in smaller quantities. They include tomato, cucumber/cantaloupe, and tomatillo or ground cherry. Mustard seeds were probably used as part of a condiment or as an ingredient of all kinds of pickles, such as cucumber pickles, tomato pickles, etc. (Cummings 1993:7.21–7.40).

The examination of biomass from an archaeological site becomes important when figuring out the relative importance of meat. Biomass is calculated by examining the relationship between bone weight and the total live weight (which includes the bone and meat). Placing the bone weight in a regression formula, a zooarchaeologist can calculate the meat weight in relationship to the existing bones. The zooarchaeologist can then calculate the relative importance of specific meat in a household's diet based on these biomass calculations.

Faunal analyses suggest the Hursts relied on fish for part of their diet (Table 7). The known species include sucker, bass, sunfish, bluegill, and smallmouth bass (Burk 1993c:16.3). All of these fish resided in the Potomac and Shenandoah rivers. Based on biomass calculations, the Hursts favored sucker over the other fish.

Table 7. Summary of Faunal Assemblage from the Hurst Privy[a]

Taxon	No.	Pct.	MSI	Pct.	Meat Weight (lbs)	Total Meat Wt. (lbs)	Pct.	Weight (gms)	Pct.	Biomass (kg)	Pct.
Calsses Aves (bird)	238	34.5	0/ 0	0.0	0.0/ 0.0	0.0	0.0	94.2	6.4	0.33	6.4
Meleagris gallopavo (Turkey)	3	0.4	1/ 0	5.3	7.5/ 7.5	7.5	0.7	42.8	2.9	0.16	3.1
Gallus gallus (chicken)	18	2.6	2/ 0	10.5	2.5/ 1.0	5.0	0.5	18.6	1.3	0.08	1.5
cf. Gallus gallus (chicken)	6	0.9	0/ 0	0.0	0.0/ 0.0	0.0	0.0	0.2	0.0	0.00	0.0
Class Mammalia (mammal)	55	8.0	0/ 0	0.0	0.0/ 0.0	0.0	0.0	0.2	0.0	0.00	0.0
Class Mammalia I (large mammal)	7	1.0	0/ 0	0.0	0.0/ 0.0	0.0	0.0	129.3	13.6	0.72	14.1
Class Mammalia II (med. mammal)	53	7.7	0/ 0	0.0	0.0/ 0.0	0.0	0.0	200.8	13.6	.72	14.1
Class Mammalia III (s. mammal)	24	3.5	0/ 0	0.0	0.0/ 0.0	0.0	0.0	83.2	5.6	0.33	6.4
Marmota monax (woodchuck)	1	0.1	1/ 0	5.3	0.0/ 0.0	0.0	0.0	0.6	0.0	0.00	0.1
cf. Pitymya pinetorum (pine vole)	1	0.1	1/ 0	5.3	0.0/ 0.0	0.0	0.0	0.1	0.0	0.00	0.0
Rattus spp. (Old World rat)	39	5.7	5/ 0	26.3	0.0/ 0.0	0.0	0.0	15.8	1.1	0.07	1.4
Sue scrofa (dom. pig)	202	29.3	6/ 0	31.6	100.0/50.0	600.0	54.7	784.6	53.0	2.46	48.1
cf. Sue scrofa (dom. pig)	38	5.5	0/ 0	0.0	0.0/ 0.0	0.0	0.0	52.1	3.5	0.22	4.2
Boe taurus (dom. cow)	2	0.3	1/ 1	10.5	400.0/50.0	450.0	41.0	1.5	0.1	0.01	0.2
cf. Boe taurus (dom. cow)	1	0.1	0/ 0	0.0	0.0/ 0.0	0.0	0.0	46.6	3.1	0.19	3.8
Ovis aries/Capra hircus (sheep/goat)	1	0.1	1/ 0	5.3	35.0/ 15.0	35.0	3.2	4.4	0.3	0.02	0.4
						Total			Total		Skeletal
Totals	689	100.0	19	100.0	—/ —	1097.5	100.0	1481.5	100.0	5.12	100.0

(N) number of bones identified to that taxon; Minimum Number of Individuals. The number before the slash is the number of adults and the number of immature specimens follows the slash. (Meat Weight) meat weight of the entire animal (adult/immature). Total Meat Weight derived by multiplying the MNI by the Meat Weight and then adding the two sides of the slash together. (Weight) weight of the actual archaeological bones. (Biomass) sketal weight.

[a]from Burk 1993:16.6

The only two bird species identified are turkey and chicken. Based on biomass calculations, the Hursts consumed a much higher percentage of turkey (3.1 percent for turkey and 1.4 percent for chicken) (Burk 1993c:16.3–16.4).

Pig, cow, and sheep/goat are well represented in this assemblage and unexpectedly, pig comprises over half (51.6 percent) of the biomass for the entire assemblage. Cow has the second largest biomass value, but trails pig considerably (3.9 percent), followed by sheep or goat (0.4 percent) (Burk 1993c:16.4–16.5). Although the largest proportion of meats eaten by the Hurst household is pig, almost 87 percent of these remains are foot and wrist or ankle elements (Burk 1993c:16.5–16.7) (Table 8). The high number of foot and wrist or ankle elements is puzzling because these tend to be one of the least expensive cuts of meat. It is unlikely that these elements represent butchering refuse. Many considered the Hurst's yard a showplace, and butchering probably would not have occurred there. Few butchering marks and other identified modifications are evident on the

Table 8. Element Distribution for Domestic Pig from the Hurst Privy[a]

Element Type	No.	Percent
Skull	0	0.0
Antler	0	0.0
Mandible	0	0.0
Tooth	1	0.4
Vertebra	4	1.7
Rib	0	0.0
Innominate	1	0.4
Acapula	0	0.0
Humerus	0	0.0
Ulna	0	0.0
Radius	2	0.8
Carpal	2	0.8
Metacarpal	10	4.2
Femur	0	0.0
Tibia	2	0.8
Fibula	2	0.8
Tarsal	29	12.1
Metatarsal	15	6.3
Metapodial	51	21.3
Phalange	101	42.1
Sesamoid	0	0.0
Other	20	8.3
Total	**240**	**100.0**

[a]from Burk 1993c:16.5

pig bones. It is likely that the Hurst family considered pigs' feet a favorite cuisine. Contemporary books often spoke of pigs feet as a treat. For instance, one book instructs:

> In considering spareribs and pigs feet, the latter will need no special description since they are easily enough recognized by their shape. They may be purchased pickled or fresh and on a fall day with a snap in the air provide a simple kind of eating pleasure that can be as welcome in its way as chicken and turkey are on other occasions. (Cullen 1976:168)

If the Hursts enjoyed pigs feet, since it consisted of a majority of their meat consumption, its preference runs counter to our preconceived notions of an upper class family's cuisine in the late 19th and early 20th centuries. Although the Hursts dressed their table with the most fashionable ceramics, kept a well-manicured landscape, and were highly respected citizens, they consumed a food that is traditionally considered by historical archaeologists to be associated with a lower socioeconomic group (Schulz and Gust 1980). There is no doubt that some members of all social groups consumed pigs' feet, but it is surprising that the largest portion of meat found in the Hurst's privy is pigs feet. Perhaps the faunal material from the Hurst household provides a cautionary tale about placing predetermined boundaries and preconceived notions about material culture and diet on a particular class. Other cultural factors need to be considered, including individual choice.

Based on the historical archaeological record it is easy to imagine the Hursts' formal dining as they entertained the major entrepreneurial families from Harpers Ferry and the surrounding region. For starters, they placed oysters at each place on the table and the oyster plate rested on a matching dinner plate. Butter pats and various condiment dishes surrounded the table. They served a light soup at the next course. After the soup, the relishes were passed among the Hursts and their guests. The Hursts, like many Americans in the 1890s, were fond of olives, radishes, and celery. The fish came next, possibly sucker or bass, followed by the entree. The servant carved the roast behind a screen, and the meats were placed on the platter with a serving fork and spoon. "It is a custom borrowed from the French, to serve after the roast a single vegetable like asparagus or artichoke, with its appropriate sauce, after which comes the game" (Schuyler 1893:26). The Hursts would have included tomato among their vegetables. They served salad with the game. Afterwards the servant cleared the table for the dessert and demitasse. Following the dessert, fruits, such as cantaloupe, were served. They were "set upon as handsome plates as the hostess may possess with a dainty doily between the bowl and the plate" (Schuyler 1893:26).

For the everyday dinner the Hursts had a centerpiece, either a "fernery" or a bowl of fruit. A dinner plate, thickly cut pieces of fresh bread, mismatched tumblers filled with water, napkins, knives, forks, and spoons at each place setting. Soup plates were stacked at the side table. Mrs. Hurst distributed the soup from the tureen and the servant set each bowl on the dinner plate. After the soup course, the under plate remained for hor d'oeuvres. The plate was then exchanged for a hot plate of either fish, roast, or pig (Schuyler 1893:26). After dinner, the Hursts had either tea or coffee with dessert.

CONCLUSION

After the Hursts died, their lot was willed to Elizabeth's siblings. In 1928, Mary Ellen Doran purchased the Hurst's house. In 1931, Mary Ellen Doran won a prize from the Women's Club 3rd Annual Garden Contest for the "Hurst site." Apparently Doran kept the exterior in excellent condition, much like her predecessors. Whether Mary Ellen Doran lived in the Hurst house for a short time is unknown, but the building was given to Josephine Delauder, her niece, as a wedding present. In 1955, the National Park Service acquired this building along with the rest of Lower Town.

The National Park Service interprets this urban lot as playing a significant role in the development of the armory and also serving as a headquarters during the Civil War. The history of the Hurst property runs counter to the established public memory developed by the federal government. Research on this household is about a wealthy entrepreneur and provides some interesting information about lifestyles of an elite family in Victorian Lower Town Harpers Ferry at the turn of the 20th century. The archaeological assemblage suggests that they followed national trends and subscribed to fashionable dinner formalities. These national trends played a significant role in the local community.

There are also some details that run counter to the stories told about this elite Harpers Ferry household. For instance, the Hursts had a high percentage of pig in their diet, and a high proportion consisting of foot and wrist elements. Also, although the Hursts helped to market Harpers Ferry as a pleasant and healthy place to live and visit, they had a high concentration of parasite eggs in their stools. Although children tend to have a higher rate of parasites, there were none who lived in the Hurst household. Since a local newspaper noted that they had one of the most beautiful yards in Harpers Ferry, it was likely that they fertilized their lawn and garden with organic materials from the privy. If this were the case, the parasites, under the right conditions, could survive in the ground for several years, and it is likely that the Hursts may have reinfected themselves by eating unwashed vegetables from their garden.

While historical context provides some of the necessary background to understand this household as a leader in the community's economic and tourist industries, the contradictions that emerge from the site also allow for additional ambiguities in the interpretation of the archaeological record. These contradictions challenge us to look at the way our memory of the past is created. These contradictions allow us to look at the past in different ways and challenge the established public memory. It encourages us to look at the world around us, and persuade us to dissolve preconceived notions of people and groups.

"The Natural Limits of Human Endurance"

Brewery Workers, Bottlers, and Labor Unrest

BREWING AND BOTTLING

Part of Harpers Ferry's Victorian revival included the development of both large and small scale industries. At the close of the 19th century the town contained many architectural styles that spanned the entire century. When looking at early 20th-century landscape photographs, it is easy to see a mix of contemporary and older architecture throughout the town. Some townspeople built a new town with modern Victorian architecture while other resourceful entrepreneurs used existing buildings to accommodate new functions.

Photographic images along with historical documentation also show the impact of small industry on the landscape. It is easy to imagine the working conditions that existed in the town. They were probably similar to working conditions in other small industrial towns. Harpers Ferry, once predominantly occupied by skilled armory craftsmen and their families, now consisted of mostly merchants, boardinghouse keepers, and immigrant wage laborers.

The National Park Service landscape, which has been created to commemorate the Civil War and the armory industry, ignores the histories of the late 19th-century workers and their families. Much of the contemporary landscape contains well-manicured green lawns with occasional outlines of building foundations. There is often space between these marked foundations, and the visitor does not get the impression of the crowded town that is evident in the turn of the century photographs. The building outlines are the remains of those that were constructed before the Civil War and thus it is easy to lose the feel of the once vibrant Victorian town. It is time freezing at its best, similar to places like Colonial Williamsburg and Mount Vernon. The National Park Service knows the locations of postbellum structures, whose foundations are not outlined, that are noticeably absent from the landscape. The National Park Service commemorates the town's prewar industrial past and Civil War history while ignoring the lives of the Victorian era workers and their families. Visitors are told about industrial advancements, although the memory of oppressed working conditions, a major part of our American history, is ignored.

One such example is the bottling and brewery complex that began in the 1880s. James McGraw decided to capitalize on the growing consumer demand for carbonated beverages and the increased demand for beer in both the region and the United States. The complex began as a very small operation, bottling beer and soft drinks. It occupied one building and employed only a few workers at low wages, but eventually expanded to a large building where brewing and bottling occurred.

The carbonated drink bottling industry in the United States grew from 100 plants in the 1850s to more than 1,400 by 1890 (Riley 1972:116). Franchise drinks began to appear in the 1870s, including Hires Root Beer (1876), Vernor's Ginger Ale (1880) Coca Cola (1886), and Pepsi Cola (1896). Soft drink bottlers, like McGraw, could bottle their own brand, or bottle a franchise product (Hull-Walski and Walski 1993:17.3). When the Harpers Ferry bottling works expanded into beer brewing in the mid-1890s, there were more than 1,700 breweries in the United States, three times more than midcentury (Friedrich and Bull 1976:306, 308). New and larger entrepreneurial endeavors developed, leading to the expansion and industrialization of the brewing craft and to the creation of new labor practices.

Bottling Technology and a Division of Labor

Bottling technology (washing, filling, and capping) remained a manual operation in the late 19th century. Eventually, new labor-saving devices allowed for a decrease in manual labor. By the beginning of the 20th century the process had become fully automated; the bottlers became machine tenders.

For instance, in the 1880s, workers cleaned bottles by hand. Even after the introduction of semiautomatic bottle washing machines, there was still a need for workers to soak the bottles to remove labels and soften any interior dirt. The bottles would then be loaded into a machine where their interiors would be scoured by brushes or lead shot. Workers then removed the bottles to rinse and dry (Paul and Parmalee 1973:51–54). By the early 20th century workers loaded bottles on a conveyor belt, which took them to a vat to soak. After soaking, the bottles were removed by workers and placed in the washing machine (Riley 1972:110). By the 1920s the process had become fully automated, including soaking, cleaning, rinsing, and draining (Hull-Walski and Walski 1993:17.4).

The bottle-filling process was the next step. Until the 1860s, workers performed this process manually. For carbonated drinks the worker held the bottle, used a funnel to pour the product into the bottle, then pounded a cork into the top with a mallet. Since the contents were under pressure, they could easily explode in the bottler's hand (Paul and Parmalee 1973:47). A bottling table, developed in the 1860s, provided some safety for the bottler. It controlled the flow of liquid and it also inserted the cork. A screen protected the bottler (Hull-Walski and Walski 1993:17.4–17.5), and a siphon extracted the beer from the keg. By 1910, filtered air or carbonic acid helped the process (Wright 1892:435). Many bottlers had semiautomatic and automatic machines in place by the 1920s.

In the next step the bottle was sealed. Between the late 1880s and early 1900s entrepreneurs developed thousands of bottle closure patents. The Hutchinson-style internal stopper was a popular type of bottle seal. Patented in 1879, it had a large wire loop—outside the bottle, attached to a rubber disk—inside the bottle. The loop prevented the disk from falling inside the bottle. Once the bottle was filled the loop was pulled back, sealing the bottle (Riley 1972:97). Other popular stoppers included the swing type stopper (Lief 1965:150). These stoppers were attached to a wire loop. They could be lifted out of the bottle or clamped into place by the wire fulcrum (Paul and Parmalee 1973:14).

The crown cap, patented in 1892, became the most popular bottle closure in the 20th century. A metal disk, lined with cork, kept the contents away from the metal. The disk was crimped tightly into place with the aid of a foot-powered crowning machine. The crown cap could be easily disposed of, and wire clamps and rubber disks did not interfere with washing and cleaning (Paul and Parmalee 1973:14–18). Not until the bottling process became fully automated—almost 30 years later—did the crown cap become universally accepted for both soda and beer (Hull-Walski and Walski 1993:17.10).

AN ARCHAEOLOGY OF THE INDUSTRIAL ERA

As more historical archaeologists turn their attention to industrial era sites, the interpretation of workers' domestic households will be recognized as contributing to issues of the development of a working-class society (see for instance Hardesty 1988; Paynter 1988; Shackel 1996). The archaeology of 19th-century American sites is important for understanding the development of capitalism and the impact of the industrial revolution on our daily lives. An archaeology of this era is exciting because it provides insights into the root of our mass consumer and mass producer society. Although the 18th century, and even earlier, may be the time in which to trace the development of capitalism (Leone 1988, 1995; Shackel 1993a; Johnson 1996), the 19th century is the era in which to address how capitalism was implemented, operated, and resisted in America by different interest groups and individuals (see Shackel 1996).

The workers' response to the new industrial conditions is a story that is often overlooked in projects and museums sponsored by the federal government. For instance, although the National Park Service exhibit at Lowell, Massachusetts strives for a more inclusive story of labor, other National Park Service exhibits at Saugus, Massachusetts, and Hopewell, Pennsylvania, fail to discuss the conflict between labor and capital that developed with the new industrial order. By recognizing the horrors and exploitation associated with industrial labor, we can change the public memory currently associated with industrial development and make people more aware of some of the poor working conditions that still exists today in industries around the world, especially in developing countries (see, for instance Bales 1999). Becoming aware of these conditions allows us the opportunity to change public memory of our own industrial past and it gives people a choice as to whether they want to sponsor and support these conditions by "buying into them" today.

Robert Paynter's (1989) work is important when looking at the development of ideologies related to modernizing industrial conditions and the formation of a working-class society. New ideologies related to factory discipline were created, imposed, and sometimes resisted. Tensions that developed "between cores and peripheries, civil and kin groups, rulers and ruled, merchants and lords, men and women, and producers and extractors evoke an unwieldy tangle of processes . . . "(Paynter 1989:558).

The introduction of industrial capitalism meant a new work discipline, the abandonment of a craft-ethos, and the adherence to a new factory discipline. Paynter (1989:386) recognizes that resistance in a capitalist world could take on several forms, including malingering and sabotage (see, for instance Juravich 1985; Scott 1985).

For instance, in the early 19th century Harpers Ferry armory, resistance to the implementation of systematic manufacturing and the suggestion of transforming craftsmen into wage laborers did not happen quietly at Harpers Ferry either. The town has a long labor history of malcontent between labor and capital. In the early 19th century many armorers and their supervisors resisted new and highly productive machinery and time discipline, spurned as "Yankee notions," regardless of how productive such techniques and organizations were. Technical and organizational innovations, often found in northern industries, threatened the armorers' craft in Harpers Ferry. The armory sometimes refused to employ New Englanders, and those who did work at the armory were often poorly treated, both by their fellow armorers and by the townspeople. Harpers Ferry armorers clearly feared becoming mere tenders of machinery, which is how they perceived their counterparts in the Springfield Armory (Smith 1977:102–137, 158; Shackel 1996).

From 1829 on, the armory slowly changed from a craft system to a factory system, although this change did not go uncontested. A new superintendent of the facility tried to enforce a labor discipline by prohibiting loitering, gambling, and alcohol consumption on armory grounds. He also refused to rehire workers who were previously fired for incompetent work. As a result, tensions developed in the armory that rapidly escalated into violence. Armorers often harassed the new superintendent outside the armory gates. Within six months of the introduction of labor discipline, the superintendent was murdered by an armorer. Although the assassin was hanged for his crime, armory workers hailed him as a hero and he became a symbol of their resistance against the new work discipline (Barry 1988 [1903]:25–35; Smith 1977: 256–257; Shackel 1996).

Sometimes these forms of resistance are visible in the archaeological record. Workers' acceptance of the new factory discipline varied between workers and factories. Michael Nassaney's and Marjorie Abel's (1993:251) analysis of the material remains at the John Russell Cutlery Company in the Connecticut River Valley describes discontent over the new factory system. Using James Scott's (1990) analysis, they recognize that discontented workers can challenge the existing power structure through a "hidden transcript." Nassaney and Abel (1993:263–274) found a large quantity of artifacts related to interchangeable manufacturing along the river bank near the former cutting room and trip hammer shop. These discarded materials consisted of inferior or imperfect manufactured parts. Nassaney and Abel recognize that the discarded materials may represent a form of defiance against the implementation of the new system.

Resistance may create other archaeological signatures. For instance Mrozowski et al. (1996:71–74) suggest that alcohol bottles found around an outbuilding implies that the users "tried to conceal the evidence of their drinking from prying eyes."

Archaeological evidence may show that resistance can take various shapes, in either explicit or implicit forms. The former can be seen with the damaging of goods, or the assassination of a supervisor. The latter can arise by secretly disobeying rules and regulations by concealing drinking habits. An examination of the archaeology at the Harpers Ferry brewery and bottling works shows that both explicit and implicit forms of resistance occurred to protest work conditions. By looking for these signatures in the archaeological record we can become aware of the tragedies associated with industrialization and thus create a new memory of postbellum labor in this small Victorian town.

THE DEVELOPMENT OF THE MCGRAW COMMERCIAL LOT

The Harpers Ferry bottling and brewery complex serves as a good example of resistance in the work place. James McGraw developed his bottling and brewery complex soon after he established a successful hardware store in Lower Town Harpers Ferry. At times he advertised salt, coal, and nails for sale. One early advertisement, which was repeated for several years, read (*Virginia Free Press* 17 December 1872:3):

> Salt, Coal, and Nails
> I have on hand for sale 590 Sacks of Liverpool G.A. Salt, 200 Sacks of Fine and 500 small Sacks of Dairy Salt. 100 Tons of George's Creek Valley Lump Coal, and 50 Tons of Anthracite Coal, and 100 Kegs of Nails, which I will exchange for Corn.
> Harpers Ferry, W.Va. Nov. 20, 1875–3t. James McGraw.

Coal sheds lined his backyard and McGraw received 1,000 tons at a time (*SoJ* 22 January 1884:3). McGraw prospered in the 1880s and early 1890s. The *Spirit of Jefferson* often publicized his affluence. On one occasion, the paper declared the interior of McGraw's house "is probably not excelled by any in the Shenandoah Valley" (28 January 1890:3).

McGraw began a beer bottling operation in 1885. He advertised in the *Spirit of Jefferson* (28 April 1885:2) that he received Milwaukee Lager Beer in refrigerated cars, and he would be bottling this beer for trade (Figure 28). Three years later he advertised Schlitz Milwaukee Beer for sale (*SoJ* 26 June 1888:2). That same year McGraw constructed a bottling plant with a two-storey deep basement for cold storage, next to and behind his house. Only a porch separated the operations from his residence. He added a boiler for heating water for bottle washing or for beer pasteurization (Hull-Walski and Walski 1993:17.15).

Americans preferred ale until German immigrants introduced lager beer in the mid-19th century. The lager had a slightly sweeter, heavier and stronger flavoring of hops. Americans took to this new beer. By the 1870s lagers outsold ales, and Germans dominated the brewing industry (Wallerstein 1950; Baron 1962:189).

During the early 1890s McGraw advertised that he served as an

Figure 28. McGraw's bottling plant consisted of the central clapboard structure with a deep cellar and converted carriage house (structure to the left). Shipments were received from the railroad (far left) and bottled in the plant. (Photograph by Paul A. Shackel)

agent for Sachs Puden Ginger Ale, Pilsner Export Beer, and Papst Milwaukee Beer. One advertisement noted that the beer was "Pure, Healthful, Nourishing and—Refreshing Papst's Milwaukee Beer . . . As a beverage unsurpassed, As a Tonic unexcelled, As a Nervine unapproachable is Papst's Beer" (*SoJ* 5 July 1892:3).

In 1890, James McGraw's son, James C. McGraw, succeeded his father in the beer bottling and ginger ale business. He advertised that he existed as the exclusive local agent for Sachs Pudens Famous Ginger Ale (*SoJ* 13 May 1890:3). James McGraw, Sr. died in 1893. His estate, valued at $155,000, remained undivided between his son, James, and two daughters, Catherine and Margaret. His son continued to invest in the bottling operations. In 1894 he purchased an ice machine, one compressor, one gasometer, one Hutchinson attachment, one saccharometer, and three graduated cylinders (4 oz., 8 oz, and 16 oz) (*SoJ* 10 June 1894:3; *JCDB* 77, 25 April 1894:47; see Hull Walski and Walski 1993:17:17). He incorporated the Harpers Ferry Brewery Company, and constructed a large brewery, which cost $30,000. He built it along the Shenandoah River, about 150 feet from his house(*SoJ* 4 June 1995:2) (Figure 29). He continued to operate a

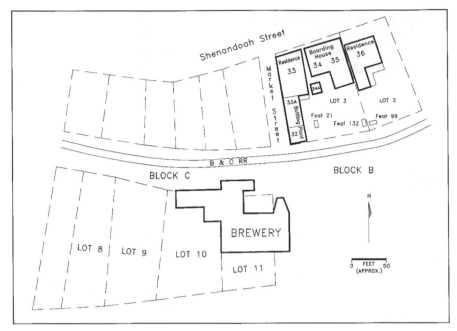

Figure 29. McGraw's 1895 brewery existed 150 feet from his residence (Building 33). The bottling works continued to operate in its original location through the early 20th century. (Drawn by John Ravenhorst)

steam bottling plant in the building next to his house and the company bottled both beer and soda (*JCDB* 83, 1 October 1897:494).

The central portion of the brewery consisted of four storeys and was typical for small and mid-sized breweries. The brewing process conformed to the tower principle of brewery construction. During the various brewing processes the product would descend from the top storey to lower levels, rather than being pumped up to higher levels. The brewery produced 10,000 barrels per year and had the capacity to brew up to 30,000 barrels (Hull-Walski and Walski 1993:17.24). Unfortunately, much of McGraw's investment came during the Panic of 1893, an economic downturn that lasted for three years (Brands 1995:272). McGraw secured a loan for $14,000 in October 1895. In 1896, his land was mortgaged again as collateral for loans (*JCDB* 80, 26 October 1895:112; *JCDB* 81, 27 July 1896:475–476).

To help with the new enterprise McGraw hired Fritz Jensen of Chicago as his brewmaster. Jensen came "with one of the best recommendations in this country" (*SoJ* 4 June 1895:2). Hiring Jensen may have come too late for McGraw's business effort. McGraw needed to secure additional loans to keep the operations functioning. In July 1897 the brewery burned, causing $6,000 worth of damage (*Western Brewer* 1897:3). Although economic prosperity returned to America by early 1897 (Brands 1995:85), it was not soon enough to change McGraw's declining fortunes. By October 1897, McGraw declared bankruptcy and by December the brewery was for sale.

The brewery and bottling enterprise survived into the 20th century under various other ownerships including Krueger and Schafer (1898) the Belvidere Brewing Company (1898–1903), and the Leder–Weidman Brewing Company (1903–1906). In 1906 a fire forced Leder–Weidman Brewing Company to sell the complex to the Jefferson Ice and Cold Storage Company (1906). They in turn sold the enterprise to the Jefferson Brewing Company (1906–1909) that same year. The plant burned again in 1909 and the company sold it to the German Brewing Company (1909–1916).

The German Brewing Company did not reroof the burned part of the building. The central portion no longer had its four storey tower, and the western half remained vacant. But part of the brewery survived including "the bottling department, a frame building where also soft drinks are manufactured along with the stable" (*FA* 16 January 1909:2) (Figure 30). With the onset of prohibition the facilities were solely used as a soda bottling works from 1914.

Charles Smith purchased the bottling operations, and he formed the

Figure 30. Harpers Ferry bottlers in front of the building works (formerly the brewery) after the 1936 flood. (Courtesy, Harpers Ferry National Historical Park, HF-96)

Harpers Ferry Bottling Works (1914–1927). He partially reconstructed the
building and later sold it to Harry Longbrake and James Grimes who
operated Gateway Soda (1927–1942). Gateway Soda continued to operate
into the 1940s despite the disastrous 1936 flood. Finally, the 1942 flood
destroyed the entire building and Gateway Soda left Harpers Ferry (Hull-
Walski and Walski 1993:17.13–17.32) (Figure 31).

The Harpers Ferry Brewery and Bottling Workers

The 1900 Census shows that Brewmaster Jensen, whom McGraw
hired in 1895 no longer worked at the brewery. In 1900, the Belvidere
Brewing Company employed 12 men, half of whom resided in boarding
houses, and the other half boarded in private homes. The employees included one engineer, two clerks, four laborers, two bottlers, one brewmaster,
one second man, and an apprentice. Four of the employees were foreign
born: one from England (a bottler) and three from Germany (brewmaster,
second man, and apprentice) (U.S. Census 1900).

The transient nature of the brewery laborers is evident. In 1910 only
two members of the 1900 brewery staff still lived in Harpers Ferry, but

Figure 31. Gateway Soda bottlers in Harpers Ferry. (Courtesy, Library of Congress,
802527 Z62 07545)

they claimed different occupations. One identified himself as a mill laborer and the other a saloon keeper. A deed of trust signed in 1903 also shows that the brewery complex had an office and a "brewery residence house" (*JCDB* 92, 17 February 1903:506). While supplying some housing for their workers may have been common for breweries, it did not encourage a state of permanence among the employees. By having the workers live in the complex also allowed supervisors and owners to keep a watchful eye over their employees.

Work in 19th-century industries was long, arduous, and unhealthy compared with today's standards. During the first half of the century, Harpers Ferry amory workers continually fought to have their work days shortened from 12 to 10 hours (Smith 1977). Exact working conditions are not known at the Harpers Ferry Brewery, but the enterprise probably subscribed to the national average of 14–18-hour work days, six days per week. On Sundays the work day consisted of six to eight hours (Schulter 1910:92-93). Between 1890 and 1910, unions gradually decreased the work day to 10 hours.

No doubt, the Harpers Ferry brewery workers were subject to the same health conditions as other brewery workers. They were constantly exposed to radical temperature changes and they breathed contaminated air. The brew house had an average temperature of 68 degrees, while the cooling room averaged 41 degrees and the malt kiln rooms reached 176 degrees. The Harpers Ferry Brewery did not have heat until after 1907 therefore the brew house maintained much colder temperatures in the winter (Hull-Walski and Walski 1993:17.34–35; 1994).

The brewery's air contained contaminants, such as carbonic acid, and sulfuric acid, and diseases, such as tuberculosis, were prevalent among brewery workers. In the first decade of the 20th century, brewery-related accidents were almost 30 percent higher than those of other industrial trades. This rate increased over the decade because of the "higher speeding of machinery." The excessive use of alcohol by workers under the "free beer system" may have contributed to this high casualty rate (these rates are calculated for only those workers unemployed for at least 13 weeks) (Schulter 1910:259–263).

On the national scene a union spokesman remarked that conditions in the brewery were

> As bad as can be imagined. It was not only that the wages paid were the smallest possible and that the working time was confined only by the natural limits of human endurance, but besides this the treatment of the workmen was such a kind that it seems impossible today to understand how they could submit to it. Cuffs and blows were everyday occurrence. (Schulter 1910:89)

Brewery workers began to unionize in the 1870s, and in 1886 the National Union of the Brewers of the United States was established (Baron 1962:281–83). A 1899 investigation of Baltimore brewing processes revealed that some brewery workers labored 18 hours per day. The brewery workers went on strike until they were promised better conditions (Hull-Walski and Walski 1993:17.36). The brewery workers and the owners agreed with the following stipulations:

> Engineers should be on duty 12 hours; that the work day for the brew-workers should be 9 hours from October to March and 10 hours for the remainder of the year, or the summer season . . . the wage scale gave the brew-workers at kettles $15 a week; in the fermenting rooms and storage and packing cellars $15 a week; in the wash-house $13; apprentices $9; regular drivers $12; engineers not less than $18; oilers and helpers $2 a day. (Kelley 1965:548)

Prior to the 1899 strike, bottlers worked the same long hours as their brewery workers' counterparts. The bottlers' job "could be hazardous; attempting to seal a bottle whose contents were under pressure was a dangerous occupation, especially when most of the work was done by hand" (Hull-Walski and Walski 1993:17.37). The bottlers were not as well organized as the brewery workers because they consisted of mostly young men and boys doing repetitive and unskilled labor. While their brewery counterparts received some concessions during the strike, the bottlers did not. Brewery owners claimed that they received little profit from the bottling industry. Therefore, higher pay to these workers would wipe out any financial gains (Kelley 1965:548).

Brewing and bottling at Harpers Ferry operated much like any other industrialist ventures of the late 19th century. The entrepreneur had to worry about competition and encourage high productivity. He also encountered growing discontent among workers' who faced long hours in the brewery under poor conditions. Slim profit margins were difficult to achieve at the Harpers Ferry brewery and entrepreneurs encountered many financial failures. Unionization at the Harpers Ferry brewery did not occur until 1903, and workers were able to secure better wages and working conditions (*FA* 31 October 1903:2).

The archaeological record provides some clues regarding working conditions and work attitudes related to the bottling works and brewery. For instance, the boardinghouse privy documents a single dumping episode of 49 late-19th-century bottles related to J.C. McGraw's ownership of the brewery and bottling works. All these bottles were marked with "THIS BOTTLE/NOT TO/BE SOLD," "THIS BOTTLE NOT/TO BE SOLD," or "THIS/BOTTLE/IS NEVER SOLD." This wording was commonly found on bottles of the era since these bottles remained the property of the bottler. Customers usually returned the bottles for refilling because the cost of the bottle was not included in the price of the product. For instance, if the bottle were disposable, its price would have increased the cost of soda to the consumer by 50 percent (Busch 1987:71–72).

Hull-Walski and Walski (1993:17.51) conclude that this dumping episode may be a product of a new brewery ownership disposing of unwanted embossed bottles of the McGraw brewery or, a simpler reason may be the boarders consumed the beer and disposed of these bottles into the privy. Such scenarios are possible but other explanations are also likely. For instance, because the cost of these bottles made their return a common practice, and because the bottling work sat fewer than 100 feet away from the boardinghouse, then the dumping of McGraw's bottles might be associated with some sort of workers' dissatisfaction. Sabotage, a common form of resistance among workers in many industrial circumstances (see, for instance Paynter 1989), may be a likely verdict.

The case for sabotage becomes even stronger when other evidence is considered. For instance, during the restoration of the bottling works building by the National Park Service in 1995–1996, archaeologists found close to 100 empty beer bottles stashed behind the wall lathing in the former bottling room. Bottlers may well have consumed the beer and hid the empty bottles from the supervisors and owners. Other evidence includes more than 1,000 beer bottles found in the basement of the bottling works' elevator shaft, most of these broke after falling more than two storey. In both cases, workers probably drank the owners' profits and concealed their actions by disposing the bottles in walls and down elevator shafts. The bottles found in the boardinghouse privy may also be a product of the dissident behavior.

These bottles all date to the 1890s and the early 1900s—the same era when brewing unions made major strides to improve the conditions of the workers. If owners did not make working conditions on par with other national breweries, they would have incited this labor unrest. The burning of the brewery in 1897, 1906, and 1909 may have been a coincidence, or it likely was related to some general workers' discontent. Newspaper accounts are inconclusive about these events, but sabotage is very plausible, especially considering the existing poor working conditions.

TEMPERANCE AND THE END OF BREWING IN HARPERS FERRY

Successful operations of the brewery complex were complicated by the town's strong temperance movement. Temperance organizations existed as early as 1831 in Harpers Ferry and continued to be active into the 20th century. In 1912, citizens circulated petitions advocating the close of local liquor establishments. The brewery felt some of this pressure because they had to acquire liquor licenses to sell wholesale beer (*SoJ* 17 May 1910:2; *VFP* 19 December 1912:5). Election campaigns were represented by "Wet" and "Dry" candidates. The "Wets" won the 1911 local elections, although the rest of Jefferson County (except Charlestown) became dry. This election victory did not mean much because the county court refused to issue any liquor licenses between July 1911 and January 1913. A new county commissioner reversed this policy in 1913 (*VFP* 13 April 1911:3; *VFP* 9 October 1913:2). The policy lasted only for a year since the state of West Virginia became dry in 1914, six years before the national prohibition in 1920 (Fenicle 1993:3.5).

The brewing operations continued in Harpers Ferry until the 1909 fire. After that, entrepreneurs used the remaining complex for bottling beer and soft drinks and as a redistribution point for the German Brewing Company. After the State of West Virginia banned alcohol in 1914, the company used the brewery building as a soft drink bottling works. It operated under various ownerships until 1942—as the last remaining manufacturing industry in Harpers Ferry (Hull-Walski and Walski 1993).

MAKING A CONSCIOUS CHOICE

The National Park Service outlined building foundations on the landscape that they believed are important for telling an important national story, but there are many structures that are noticeably absent. For instance, the brewery building and many of the boardinghouses are missing from the landscape. This omission occurs for two reasons. First, these buildings, the brewery workers and their families, as well as other Victorian era wage laborers, existed after an era the park sees as significant, the armory era (1796–1861) and the Civil War era (1861–1865). By omitting the history of these people by not commemorating them on the landscape the National Park Service is explicitly conveying to the visiting public what they see as important. The wage laborers of the Victorian era are absent, their history plays a subservient role to the "great men" histories and the notion of industrial progress.

Knowing and understanding the roots of American industrialization is often clouded by the image of material growth and industrial advancements. Although many appreciate new consumer goods and new technological advancements, we often overlook the conditions in which they were produced. The struggle between labor and capital is never ending. It is when we are able to see the historical conditions of industry that we become aware of the industrial circumstances that exist in the world today. We can then decide if we want to support inhumane conditions found in developing countries, and if not, we can find an alternative product, or purchase goods that may cost more but are made under more humane conditions. Industrial labor and the purchasing of industrial goods is inevitable, but we the consumer have a choice of industry and labor condition that we choose to support. Making workers part of our national landscape, such as a national park, is important because it can make us aware of the historical conditions of labor and the contemporary practices in which it now exists.

"A Miserable Mockery of a Home"

Boardinghouse Life in the Lower Town

INTRODUCTION

After the Civil War, boardinghouses developed rapidly in industrializing urban areas and often became associated with the urban poor population. There is very little on the contemporary landscape at Harper Ferry that would indicate more than 25 percent of the town's population lived in boardinghouses that after the Civil War. Many of the postwar boardinghouses are now interpreted by the National Park for their prewar functions. Those buildings which once held multiple families are now used to house exhibits that are not related to either domestic life or the plight of boarding in a small industrial town. Some may see this situation as good adaptive reuse, while others can see these actions as ignoring an important part of human history. Therefore, I think it is important to remember a forgotten part of our urban domestic industrial heritage. Historical archaeology provides a picture of boardinghouse life that cannot be procured solely from the written records.

With the rise in popularity of boardinghouses came an increase in etiquette manuals that dictated rules and regulations for behavior in these establishments. The manuals demanded that families have a single (male) wage earner, and they wanted women to stop operating these ventures. By the end of the 19th century, social reformers called for the end of boardinghouses.

Industrial enterprises in Harpers Ferry flourished from the 1890s through the early 20th century, and a transient labor class needed accommodations. Boardinghouses served this need. Examination of a late 19th-century Harpers Ferry boardinghouse reveals how townspeople survived and reveals how they perceived the many rules established by contemporary social and health reformers.

BOARDINGHOUSE LIFE

While McGraw's beer bottling and eventually the brewing business thrived in the late 1880s and early 1890s, he constructed a "first-class" boardinghouse on Shenandoah Street, in the heart of the Lower Town commercial district. It catered to working and middle class households. The construction of this building in Harpers Ferry at the height of the Victorian era poses some interesting questions about lifestyles in this small industrial and tourist town.

The growth of boardinghouses is related to the development of a wage-labor system. Boarders paid for a service—room and board—something they could do only in a wage system. By 1860 boarding became so common in the industrializing United States that one contemporary historian came away with the impression that "nearly all Americans lived in hotels or boarding-houses" (quoted in Strasser 1982:148; see also Martin 1942:148–149). Many Americans, who chose not to stay at boardinghouses, and who had the means, could stay at hotels. Hotel accommodations that served room and board, became known as the American Plan (Strasser 1982:148).

A 1869 guide book described boardinghouses as containing single men and women and married couples—an unacceptable mixture in Victorian society. Critics viewed any kind of cooperative living as a threat to the family. The household lacked privacy and the living situation facilitated contact with strangers who may have had different morals and values (Figure 32). A contemporary New Yorker found living in a "boardinghouse, at its best, is but a miserable mockery of a home." Another citizen commented that a boardinghouse had "Nothing like comfort or content anywhere, but the opposite of what you mean when you talk of home" (from Cromley 1989:21) (Figure 33).

Group living, suggested contemporaries, weakened family bonds. "[T]he husband is but half husband, the wife but half a wife, the child but half a child, when all three reside in some huge caravanserai in common with . . . other persons, separated from them by different tastes, feelings, opinions—yet congregated with them by self-imposed necessity" (quoted in Cromley 1989:21).

The intimacy of boardinghouses distressed housing reformers. Junius Browne (1869:398) noted the immorality of group living and wondered "How many women can trace their first infidelity to the necessarily demoralizing influence of public houses—to loneliness, leisure, need of society, interesting companions, abundance of opportunity, and potent temptation."

In 1899 S.T. Rorer in *The Ladies' Home Journal* (1899:29) acknowl-

How my maiden neighbors learned my secrets.

Figure 32. Boardinghouse living arrangements often lacked privacy. (*Harper's Weekly,* 9 January 1858:21. Courtesy, The Winterthur Library: Printed Books and Periodical Collection)

edged that boardinghouse life was almost unavoidable in society. The column lectured readers on what to expect concerning quality of room and board. Most important, the article relayed that the conditions of the boardinghouse were not necessarily the fault of the boardinghouse mistress who was trying to eke out a living. Tenants expected too much for their money, and they should not expect to feast every night. "People complain, not because the food is bad, but because it seems to be natural to complain about and criticize the boarding-house table" (Rorer 1899:29). Although most families ate meat once a day, boarders expected it three times a day at a boardinghouse. Because of newly developed transportation systems, most people in large cities had become accustomed to having the freshest vegetables and meats. However, when they left the city for the summer and stayed at a boardinghouse, they said "we meet with our first surprise—inferior meats badly cooked, vegetables that have been kept all winter long; a perfectly natural thing under the existing conditions" (Rorer 1899:29).

Rorer's article continued to state that generally, the boardinghouse

Jovial Neighbor (Time 2 a. m.) -"Could you O-O-Obligaf La' with light?"

Figure 33. The jovial boardinghouse neighbor. (*Harper's Weekly,* 12 July 1873:21. Courtesy, The Winterthur Library: Printed Books and Periodical Collection)

keeper was an untrained housewife who was in need of earning a living, although she was not "especially adapted to it" (Rorer 1899:26). Servants in the boardinghouse were also not well trained, he claimed, and they were wasteful. Lodgers always tried to get their money's worth at boarding-houses. However, they often forgot the expenses of servants, fuel, rent, and wear and tear on the furniture. On the whole, boardinghouse keepers did not make much of a living, but rather survived a "miserable existence" (Rorer 1899:26).

With the development of boardinghouse culture in the late 19th century came a proliferation of household management literature. One author, Helen Campbell, justified the creation of household manuals for women. According to her, women, if not taught by their mother's, find that house-keeping, "is a combination of accidental forces from whose working it is hoped breakfasts and dinners and suppers will be evolved at regular periods, other necessities finding place where they can" (Campbell 1881:35).

Generally, women's place in this new industrial economy was perceived as uncharted, and providing instructions for household management practices became necessary. The development of household management became a concern since women increasingly pursued higher education outside of the household in the late 19th century. One author noted "in doing this (pursuing higher education) they neglect the lowlier, but not less noble, study of domestic science, and so enter upon life unprepared for duties that usually awaits them" (The Kitchen–Garden Association 1882:iv).

Housework, according to contemporary household management authorities, needed to be done in a systematic fashion (Harland 1899:30). Maria Parloa's 1893 article, "Division of Household Work," in *The Ladies' Home Journal* (1893a January:19), is one of the first to mention dividing the housework over the week and performing housework in a systematic fashion (also see Parloa 1993d). Her article includes such topics as "What to do in the morning, special work for special days, and cleaning a room by system" (Parloa 1893a:19).

Others also believed women were ill trained for domestic life and that significant waste occurred frequently within the household (Figure 34). One household management writer claimed, "Somebody has said that a well-to-do French family would live on what an American household in the same condition of life wastes, and this may not be a great exaggeration. Here, the greatest source of waste is the blunders and experiments of the inexperienced" (*Buckeye Cookery* 1877:v). *The Ladies' Home Journal* (1889 October:7) also reinforced the image of a French servant being a worthy investment since she is relatively refined, and frugal within the household. "Yes, though a lady born and bred, refined, elegant and agreeable in society, a belle in her way, yet she does not think it beneath her dignity to lighten the household expenses by practical economy and activity. . . . No French woman will spend a cent to save herself."

The belief that American women needed to be taught household management techniques seems quite interesting, especially since women's roles at the home have traditionally focused on domestic activities, like rearing children, preparing meals, and tending to daily domestic chores (see for instance Campbell 1897:15). Not every woman could stay at home and care for their household. Many lower class women found employment in factories, or as domestic servants in private households or in boardinghouses, to help their families survive. Employment meant that she neglected at least some of her domestic duties as wife and mother. The myth of the single income household was just that—a myth.

DOMESTIC REFORM MOVEMENT

The introduction of new technologies into the home increasingly devalued household work. Much like the men's factory work, women's work also became deskilled in the 19th century. For instance, canned foods, and

Figure 34. The drudgery of housework extended to the boardinghouse. (*Ladies' Home Journal* 1889. Courtesy, The Winterthur Library: Printed Books and Periodical Collection.)

later cake mixes, changed cooking from a craft to unskilled labor. The skilled craft of housework became a menial task and the status of housework declined through the 19th century (Matthews 1987).

In the late 19th century Melusina Fay Peirce (1884) suggested the development of cooperative stores to help relieve some of the drudgery of domestic life, provide cheaper goods, and allow women to find some relief from constant housework. Peirce (1884:56) noted " . . . –into harmony with the spirit of their own generation. In other words, ORGANIZE IT!–these house-hold buying on the basis of the Co-operative Store." Though the husband controlled household capital, housekeepers still had the power to create cooperative stores, kitchen, laundries, and sewing rooms. Peirce proposed women take their savings, open small cooperative stores, and reinvest their profits until the stores were large and thriving. She reasoned women were naturally disposed to running a cooperative store, since "men are the natural earners and accumulators of the world" (Peirce 1884:61), so naturally they would be under stress always to increase their profits. However, women were perceived as being "distributors of society. Thus they are removed from the arena of strife and competition, and since the function of every modern woman is that of buyer for her family, her chief anxiety is, or should be, how to make the funds entrusted to her go farther" (Peirce 1884:62).

The ultimate goal of these cooperatives, according to Peirce, was to run the small retailers out of business, and change the large retailers into wholesalers. Male clerks would disappear along with their "ignorance, meanness, daily lying and dishonesty–in fine, with every attribute of manhood wanting, being compelled, greatly to the benefit of the species, into more manly occupations" (Peirce 1884:67–68). Men belonged outdoors cultivating the soils "where the energies of the stronger sex, both physical and mental, are needed" (Peirce 1884:68).

The ultimate goal would be a more equal distribution of wealth:

> The profits of the household trade would be distributed among households in proportion to their consumption, and thus many of the gigantic fortunes which now tower over society so menacingly, would not be building up, as they daily are, out of the retail profits wrung from the family and the sewing-girl. Co-operative housekeeping, in fact, and without any governmental interference whatever, would equalize the wealth of the community as no other agency by any possibility can. (Peirce 1884:68)

Pierce (1884:72), remarked that men, in industrial society, perform most of their work outside of the house. When they return home at the end of the day, it is for them "the place of ease, refreshing and happiness." However, for the women, the home is a place of "her labor, care, disappointment, and fatigue" (Pierce 1884:72). Therefore, Peirce (1884:73) concluded, why should women not carry on "their feminine vocation of house-keeping, *together*, outside the house, and keep the home, the family circle, as the delightful place of order and beauty, of rest and seclusion for the wife as for the husband—for the daughters as for the sons?"

The idea of cooperative organization was not new since they had thrived in the earlier part of the century at places such as Brook Farm, the Oneida Community, and many other Shaker Communities. The idea of urban cooperatives did blossom in the 1870s and 1880s. In 1879 the concept of French socialists George and Charles Fourier became popular in American culture with the 1877 publication of Henry George's book, *Progress and Poverty*. As a utopianist George championed and popularized Fourierism, which waxed and waned in the 1840s. In the early 19th century, Fourier advocated cooperation over competition and union over individualism. Fourier proposed that society could be divided into smaller groups which he called phalanges. People should inhabit phalansteries, or common buildings, and survive cooperatively.

In 1888 the *Tribune* published a regular column by Edward Brisbane, a popular and influential Fourierist. Another popular novel written in 1888 by Edward Bellamy, *Looking Back*, proclaimed the rewards of cooperation. The novel described a crime-free Boston in the year 2000 with central kitchens and communal dining rooms (Hawes 1993:56-57). Hellen Campbell also published a column in *Good Housekeeping* in 1889 through the 1890s that promoted Women's Exchanges.

Cooperative apartments, in the form of a joint stock company developed around 1880. They were constructed by Philip Hubert, a utopianist. Much of the contemporary literature stirred his intellectual hopes. The firm of Hubert, Pierson, and Company constructed cooperatives, known as Hubert Home Clubs. The Hubert Home Clubs were architecturally innovative, although a furor developed in reaction to the success of this "socialist architecture and living arrangement." Others questioned the legitimacy of a Fourierist making a handsome profit on these cooperatives. While George, Brisbane, and Bellamy's attacks on capitalism, a system responsible for American poverty, were popular, there were few people who wanted to abandon or change the system (Alpern 1975:1; Hawes 1993:57–65).

Cooperation was a powerful concept in late 19th-century American society, a time when divisions in the social and economic spheres of the country widened. This philosophy allowed for increased attention to be focused on the social and economic injustices associated with urban development. Issues such as child labor legislation, welfare and public health programs, tenement house regulations, and social settlements became prominent concerns.

In the 1880s, more and more middle-class women in the United States received a college education. The Settlement Movement, founded in 1886, was one vehicle for contemporary women to put their education and politics into practice. These women lived in the communities where they worked, and they argued for links between housing and social services in neighborhood planning to develop "more livable urban environments through neighborhood regeneration" (Wirka 1996:60). They gave slum areas a social nucleus by providing community centers. These centers became a place to discuss cooperative action on community issues (Mumford 1961:500–501). The mainstream movement pacified, rather than empowered, the settlement communities. The more radical part of the movement, headed by socialists, did help impoverished immigrants fight for better living and working conditions (Wirka 1996:60–62; also see Spencer-Wood 1987,1991).

Probably the most studied settlement house is the Hull House in Chicago. There, Jane Addams wrote about the plight of the factory worker who was driven to alcohol abuse and suicide because of the tedium of labor. She accepted the industrial process and believed alienation of labor was inevitable. However, she thought that if the worker could see how their labor articulated with the manufacturing process, and realize how their work helped to create a product, they would be spiritually uplifted (Addams 1990 [1910]). By encouraging teamwork, the fragmenting affects of the division of labor might not seem as severe. "A man who makes, year after year, but one small wheel in a modern watch factory, may, if his education has properly prepared him, have a fuller life than did the old watchmaker who made a watch from beginning to end" (quoted in Lears 1981:80). Some recent scholars have called Jane Addams and her philosophy "accomodationist," because she willing cooperated with organized capitalism (Lears 1981:80; also see Addams 1972 [1909]; Sklar 1985; Goldmark 1953; Davis 1967).

In New York, other known socialists, such as Mary Kingsbury Simkhovich, based her settlement philosophy on cooperation and collective efforts. She "formed the Cooperative Social Settlement Society in 1901, and founded Greenwich House, the first cooperative social settlement in New York City, a year later" (Wirka 1996:63). Simkhovich believed strong settlements would protect the neighborhood's interests. They could provide childcare, healthcare, and recreational and educational opportunities (Wirka 1996; see Simkhovitch 1938).

In 1889 Helen Campbell developed the "Woman's Work and Wages" column for *Good Housekeeping* (1889:237) which reported on the working accomplishments of women. She invited clubs and exchanges to send reports that may be of value and interest to any women workers. In 1890

(1890a:159–162) she reported on the development of 21 Women's Exchanges throughout the nation. The list appeared in her column in the August 30, 1890 issue of *Good Housekeeping*, and it can also be found in subsequent issues.

Some exchanges developed as consignment shops. A woman would consign a product at an exchange and, if the item sold, she would pay a percentage to the Exchange. The process allowed the woman to earn extra income without burdening her husband. It was also a way to supplement her family's income. One writer, who needed to supplement her family's income, wrote Hellen Campbell for the addresses of Women's Exchanges in other cities. She did not want to embarrass her husband by being seen in an Exchange, since she had to work. By the early 1890s almost every large city had Women's Exchange, the most respected being in New York, Philadelphia, and Buffalo (Campbell 1890a:160–61).

The Mutual Benefit Exchange in New York housed a restaurant for meals for any time of the day. The Exchange " . . . will not consist wholly of fancy articles. Great pains will be taken to cultivate that which is useful, but different from the things commonly seen in shops, particularly the home industries of women who earn their bread, and whose work is distinguished by their care and skill" (Campbell 1890a:162). Describing some nontraditional skills developed by women, Campbell (1890a:162) reported, "Every year widens the field for women. One consignor of the Women's Exchange, known as No. 7,672, earns her living hammering silver. Potpourri jars, hair brushes, pen, card and cigarette trays, paper knives, punch bowls and silver drinking mugs, are among the pieces of repousse work done by 7,672 for the holiday trade" (Campbell 1890a:162).

Campbell told of another type of cooperative. Several women in the Dakota prairies gathered to do work for each other. They divided the chores, such as washing, sewing, and to some extent cooking. The letter in Campbell's column said "five families, all near together, as nearness on a prairie goes, all settled to give up an individual wash-day and devote it to earning the pay for it by sewing and contriving for the two who took the work. . . . By the time three months were over we had reduced the thing to a system" (quoted in Campbell 1890a:159). Everyone in the group performed duties that they enjoyed the most, and they claimed to have more time than ever before. The letter writer kept in mind the Victorian ideology which emphasized a woman's duties were within her house. Cooperatives, and shared living spaces, were inappropriate for teaching values to children and family. She explained "You can't call it a co-operation, because we wouldn't give up our individual homes for anything, but it is a kind of co-operation after all" (quoted in Campbell 1890a:160). The women were contemplating moving closer together into a single structure for their work so they could rely on each other for help and assistance in their cooperative work.

Hellen Campbell's column, "Woman's Work and Wages" came under attack almost immediately. She reported of a "western journal," which remarked it thought it was inappropriate to publish this information in what many perceived to be a magazine that catered to the domestic chores of a woman. The "western journal" reported

> We are sorry for a new departure on the part of our pet magazine, *Good Housekeeping*, which has been as good of its kind as it seemed possible for human work to be. It has introduces a department on "Women's Work and Wages," which has no possible connection with housekeeping. A medical journal might as well give a department to carpentering because men are both doctors and carpenters. We believe heartily in women doing outside work has nothing to do with housekeeping, and we begrudge the pages given to that subject. (quoted in Campbell 1890b:183)

By the turn of the century, the column no longer existed in *Good Housekeeping*.

Social reformer Charles Henderson (1897) also proposed cooperative housekeeping. He noted that for boardinghouse living, or for those who lived in tenements "Many families . . . take their meals at restaurants. But this is felt to be objectionable because it disturbs family privacy and introduces alien elements" (Henderson 1897:33). He then claimed there were good reasons for developing some cooperation between families. Henderson suggested the building of a large number of dwellings around a "common kitchen, with a common heating apparatus and janitor service, while the family could retain its own living rooms separate from all others" (Henderson 1897:33).

Cooperatives succeeded on a small scale in the late 19th century, but they did not last long in America. Those that did exist developed in the most heavily industrialized areas of the United States, such as New England. But they remained small, unlike those found in England. Both Peirce and Henderson point to Rochdale Pioneers of England as a successful cooperative program. It began in 1844 with 28 members and $140 in capital. In 1892 it had 1,459 distributive cooperatives with more than a million members and sales of more than $150,000,000. Henderson (1897:148) explained the American lack of interest in cooperatives and remarked that, until the 1890s, every American had a chance to become a capitalist. Acquiring homesteading lands was relatively easy. Because Americans could still dream of wealth, then cooperatives, and other programs to make life more manageable, escaped the minds of most citizens.

According to Cowen (1979:1–23) women did not necessarily want to see their homes as technologically efficient. Rather, they saw their homes as an escape from the systematic driving forces of industrial culture. Cowen (1983:Chapter 5) thinks women tended to reject alternatives to housework, such as the organization of cooperatives suggested by Pierce. They may have perceived these alternatives as undermining their autonomy within the domestic sphere of their household.

THE MCGRAW BOARDINGHOUSE

In Harpers Ferry, James McGraw's boardinghouse in Lower Town provides an excellent example of cooperative living in a small industrial town. Unfortunately, the National Park Service does not use this building to tell the story of boarders who were the new wage laborers in the town's post-Civil War era. McGraw also used the first floor of these buildings for his store. He modified an 1820s structure, and built an addition to it. These changes created a late 19th-century facade which blended into the rest of the streetscape on Shenandoah Street. Visitors to Harpers Ferry today learn only about the building's function before and during the war. Within the first floors of these buildings, the national park uses this space to interpret a general store from the late 1850s, and the Provost Marshall's office during the Union's occupation. The first floor of another McGraw building is used to interpret the town's history, which includes the Victorian era. The upper floor of one of the buildings, which held the boarding house dining room and boarding rooms, also has very different functions. Much of the space is used for staff offices.

One exhibit exists. It describes a boardingroom used by James Taylor, a famous correspondent and artist who covered Sheridan's Shenandoah Valley campaign. So, while we know Taylor rented an attic room in the building during the Civil War from Mrs. Stipes (see Chapter 2), the Taylor exhibit is not in the third floor room that he occupied. Rather, the exhibit is on the second floor, which is made to look like the third floor room. The exhibit designers created a cramped space with interior dormers and a sloped roof to simulate what his space would have looked like.

The archaeological record from the McGraw boardinghouse can provide information that creates a different memory about boarders in Victorian Harpers Ferry. James McGraw added a substantial addition to the rear of the old master armorer's house to operate a hotel or boardinghouse. The *Spirit of Jefferson* (28 July 1891:3) wrote in 1891:

> Mr. James McGraw, who by the way is one of the best known and most enterprising citizens of Harpers Ferry, has just erected another large house, or addition to his former residence. It is a massive building, fronting on Shenandoah Street, and besides having one of the largest

storerooms in the town, will contain thirty large rooms, for hotel or boarding house purposes. The post office is in this building, but will be moved into the room west of it, which has been nicely fitted up for the purpose.

In April 1892, McGraw advertised his new venture for rent as a "large, new stone and brick dwelling, 26 rooms, fine location. A splendid opening for a first-class Boarding House. Possession from April 1, 1892" (*SoJ* 22 March 1892:2). That same year the *Spirit of Jefferson* described the building as containing "fifty-seven doors elegantly grained in walnut and other items to correspond" (*SoJ* 17 May 1892:3). Of the doors that remain on the second and third floors of McGraw's boardinghouse, many have their numerals varnished over. This feature is leftover from when the structure served as a place for corporate living.

McGraw's construction of a boardinghouse was timely. By the 1880s, Harpers Ferry had undergone a small industrial revival. The bottling works, brewery, hotels, restaurants, paper mill, pulps mill and other enterprises employed working class families who needed boarding accommodations. McGraw's boardinghouse could accommodate some of this growing number of transient workers.

The McGraw family established themselves as leading entrepreneurs in the Harpers Ferry community. By 1897, McGraw's business expansion failed, and James C. and Catherine (Margaret had died in 1896) left town while the court auctioned their assets to satisfy creditors (Fisher 1989:31). Catherine died in Chicago in 1908 at the age of 50. That same year James C. moved back to Harpers Ferry and found work as a wood inspector at the pulp mill owned by Savery, on the Shenandoah River (*FA* 2 May 1908:2). In 1909 he became clerk for the local census enumerator, George Child (*FA* 25 December 1909:2). Sometime after this, he moved to Washington, D.C., and died there in 1913 at the age of 53 (Fenicle 1993).

After a complex set of suits in chancery, the McGraw buildings, including the old master armorer's house and the boardinghouse, were conveyed to William and Mary Ellen Doran in January 1899. William and his sister Mary Ellen operated a store in these buildings, and the 1900 census lists them as "merchant" and "saleslady" (*U.S. Census* 1900). They also continued to operate the boardinghouse.

A PROFILE OF BOARDINGHOUSE LIFE IN HARPERS FERRY

Some form of boarding had taken place in Harpers Ferry since 1796, when of the United States Armory began. The 1860–1920 census data revealed 28 people declared themselves as boardinghouse keepers. The majority were women (n = 25). After 1880, no males claimed this occupation. This figure provides a lower than actual estimate since other census data show women, who were heads-of-household, informally took in boarders, but did not declare an occupation.

Although the exact demographic composition of residents in the McGraw boardinghouse is unknown, a census survey of Harpers Ferry shows that in the late 19th and early 20th century most of the boarders were immigrants from Germany, England, and Ireland. Susan Strasser (1982:148ff) suggests a third of America's population, between 1870 and 1910, were foreign born or first generation. Most of these immigrants were landless transients, searching for an opportunity to earn money by working for others. Immigrants made up a large proportion of the boarding community. Different accommodations existed for different classes of boarders. With a limited amount of wage labor opportunities available for women, they usually operated these boardinghouses. Boardinghouse mistresses prepared food, cleaned dishes, washed bed linens, and often washed the boarders' clothes.

Some artifacts found in the McGraw boardinghouse complex provide general clues about its former occupants. The remains left by these working class residents include one copper alloy crucifix and a holy water container made of gilded hard paste porcelain (Figure 35). Black glass beads from a rosary are also present in the assemblage.

Various smoking pipes are also present in the assemblage. One of them is a short stem pipe made of salt-glazed stoneware. The short stem pipe is often associated with working class people, because it made it possible for them to smoke while doing manual labor (see for instance Trowbridge 1870). Of particular interest are the number and kinds of tobacco clay pipes which are often associated with Irish immigrants. Besides pipes showing typical Irish symbols of shamrock and harp designs, we also found a pipe with the inscription "Home Rule." This long stem pipe, constructed from white clay, has this Irish nationalist slogan stamped and facing the smoker (Figure 36). Cook (1989:227) argues that these pipes enforced a conscious ethnic identity often associated with display and ritual. While the words "Home Rule" face inward, they probably have little to do with "display and ritual" and more to do with reaffirming one's ideals. All together, the artifacts, including the "Home Rule" pipe, the holy water container, and the rosary beads, along with the fact that the boardinghouse owner was Irish, provide contextual information to indicate at least some of the residents were Irish and Roman Catholic.

The presence of an infant nursing bottle, a bottle of whooping cough remedy, and eight marbles implies children of various ages lived in the

Figure 35. Porcelain holy water container and copper alloy crucifix from the McGraw boardinghouse assemblage. (Photograph by Cari YoungRavenhorst)

boardinghouse. The nursing bottle provides some complex scenarios regarding the relationship between mother and child in the boardinghouse. By the late 19th century, nursing bottles and nipples were easily available on a national level through catalogs, such as Montgomery Ward. Eric Larsen remarks that the nursing bottle and the nipple replaced the necessity of a mother's presence in the care of an infant. "The mother's role no longer required a biological mother" (Larsen 1994:73–74). Because the

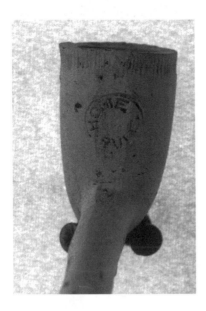

Figure 36. Home Rule pipe found in the McGraw boardinghouse assemblage. (Photography by Cari YoungRavenhorst)

mother was no longer tied to the infant, she could work in a factory, or maintain the household or the boardinghouse. Reformers feared that while the poor turned to artificial feeding, the mother would cease to mother her offspring and blur accepted gender roles (Larsen 1994:73).

Reformers denounced the use of infant foods and blamed them for the high infant mortality rate prevalent among the lower class, ignoring other issues such as sanitation conditions in urban areas. Ironically, it was the middle and upper classes who increasingly used the formulas because the high cost made bottle feeding inaccessible to the poor. The presence of the feeding bottle, therefore, may be an indication of residents pursuing middle class ideals, or it may be related to a woman needing to perform other duties during the day (Larsen 1994:74).

Health Conditions in the McGraw Boardinghouse

By the late 19th century the sanitary reform movement was well underway in the United States. Many new publications preached the virtues of basic sanitary principles (Waring 1867 1876; Bayles 1879; Griscom 1970). The national health reform movement pressured governments to fund sewage systems (Galishoff 1976:31–32; Giglierano 1976:229).

Harpers Ferry merchants and entrepreneurs, like James Garland Hurst, publicly advocated sanitary reform policies, although, archaeological data reveal that their practices contradicted what they advocated. Harpers Ferrians continued to rely on privies well into the 20th century. The city council also continued to allow pigs to run freely through the streets (*SoJ* 17 January 1873:3; *SoJ* 6 January 1891:2).

To accommodate the boardinghouse occupants, McGraw constructed a mortar-laid and shale-lined privy. It measures 8 feet x 3 feet. Stud pockets in the remaining rear wall suggest that it contained three stalls. The interior substructure is pargetted on the north, east, and west walls and the bottom 6 feet of the vault. Drainage passes through the south unpargetted wall. The unpargetted side violated health codes of the day for the containment of waste matter (Ford 1993:12.23–12.26).

Excavations in the boardinghouse yard reveals the presence of three glazed terra-cotta sewage pipes that drained across the backyard. Contemporary health experts prescribed terra-cotta for sewer pipes since it was nonporous (Waring 1876:45). The terra-cotta pipes associated with the McGraw boardinghouse carried materials away from the house to the Shenandoah River. The swift currents of the river were thought to sterilize and purify the waste.

With the construction of the boardinghouse McGraw renovated an old cistern system. The armory originally had contractors build it in the 1840s and McGraw enlarged it in 1891–1892. It served as the only water source for the boardinghouse complex until piped-in water from Loudoun Heights, across the Shenandoah River, reached town in the early 20th-century (Ford 1993:12.23–12.26).

About that time, the new boardinghouse owners, William and Mary Doran, installed indoor plumbing on the third floor. The bathroom included a sink, bathtub, and a flushing toilet. A 1903 patent date on a bathroom fixture provides a general date for installation. The date coincides closely with the introduction of water service to Lower Town Harpers Ferry (1895–1906) and the end of the privy's use (circa 1906). Several cast-iron drain pipes and ferrous water service pipes exist next to the boardinghouse, all dating to the first decade of the 20th century (Ford 1993:12.26–12.28; also, see Ford 1994).

Eric Larsen (1993:11.40–11.64) analyzed the bottles found in the McGraw boardinghouse privy (Table 9). More than 75 percent (*n* = 1154) of them are medicine bottles, while alcohol (9.8 percent, *n* = 149) and chemical (8.7 percent, *n* = 133) bottles represent a much smaller amount. The large quantity of medicine bottles is skewed by 1,061 identical small bottles. Like the medicine bottles, they are three-piece mold and were manufactured by Whitall Tatum & Co. or Carr-Lowrey Glass Co. (Figure 37). The bottles were sold in the 1880 Whitall Tatum catalog (Whitall Tatum & Co. 1880) as round, wide-mouth prescription bottles. These bottles

Table 9. Glass Vessels from McGraw's Boardinghouse Privy[a]

Vessel form	N	Percent
Tumbler	12	34
Stemware	6	17
Pitcher	2	6
Cup	1	3
Shot glass	1	3
Berry dish/sauce	2	6
Bowl (miscellaneous)	3	9
Butter dish	0	0
Salt/pepper shaker	1	3
Spoon holder	1	3
Celery holder	1	3
Cake salve	1	3
Unidentified	4	11
Total	**35**	**100**

[a]From Lucas (1993:14.20).

Figure 37. Over 1000 of these medicine bottles were found in the McGraw boardinghouse assemblage. (Photo by Cari YoungRavehorst)

were distributed throughout all layers of the privy. This distribution pattern suggests the deposition is not the product of a single depositional phase, such as the emptying of a drug store, or a very large medicine cabinet. Rather, this consistent and equal distribution suggests that the users consumed the contents over a ten-year period, the time that the privy existed.

The contents of the 1,061 medical bottles are unknown, but there is a range of possibilities for their use. The bottles are generic prescription bottles, similar to Bromo-Seltzer bottles. Prior to 1906 Bromo Seltzer and other similar products had high concentration of the crystalline compound acetanilid. "Acetanilid, having similar properties to aspirin, is used in medicine chiefly as an analgesic (for pain reduction) and an antipyretic (to prevent and remove fever)" (Larsen 1993:11.46). The product is potent and could be fatal. A 1906 explanation of the product noted that:

> Bromo-seltzer is commonly sold in drug stores, both by the bottle and at soda fountains. The full dose is "a heaping teaspoonful." A heaping teaspoonful of Bromo-seltzer means about 10 grains of acetanilid. The United States Pharmacopeia dose is four grains; five grains have been known to produce fatal results. The prescribed dose of Bromo-seltzer is dangerous and has been known to produce sudden collapse. (Adams 1905 & 1906:37)

Acetanilids, often used as headache powders, had habit-forming properties, although not as severe as opium and cocaine (Adams 1905 & 1906). Whether the bottles contained acetanilid, or one of the many other narcotics available prior to 1906, is unknown. The large quantity and even distribution of these bottles throughout the privy context suggests that perhaps the bottles contained a habit-forming substance. These bottles were not found in any yard refuse. It looks as though their users disposed of the bottles very carefully. "[A]ddictive behavior seen as a social disorder, the user may have attempted to conceal his/her habit" (see Larsen 1993:11.48–11.49).

Harpers Ferry sanitation at the turn of the 20th century was far from perfect. Samples from the boardinghouse privy further illustrate the poor health conditions of workers and their families since they contained evidence of intestinal roundworm and whipworm (Table 10) (Reinhard 1993, 1994). Clearly, sanitation problems persisted in Harpers Ferry into the early 20th century. The possibility of other fecal-borne diseases exists, and pathogen-induced diarrhea was probably another health problem at Harpers Ferry (Reinhard 1993:13.8).

Of the identified medicine bottles (Table 11), over half are either painkillers or national cures. Some painkillers include Bromo-Caffein, Bromo-Celery, and Keasby & Mattison bottles. Other painkillers include Davis Vegetable Pain Killer (Fike 1987:130) and Prof. Low's Magnetic Liniment

Table 10. Egg Concentration Values by Bag Number and Species
from the McGraw Boardinghouse Privy.[a]

Layer	T. *Trichiura* (whipworm)	A. *Lumbricoides* (intestinal roundworm)	N
E	570	570	2
E2	None	90	1
E3	None	2,260	1
E4	None	570	3
E5	570	5,090	10
E6	570	1,130	3

(N) Number of parasite eggs per milliliter of soil.
[a]From Reinhard (1993:13.2).

(Devner 1968:59). National products include Rumford Chemical Works, Andrews & Thompson bottle, Stonebraker Chemical Co., Wyeth & Bro., A.C. Meyer & Co., and Koenig Med. Co., Keasbey & Mattison. The exact content of these latter bottles is not known (Larsen 1993:11.44). Laxatives include Pitchers Castoria bottles and California Fig Syrup. Other digestive remedies were Dewitt's Colic and Cholera Cure, and Chamberlain's Colic, Cholera, and Diarrhea Remedy, both of which claimed to relieve severe stomach cramps that accompany colic (Fike 1987:152, 205–206). Dr. D. Jaynes Alterative was a universal cure that also purported to cure ulcers (Fike 1987:168). Fairchild Bros. & Foster/Essence of Pepsin is also present, it was used for settling upset stomachs (Devner 1970:11).

A graduated nursing bottle and a bottle of DeLavau's Whooping Cough Remedy, both related to child care, are also present (see Larsen 1994). Teeth and breath care bottles are represented by Van Buskirk's Fragrant Sozodont for Teeth and Breath and Rubifoam for the Teeth.

Table 11. Breakdown of Identifiable Bottles into
Medicine Types from the McGraw Boardinghouse
Privy.[a]

Medicine type	N	Percent
Digestive remedies	9	18.37
Pain killers	12	24.49
Tooth care	4	8.16
Child care	2	4.08
National cures	14	28.57
Prescriptions	5	10.20
Other	3	6.12
Total	**49**	**100.0**

(N) number of bottles; (Percent) percentage of identifiable bottles.
[a]From Larsen (1993:11.44).

Five prescription bottles from the local area are also present in the assemblage. They include a MisKimon Pharmacist bottle (Harpers Ferry), an H.V. Daniels bottle (Harpers Ferry), a George T. Light bottle (Charlestown, West Virginia), and a Baker & McMurran's bottle (Shepherdstown, West Virginia) (Larsen 1993:11.46).

BOARDINGHOUSE MEALS

The Table Setting

Michael Lucas (1993:14.1–14.36) analyzed the ceramic assemblage for the boardinghouse. Most of the ceramic vessels are refined earthenwares (74 percent, n = 59), of which almost half have transfer-printed decoration (41 percent, n = 24). The ceramics have a wide range of decorative patterns that includes decal, painted, enameled, luster, molded, and gilded wares.

The plates that once adorned the boardinghouse table range in size from 7, 7.5, 8, 9, and 10 inches (Figure 38) of which four are undecorated and four are transfer-printed. One is a gilded porcelain plate and one is a

Figure 38. A variety of plate sizes and decorations found in the McGraw boardinghouse assemblage. (Photograph by Cari YoungRavenhorst)

hand painted plate. The four transfer printed plates are dessert plates. Half (n = 10) of the tableware items are serving vessels, most of which are undecorated (Lucas 1993:14.14–14.18) (Table 12).

Cups and saucers comprise a third (33 percent, n = 26) of the entire ceramic assemblage. The majority (62 percent, n = 16) are transfer printed, and only two are undecorated. Six (23 percent) tea or coffee cups, six (23 percent) saucers, and three plates have the "Sydenham" pattern. Most of the coffee/tea wares are whiteware, an earthenware, and less than a fifth (19 percent, n = 5) are porcelains (Lucas 1993:14.18).

Six sets are present in the assemblage, the largest consisting of 15 vessels of a matching transfer print (six cups and saucers and three 7.5-inch plates) (Table 13). Another set has a transfer-printed geometrical Japanese-style design (Godden 1964:225). Two of the sets were porcelain (one gilded and one decal) (Kovel and Kovel 1986:120). The last set is decal whiteware made by Johnson Brothers (Godden 1964:355). One chamber set is present including two ewers, one chamber pot, and one basin (Lucas 1993:14.18).

Almost two-thirds of the entire dining-related glassware is drinking vessels. The glassware includes tumblers (34 percent, n = 12), other drinking vessels (17 percent, n = 6), stemware pieces (6 percent, n = 2) pitchers (3 percent, n = 1), a handled cup (3 percent, n = 1), and a shot glass (3 percent, n = 1). Other vessels include dishes or bowls, one milk glass bowl, one colorless leaf-shaped vessel, and one footed milk glass dish. Other vessel forms include a cake salve, salt or pepper shaker, a spoon holder, and a celery holder (Table 14).

The ceramics and glass tableware do not necessarily reflect any boarder's personal preferences, but rather the choice of the boardinghouse operators. As seen at other boardinghouse sites, the predominance of platters may mean food was placed in the center of the table and shared between diners (also see Landon 1989:42). Platters, plates, and bakers are undecorated at this boardinghouse. In the middle of the 19th century white undecorated dinner services had been fashionable. In England, for instance, one writer noted a possible prejudice against French white serving dishes, "but they are infinitely preferable to the 'willow pattern' and its monstrous devices" (Table Observances 1854:23). But by the 1880s white dinner services had become unfashionable (Collard 1984:135; Majewski and O'Brien 1987:123). These undecorated ceramics became known as "Thrasher's China" (Dutton 1988:91). By the late 19th century, distributors advertised Thrashers China in mail order catalog advertisements and targeted hotels and boardinghouses. Their thick, bulky construction and durability appealed to these establishments (Sears, Roebuck & Co. 1929:797).

Table 12. Ceramic Vessels from the McGraw Boardinghouse Privy.[a]

Functional category	Vessel form	N	Percent	Context A
Tableware	Plate 10 in.	2	10	3
	Plate 9 in.	1	5	1
	Plate 8 in.	2	10	3
	Plate 7.5 in.	4	20	5
	Plate 7 in.	1	5	1
	Plate daim?	0	0	0
	Platter	2	10	3
	Butter pat	0	0	0
	Bowl	0	0	0
	Sauce dish	0	0	0
	Pitcher	2	10	3
	Baker	4	20	5
	Creamer	2	10	3
	Other	0	0	0
Subtotal		**20**	**100**	**25**
Tea/Coffee	Cup	11	42	14
	Saucer	15	58	19
	Tea pot	0	0	0
Subtotal		**26**	**100**	**33**
Storage/Food preparation	Crock/Jar	2	33	3
	Bowl	1	17	1
	Pie plates	0	0	0
	Unidentified	3	50	4
Subtotal		**6**	**100**	**8**
Personal	Chamber pot	1	10	1
	Ewer	2	20	3
	Basin	1	10	1
	Slop jar	1	10	1
	Tooth brush holder	1	10	1
	Soap dish	1	10	1
	Chamber lids	2	20	3
Subtotal		**10**	**100**	**13**
Other vessels	Flower pot	10	55	13
	Flower pot Saucer	5	27	6
	Unidentified	3	17	4
Subtotal		**18**	**100**	**23**
Total		**80**	**NA**	**100**

(N) number within feature; (Percent) percentage withing functional category; (Context A) percentage within context A.
[a] From Lucas (1993:14.17).

Table 13. Ceramic Sets Present in the McGraw's Boardinghouse Privy.[a]

Set	Ware	Decoration	Forms	Potter/Date	Source
A	Whiteware	Transfer	1 Saucer, 1 Platter	Dunn Bennet & Co. 1875–1890	Godden 1964 pg. 225
B	Whiteware	Transfer	6 Cups, 6 Saucers, 3 Plates	Unidentified G & O	—
C	Porcelain	Guilded	1 Plate, 1 Saucer	Unidentified	—
D	Porcelain	Decal	2 Cups	Jager & Co., ca. 1902	Kovel 1986 pg. 120
E	Whiteware	Decal	1 Saucer, 1 Pitcher	Johnson Bros. after 1900	Godden pg. 355

[a]From Lucas (1993:14.18).

Items like bowls used for stews and soups are surprisingly absent from the boardinghouse assemblage (Lucas 1993:14.22–14.24).

The presence of many decorated pieces and matched sets, and porcelain tea sets may have been recycled by the boardinghouse owners, although, Lucas (1993:14.24) notes in his analysis that these fancier items show less wear than the "Thrasher's China." They might have been reserved for the boardinghouse keepers and their families.

A high percentage of cups and saucers seem common among boardinghouse assemblages, especially since coffee had become an important part of late 19th-century working-class culture (Levenstein 1988:100). At the Boott Mills boardinghouse in Lowell, Massachusetts, tea and coffee wares comprise 29.3 percent of the ceramic assemblage (Dutton 1988:92). At the McGraw boardinghouse in Harpers Ferry, these coffee and tea

Table 14. Glass Vessel Counts From the McGraw Boardinghouse Privy.[a]

Container type	N	Percent
Medicine*	1154	75.6
Alcohol	149	9.8
Chemical	133	8.7
Food	3	0.2
Ink	8	0.5
Personal	8	0.5
Other	71	4.7
Total	**1526**	**100.0**

* includes 1061 three piece mold unmarked bottles; (N) total number of containers; (Percent) percentage of containers.
[a]From Larsen (1993:11.43).

wares comprise 33 percent of the entire ceramic assemblage, suggesting that the structure contained working-class occupants.

The glass tableware was all probably purchased through a mail order catalog (see for instance Sears Roebuck and Co. 1970:1092). By the turn of the century full glass sets such as pitchers, berry dishes, and spoon holders were commonly advertised in catalogs (Lucas 1993:14.24–14.25).

Fruits and Vegetables Consumed in the Boardinghouse

Evidence of fruits and seeds can be identified by examining the fecal matter in the privy. Compared with other late 19th-century sites in Harpers Ferry, the diet of the boardinghouse members lacks variety. Only six different seeds from fruits and vegetables are present. More than 50 percent of the entire macrofloral assemblage is raspberry seed. Also found in large amounts are tomato seeds. Fig, strawberry, grape, apple, and blueberry also exist, but in smaller quantities (Table 15). The presence of a buffalo burr seed in the privy, a weed found in the surrounding boardinghouse yardscape, may mean soil was shoveled into this privy to dampen the foul odor (Cummings 1993:7.36–7.40).

By the late 19th-century, fruits had become an essential component of the American diet, based not on their nutritional value, but rather "as an agreeable stimulant to digestion" (Peltz 1883:201). Kitchen manuals proscribed a jelly bag for every kitchen, and they provided recipes for various jellies (Peltz 1883:201). Many canned fruits and vegetables became accessible after the mid-19th century as canning developed into a major industry (Ward 1882:32–33). From 1890 to the first decade of the 20th century, the output of canned goods increased by almost 10 times (Powell 1917:11). Some of the fruits identified from the boardinghouse privy were likely from this new mass production, although it is equally probable that they could have been eaten fresh or as jellies and preserves (Cummings 1993:7.42–7.46).

Meats Consumed in the Boardinghouse

Brett Burk (1993a:15.1–15.12) identified the boardinghouse faunal materials. The assemblage contains 2,101 bone elements from 29 taxonomic groups: 11 fish, 5 birds, and 13 mammals.

The fish includes alewife, Atlantic herring, minnow or carp, carp, sucker, catfish, channel catfish, haddock, sunfish, and smallmouth bass. Only the Atlantic herring and the haddock are not freshwater inhabitants. The majority (192 of 208, or 92.3%) of the identified elements are predominantly from the sucker and carp or minnow families (Table 16). Appar-

Table 15. Macrofloral Remains Recovered from the McGraw Boardinghouse Privy.[a]

Identification	Part	Char whole	Char frag	Unch whole	Unch frag
1907: Layer E					
Ficus (fig)	Seed			987*	
Ficus/Fragaria	Seed				37*
Fragaria (strawberry)	Seed			680*	
Lycopersicor (tomato)	Seed			66*	10*
Malus sp. (Apple)	Seed			2	
Rubus (raspberry)	Seed			1006*	26*
Vaccinium (blueberry)	Seed			16*	19*
Vitis (grape)	Seed			22	4
ca.1900: Layer E-2					
Ficus (fig)	Seed			32*	
Ficus/Fragaria	Seed				80*
Fragaria (strawberry)	Seed			8*	
Lycopersicon (tomato)	Seed			168*	40*
Rubus (raspberry)	Seed			464*	48*
Solanum cf. sarrachoides	Seed			1	1
Vitis (grape)	Seed			64*	120*
late 1890s: Layer E-3					
Ficus (fig)	Seed			300*	
Ficus/Fragaria	Seed				505*
Fragaria (strawberry)	Seed			40*	
Lycopersicon (tomato)	Seed			582*	268*
Rubus (raspberry)	Seed			2710*	224
Vaccinium (blueberry)	Seed			10	4
Vitis (grape)	Seed			10*	27*
1890s: Layer E-4					
cf. Carya (hickory)	Nutshell				7
Ficus (fig)	Seed			64*	
Ficus/Fragaria	Seed				
85*					
Fragaria (strawberry)	Seed			8*	
Rubus (raspberry)	Seed			1251*	136*
Solanum cf. rostatum (buffalo bur)	Seed			1	1
Vitis (grape)	Seed			47	102*
1890s: Layer E-5					
Ficus (fig)	Seed			25*	
Ficus/Fragaria	Seed				
48*					
Fragaria (strawberry)	Seed			5*	
Lycopersicon (tomato)	Seed			32*	78*
Vitis (grape)	Seed			16*	88*

Table 15. *Continued*

Identification	Part	Char whole	Char frag	Unch whole	Unch frag
1890s: Layer E-6					
Ficus (fig)	Seed			30*	
Ficus/Fragaria	Seed				192*
Fragaria (strawberry)	Seed			3*	
Lycopersicon (tomato)	Seed			432*	27*
Malus sp. (Apple)	Seed			1	
Rubus (raspberry)	Seed			2304*	150*
Sambucus (elderberry)	Seed			1	
Solanum rostratum (buffalo-bur)	Seed			1	
Vitis (grape)	Seed			4	18

*indicates an estimated seed or seed fragment frequency based on sort of a portion of the total volume floated.
ªFrom Cummings (1993:7.37).

ently the boardinghouse keeper relied on the town's riverine environment for food resources, rather than relying solely upon a larger regional provisioning system (Burk 1993a:15.4). By the late 19th century carp was no longer considered a delicacy. Cassell's (1875:340) noted that "In many parts of the Continent it is still held in more esteem than, in our opinion, its culinary merits entitle it to. It is, in fact, a fish to keep in ponds, as we keep pretty birds in cages—to look at and not to eat."

The birds eaten at the boardinghouse include duck, goose, chicken, and turkey. Chicken comprises most of the identified bird remains. The presence of chicken beaks (n = 3) may mean the boardinghouse keeper raised and butchered the birds on the site (Burk 1993a:15.4). Chicken would require a small amount of space to raise and they provide eggs and meat (see Landon 1987:130)

Wild mammals in the assemblage include Opossum, Eastern Cottontail, Eastern Gray Squirrel, and Old World Tat. The first three are food sources to supplement market purchased domestic meats such as cow, pig, and sheep/goat. These domestic animals make up 40 percent of the boardinghouse's total biomass with cow contributing almost 34 percent (Burk, 1993a:15.4–15.6).

Of particular interest is the large number of calf skulls identified (Figure 39). More than 57 percent (n = 68) of the cow elements are skull and mandible pieces. They were all cut down the center (Burk 1993a:15.11). Although unappetizing to our modern western palates, recipes for cooking calf skulls are often found in period cookbooks.

Table 16. Summary of Faunal Assemblage for the McGraw Boardinghouse Privy.[a]

Taxon	N	Percent	MNI	Percent	Meat Weight (lbs)	Total Meat Wt. (lbs)	Percent	Weight (gms)	Percent	Biomass (kg)	Percent
Class Osteichthyes (bony fish)	3	0.2	0/ 0	0.0	0.0/ 0.0	0.0	0.0	0.3	0.0	0.00	0.0
Anser anser (dom. goose)	1	0.1	1/ 0	2.9	6.0/ 6.0	6.0	0.6	2.0	0.0	0.01	0.0
Anas spp. (dabbling duck)	1	0.1	1/ 0	2.9	0.0/ 0.0	0.0	0.0	0.5	0.0	0.00	0.0
cf. Family Phasianidae	11	0.7	0/ 0	0.0	0.0/ 0.0	0.0	0.0	3.3	0.0	0.02	0.1
Gallus gallus (chicken)	169	10.2	5/ 8	37.1	2.5/ 1.0	20.5	2.2	251.3	3.4	0.81	3.5
cf. Gallus gallus (chicken)	5	0.3	0/ 0	0.0	0.0/ 0.0	0.0	0.0	4.2	0.1	0.02	0.1
Class Mammalia (mammal)	433	26.2	0/ 0	0.0	0.0/ 0.0	0.0	0.0	975.2	13.0	3.00	13.1
Class Mammalia I (large mammal)	96	5.8	0/ 0	0.0	0.0/ 0.0	0.0	0.0	1966.1	26.3	5.63	24.6
Class Mammalia II (med. mammal)	77	4.7	0/ 0	0.0	0.0/ 0.0	0.0	0.0	502.4	6.7	1.65	7.2
Class Mammalia III (sm. mammal)	139	8.4	0/ 0	0.0	0.0/ 0.0	0.0	0.0	146.7	2.0	0.55	2.4
Didelphis virginiana (opossum)	3	0.2	1/ 0	2.9	8.0/ 8.0	8.0	0.9	21.1	0.3	0.10	0.4
Sylvilagus floridanus (cottontail)	19	1.2	2/ 0	5.7	2.0/ 2.0	4.0	0.4	17.2	0.2	0.08	0.3
cf. Sylvilagus floridanus	2	0.1	0/ 0	0.0	0.0/ 0.0	0.0	0.0	2.4	0.0	0.01	0.1
Sciurus carolinensis (gray squirrel)	12	0.7	2/ 0	5.7	1.0/ 1.0	2.0	0.2	8.8	0.1	0.04	0.2
cf. Sciurus carolinensis	2	0.1	0/ 0	0.0	0.0/ 0.0	0.0	0.0	0.8	0.0	0.01	0.0
Rattus spp. (Old World rat)	16	1.0	3/ 0	8.6	0.0/ 0.0	0.0	0.0	5.5	0.1	0.03	0.1
Felis domesticus (dom. cat)	21	1.3	0/ 3	8.6	0.0/ 0.0	0.0	0.0	33.6	0.4	0.15	0.6
cf. Felis domesticus (dom. cat)	14	0.8	0/ 0	0.0	0.0/ 0.0	0.0	0.0	6.6	0.1	0.03	0.1
Order Artiodactyla II	9	0.5	0/ 0	0.0	0.0/ 0.0	0.0	0.0	61.5	0.8	0.25	1.1
Sus scrofa (dom. pig)	47	2.8	2/ 1	8.6	100.0/ 50.0	250.0	27.0	324.8	4.3	1.11	4.9
cf. Sus scrofa (dom. pig)	3	0.2	0/ 0	0.0	0.0/ 0.0	0.0	0.0	35.5	0.5	0.15	0.7
Bos taurus (dom. cow)	86	5.2	1/ 4	14.3	400.0/ 50.0	600.0	64.8	2251.9	30.1	6.36	27.8
cf. Bos taurus (dom. cow)	33	2.0	0/ 0	0.0	0.0/ 0.0	0.0	0.0	519.7	6.9	1.70	7.4
Ovis aries/Capra hircus (sheep/goat)	4	0.2	1/ 0	2.9	35.0/ 15.0	35.0	3.8	61.5	0.8	0.25	1.1
					84BP - PRIVY MATTER SUMMARY CHART							
Totals	1650	100.0	35	100.0	−/ −	925.5	100.0	7489.7	100.0	22.86	100.0

(N) number of bones identified to that taxon; (MNI) Minimum Number of Individuals. The number before the slash is the number of adults and the number of immature specimens follows the slash; (Meat Weight) meat weight of the entire animal (adult/immature); (Total Meat Weight) derived by multiplying the MNI by the Meat Weight and then adding the two sides of the slash together. (Weight) weight of the actual archaeological bones; (Biomass) seketal weight.
[a]From Burk (1993a:15.7).

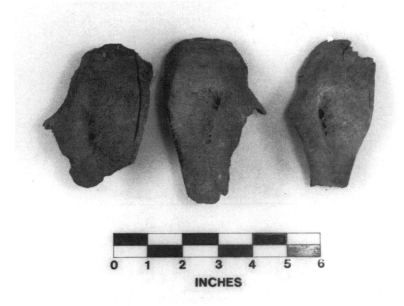

Figure 39. Calf skull remains from the McGraw boardinghouse assemblage. (Photograph by Cari YoungRavenhorst.

Calves' heads could be purchased from the butcher either skinned or unskinned. "If there are no signs of horns, the animal was too young to be wholesome as food" (Goodholme 1877:69). It could be served either whole, or hashed or stewed. Calves' heads were usually used for "Mock Turtle Soup." The calf's head was cleaned and boiled for up to four hours (Figure 40). The next day the cold meat was minced, seasoned, and then cooked in a soup (Campbell 1881:123; also, see Tyree 1879).

> On a scalded head the ear is left in its natural position, erect; the eye also remains in its entire beneath the lid. From a skinned head we always have the eye-ball removed, simply for the sake of rendering it more sightly. The iris and the crystalline lens are not the eatable parts, and, whether cooked or uncooked, are no ornament after death. The dibble portion, one of the epicure's tid bits, lies deep in the socket of the eye, and is not injured by the removal of the poor calf's ogling apparatus. (Cassell's 1875:376)

After being boiled for several hours (depending upon the size of the head), it could be served plain, with the cheek upward. Or beaten eggs could be smeared over the head, bread crumbs or biscuit raspings dusted over this, and then browned in the oven. For the parts removed prior to cooking,

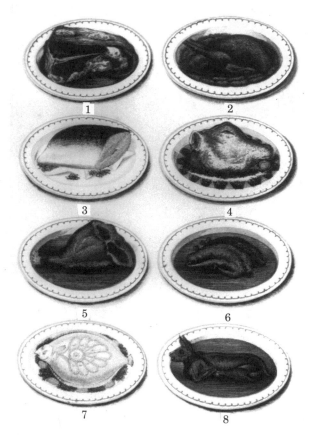

Figure 40. Calves head on a platter (second column, second row). From a late 19th-century home management guide. (Cassell's 1875, inside cover)

Cassell's (1875:377) lists other recipes such as brain sauce, brain cakes, and fine herb sauce.

The calf's head was also split and served whole on a platter. One recipe said:

> Remove the eye-ball and the cartridge of the nose; shorten the jawbones, so as to get rid of the teeth, but leaving the meat which covered them, and throw them away. . . . (Cassell's 1875:139)

The head was to boil for three hours before carrots, turnips, onions, and leeks could be added. Then it all boiled for another hour.

> When done take it up, and raise the flesh of the cheek and the part containing the glands of the neck off the bones, keeping them entire.

Trim this lump of meat freely into shape, and set it aside for another day. The trimmings, the eye, and the fore part of the head, served with vegetables, will make a nice dish. (Cassell's 1875:139)

In 1878, Henry Allen (1878:74) wrote about the different quality of meats found on the calf's head. He said the area nearest the end of the jawbone was considered the choicest part. The meat found in the under-part of the lower jaw is also considered to have tasty meat. The part above the ear has some fat and it is a bit gristly, but it is also a desired part. The part nearest the neck, Allen described, is considered inferior and it is not worth eating. Some people like the eye, which should be cut out with the point of a knife, and divided into two before consuming. Recipes for lamb's head and pig's head are also provided (Allen 1878:82–83).

Generally, the ceramics from the boardinghouse consist of a large quantity of platters rather than bowls. This evidence suggests that much of the boardinghouse foods would not have been prepared as soups (see Lucas 1993:14.1–14.36). Generally, beef was the main staple, followed by pig. The boardinghouse keeper also procured some game. The use of wild foods would have offset the food costs incurred from running a boarding-house. Consuming wild species decreased the boardinghouse keeper's reli-ance upon the market system and gave this person some sense of au-tonomy.

Post-McGraw Use of the Boardinghouse

In 1907, Mary Ellen Doran purchased the building that had formerly housed the bottling works, along with the stable, and McGraw's former dwelling and boardinghouse. She operated a pool hall on the first floor and a restaurant on the second floor of the former McGraw residence (Figure 41). She also operated a store in the old master armorer's house. The Dorans could provide quality goods for their customers because Mary Ellen often traveled to New York to obtain the latest fashions. The board-inghouse still operated into the early 20th century; town records show a license granted to George Green to operate one in the "McGraw building" in 1907 (Harpers Ferry Town Records 1 July 1907:525). By this time the boardinghouse privy had been filled, and plumbing had been installed on the third floor. Because of new sanitation practices, the material record of residences becomes more difficult to piece together after this date. Mate-rials that would have once been deposited in a household's yard, privy, or abandoned well, now were discarded in the community dump. A new dump opened in Harpers Ferry along the Shenandoah River, in an area that once had housed several domestic structures, but was virtually vacant after several late 19th-century floods destroyed these buildings. Parts of

Figure 41. The Dorans and others in front of their residence, circa 1910 (the former McGraw residence). (Courtesy, Harpers Ferry National Historical Park)

this dump have also been eroded away during the major 20th-century floods.

The analysis of materials from the boardinghouse provides significant insight into the late 19th-century boarders in the commercial district of Harpers Ferry. By the late 19th century in Harpers Ferry, and in many cities in the United States, boarders represented a growing segment of the urban population. It is a story that is often neglected when park interpreters talk about nationally significant developments that occurred in the park.

In the first half of the 19th century, boardinghouse arrangements in Harpers Ferry were small and informal. Individual households often supplemented their income by taking in one or two boarders. But, after the Civil War and with the redevelopment of industry, such as the flour mill, brewery and bottling works, and the pulp mill, wage laborers from the outside flocked to these industries. Many tourists also came to town for rest, amusement, and to visit Civil War sites. Many nontourist boarders were immigrant working-class families. While national reformers wanted board-inghouses abolished, entrepreneurs continued to build and operate them in Harpers Ferry and in other areas around the country. McGraw's board-inghouse received indoor plumbing in the first decade of the 20th century. The building served as a multifamily dwelling into the 1930s. After the 1942 flood, much of Lower Town Harpers Ferry was vacant, with only a few dwellings occupied. With the major industries no longer operating, the need to house workers and their families decreased substantially. Tourists stayed in the Upper Town areas that were not subject to flooding. The McGraw boardinghouse stood vacant.

Guidebooks may have provided some general directions for everyday behavior, but archaeological analysis of the material from Victorian Harp-ers Ferry indicates people did not necessarily follow the advice. Household reformers proposed Victorian ideals, suggesting women should not partici-pate in boardinghouse life. These conditions, they warned, only led to the breakdown of family values. Despite this advice, women and children continued to participate in boardinghouse life in Harpers Ferry.

The fact that McGraw constructed a boardinghouse in 1890s Harpers Ferry while national reformers advocated the abolition of these establish-ments, highlights the contradiction between the written and the material record. For this reason, it is important to recognize that when creating a public memory of our past we need to go beyond the written record. Archaeology is one way we can provide a history of people who have been traditionally overlooked by the recorders of history. In the case of Harpers Ferry, archaeologists collected and analyzed a boardinghouse assemblage and used this information to shed light on the story of these otherwise unknown people. Archaeology provides a venue through which we can gain a fuller picture of late 19th-century life. Because of these archaeologi-cal excavations, and the emphasis placed on them during this research, they now occupy a spot in a new interpretive exhibit of the town. Archae-ology can be a powerful tool that can help change the public memory of a place.

The Assassination
of Plurality
Material Wealth and Consumption in Victorian Harpers Ferry

REMEMBERING HARPERS FERRY

Memories can be individual or collective experiences by people who have shared histories. Whether internally coherent, or contradictory to the dominant view, memories validate the holders' version of the past. Collective memories can serve the dominant culture and support the existing hierarchy, although, subordinate groups can challenge and subvert dominant meanings. As a group, people decide not only which experiences to remember and which ones to forget but also how to interpret these experiences.

This archaeology project at Harpers Ferry began as a data recovery project made necessary by the 1966 National Historic Preservation Act, as amended. Archaeology at Harpers Ferry National Historical Park performed before, as well as after the creation of this act, concentrated on what contemporaries perceived as nationally significant issues, the Civil War and the United States Armory. The goal of archaeology was to help recreate and interpret an 1850s townscape. However, many archaeologists who excavated Victorian deposits in the 1960 and 1970s often discarded these remains, justifying that the materials could not enhance the interpretation of the park (see introduction). It was not until the 1980s that this national park began to broaden its perspectives about its past. It began to incorporate a more inclusive history and archaeology into its mission. The Lower Town archaeology project in Harpers Ferry performed in the 1990s, had more inclusive research goals than previous archaeology programs. This archaeology project is part of a growing national trend which demands a more inclusive history that recognizes cultural diversity. Although, by no means, is every park or federal institution eagerly joining in on this new paradigm.

Therefore, when we think about how we shape our national histories we must recognize people develop a collective memory by molding, shaping, and agreeing on memories. The archaeology of the Victorian era in Harpers Ferry is, I believe, an important program that is helping park managers to create and expand our views of our national story. Much of the archaeology presented in this book has been incorporated into a new park exhibit that documents the history of the town. Archaeology has contributed significantly to expanding the boundaries of the park's interpretation of the town. This archaeological analysis also provides a fruitful context for understanding why some of the town's histories are remembered while others are ignored.

THE ASSASSINATION OF PLURALITY

Harpers Ferry's postwar redevelopment occurred in an era when Americans were becoming increasingly divided along social, economic, ethnic, and racial lines. In his introduction to *The Land of Contrast:1880– 1901*, Neil Harris (1970) makes important observations on how Victorian society developed during the last quarter of the 19th century. To illustrate the changing Victorian attitudes, Harris contrasts Americans' reactions to the assassinations of two American presidents. His analysis provides a barometer of changing attitudes and shifting social values in what increasingly became a land of contrast.

Harris begins his description with the assassination of President James Garfield, which happened on a Washington, D.C., railroad platform on July 2, 1881. The actions of the assassin, Charles J. Guiteau, created shock waves throughout the country. Guiteau, was a devout believer of the doctrines of John Humphry Noyes, "a perfectionist contemporary of Emerson and Thoreau. . . . [He] was converted by Noyes's mystical writings and his promise of freedom from sin" (Harris 1970:4). Guiteau joined the famous Oneida Community in New York and stayed for a short time. An enthusiast for new causes, he was a remnant of the day of earlier utopian communities of New Harmony, Nashoba, Oberlin, and Brook Farm. He was a misfit by 1880. Many of the reformers he subscribed to (Ralph Waldo Emerson, Wendell Philips, Harriet Beecher Stowe, and James Russell Lowell) were still alive, although their popularity had diminished significantly. Despite prominent physicians testifying he was in a deranged state, the court tried him and insisted on statutory punishment (Harris 1970:4; also, see Foote 1997:37–41).

In contrast, twenty years later, Leon Czolgosz, a self-proclaimed anarchist, assassinated President William McKinley (see Foote 1997:41–47). Although the public handled the Garfield assassination with controlled anger, Americans reacted to the McKinley assassination with an outburst of fear and anxiety. Czolgosz, though born in America, became associated with Southern and Eastern Europe immigrants, who were perceived as not having the same values as middle-class white Protestants. White American Protestants did not celebrate pluralities, and many upper class members viewed group differences based on wealth, race, occupation, and religion as a threat to the collective security of the country.

> The American Protective Association campaigned to reduce Catholic influence in politics and education; patrician New Englanders organized to limit immigration to favored races; Southern mobs terrorized black men with rope and fire; Californians discovered an Oriental menace. Cataclysm and disaster became popular themes [in American culture] . . . Orgies of bloody violence and the end of civilization seemed near at hand. (Harris 1970:17)

Laws limited the activities of political radicals. "[A]ngry patriots decried the dangers of unlimited immigration, newspaper editors thundered against unnamed terrors subverting society, mobs wrecked immigrant newspapers and attached foreigners in the streets" (Harris 1970:5). Although the McKinley assassination took place at the 1901 Buffalo Exposition, a pageant that proclaimed American unity and greatness, in actuality America had explicitly become a nation with many rifts along the lines of class, ethnicity, and race.

These rifts became accentuated with the development and growth of the new information age. For instance, curiosities during the 1876 Centennial in Philadelphia, the typewriter and the telephone revolutionized information processing over the next 20 years. Manufacturers established typing schools for a new generation of female secretaries. Women had entered the business sphere, which had formerly been occupied by men only (Harris 1970).

Mergenthaler's linotype and Edison's mimeograph helped the flow of information. The 1880s and 1890s saw the development of the visual age. Pictures, prints, and cartoons were reproduced on a large scale for the first time. Visual communication contributed to the advertisement phenomenon. Companies like Ivory Soap, Quaker Oats, Sapolio, and Hire's Root Beer were among the first to exploit this new sensory media. Advertisement agencies grew rapidly (Harris 1970:8; also, see Smith 1967). Cameras also became available on a large scale.

By the turn of the century, the number of newspapers had grown to more than 2,000 dailies, reaching more than 15 million people. Magazines also flourished and appealed to a mass audience. New periodicals that developed in the late 1880s include *Cosmopolitan, Munsey's Magazine, McClure's, The Ladies' Home Journals,* among others (Harris 1970:10).

The new growing media and transportation and communication links helped to foster and reinforce stereotypes and cultural differences. It also helped to create a popular past that was dictated by a new mercantile elite.

Harris (1970:22) quotes Henry James' perception of the 1890s: "We may have been great fools to develop the post office, to invent the newspaper and the railway; but the harm is done—it will be our children who will see it; we have created a Frankenstein monster at whom our simplicity can only gape."

Farmers in the Great Plains states found it difficult in the 1880s and 1890s to make ends meet. Low prices, overproduction, inept management, and crippling mortgages all contributed to their financial difficulties. Many Americans faced prolonged agricultural depression and financial hardship (Bailey 1973:455–459). Many left the farm and joined the factory labor force.

Labor increasingly questioned the practices and intent of capitalism. Workers complained about the physical dangers of the industrial environment and the speeding-up process. Workers blamed unemployment on industrialization. Strikes became major disruptions, and bloodshed was often one of the byproducts. Workers continually fought for higher wages and decreased hours of labor, from 16 hours, to 12, to 10. The Haymarket riots (1886), which grew out of labor disputes at the McCormick Harvest factory in Chicago, and the Pullman strike (1894), at the Pullman Palace Car (sleeping car) Company, rocked America's myth of a stable and united society (Figure 42). Conflict between labor and capital had developed into bloody clashes and destruction, and they were blamed on unions and radicals. A financial depression swept through the country in 1893.

Between 1870 and 1910, 20 million immigrants came to the United States. A third of the American population were either foreign born, or first generation Americans. In 1882, President Arthur signed a bill that restricted immigration by excluding paupers, convicts, and defectives. Americans had forgotten the conditions of their ancestor's early migrations to the New World. Immigration laws excluded the Chinese from entering the country for ten years (Miller, 1969). Nevertheless, there was still a large influx of immigrants. Americans feared this new cheaper labor would successfully compete against them for jobs (Figure 43). Patriotic societies developed to preserve and celebrate ethnic purity.

Americans created clubs and organizations at a rate never seen before or after in American history. Associations developed for group protection, and the wealthy increasingly excluded other groups. The *Social Register* was first published in the 1880s. The elite could check social credentials and prevent impostors from attending their social events.

It was an era that saw a passion for genealogies using an aristocratic

Figure 42. The Haymarket Riots in Chicago, 1886. (*Harper's Weekly*, 15 May 1996:312–313. Courtesy, The Winterthur Library: Printed Books and Periodical Collection)

criterion of descent. Genealogy became primarily a female pursuit. One group that helped to define the memory of a native white and overwhelmingly Protestant group was the Daughters of the American Revolution (DAR) in 1890. The DAR became a stronghold in established wealthy areas in Connecticut, New York, and Pennsylvania, and among the millionaires of Chicago (Hobsbawm 1983:292–293). Other social groups developed that established a memory that created an image of long-term domination in politics and society, thus justifying the established hierarchy. These organizations include the Society of Colonial Wars, the Order of Founders and Patriots, and the Mayflower Descendants, among many others (Harris 1970:17–19).

Although the Victorian era is often thought of as a healing period between the North and the South, greater schisms developed in this country that divided people along lines of class and ethnicity. These groups consciously created explicit boundaries. The weapon used to exclude outsiders was the creation of new, rigid rules of behavior and household management advice guides which influenced the behavior of groups and classes of people. They designed an order of behavior that mirrored European aristocracy, a behavior that the new republic fought against. They

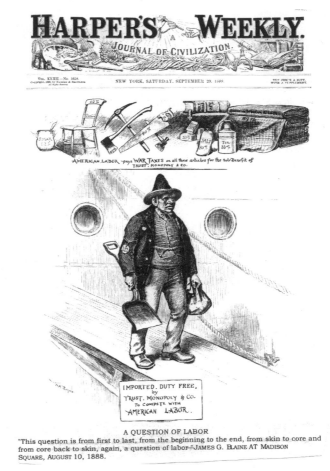

Figure 43. In the late 19th century, American feared immigrant labor would take jobs from them. (*Harpers Weekly,* 29 September 1888:727. Courtesy, The Winterthur Library: Printed Books and Periodical Collection)

started this new tradition, justifying that it was part of the root of the upper class.

WHY RULES OF ETIQUETTE?

Americans created new exclusionary groups because they feared the tremendous immigrant influx and the shift of the American population from the countryside to the cities. Etiquette became a necessary tool which allowed the new industrial class to maintain control of a new and unstable population. Arthur Schlesinger (1968:29–47) observed that the rate of new advice manuals doubled during the post-Civil War era. During the first half of the 19th century an average of three advice books were printed per year. By 1870, and through the rest of the century, the number averaged six books per year. This new and immense literature ran counter to the republican ideology of the antebellum era. While some authors tried to maintain a facade of republicanism, they also helped to usher in a new set of rules of decorum. Americans began to forget the roots of their heritage and the fact that they fought vigorously against aristocratic behavior.

Mechanisms for reinforcing a standard set of behaviors went beyond the increased printings of etiquette manuals. Women's magazines were established to advise home care to housewives (Schlesinger 1968). *The Ladies' Home Journal* along with over a dozen other women's magazines, developed to meet the real or perceived needs of this changing society. They catered to teaching manners to the new and growing middle class. Advice columns appeared regularly and preached on refinement in society.

Between 1860 and 1917 egalitarianism lost out to a more aristocratic style that catered to the new industrial elite classes. *The Ladies' Home Journal* (Holt February 1890:4) reported that the middle class observed the lower classes trying to become part of their inner circle. "In plain words, to get into society is the aim of the butcher, baker, and candlestick maker, once so happy in their lowly station,—now so eager to climb that everything in life becomes valueless" (Holt 1890:4). It was the middle classes' duty to guard from such an intrusion. Victorian etiquette protected the new postwar hierarchy that developed in the United States.

The new American Victorian behavior used European customs, specifically those found in France. Americans viewed French customs as standard among polite society on an international scale (*The Manners That Win* 1880:13). *The Social Etiquette of New York* (1883:12) said the metropolitan city of America largely chose its customs from France, modifying and adapting them according to its own situation and conditions. By the turn of the century, New York was considered the social center of etiquette and had many communities following its lead. From the 1880s many authors wrote manuals with the idea of teaching "New York etiquette" (see for example Harrison 1898; Learner 1906; *Social Etiquette of New York* 1883).

Victorian behavioral guides became more detailed regarding specific behaviors, and they aided in increased ritualized behavior. One author explained the attainment of good manners had become such a complex process that it was even more difficult than it had been in the past. "It is less distinct in appearance, far more subtle, far more difficult to attain than the old distinction; but in these days, he who does not posses it, even though he has a ducal title, need not expect to be called a gentleman by gentlemen" (Ward 1878:xvi). A typical behavioral manual included the following topics: invitations and answers, luncheons, teas, informal card parties, teas and musicals, dinner dances, theater parties, fancy dress parties, the table and its appointments, customs at the table, dinner giving, the serving of dinner, introductions, shaking hands and bowing, visiting and the use of visitation cards, engagements, wedding preparations, note-writing, hospitality, speech, traveling, appropriate dress, the etiquette of morning, and servants (see, for instance, Harcourt 1907; Hemphill 1988).

Although Americans of the early American republic viewed etiquette as a set of unofficial rules that reinforced class distinctions, Victorian citizens saw etiquette as akin to an "art." The art of behavior needed to be mastered and appreciated in order to participate in society. For instance, an etiquette book explained the true gentleman "carries himself with grace in all places, is easy but never familiar, genteel without affection" (*The Manners That Win* 1880:9). It went on: "Etiquette is to society exactly what music is to dancers. While each observes the time, the figures are all grace, harmony, and beauty, but suspend the music and what chaos and confusion" (*The Manners That Win* 1880:13). Many period manuals often have the word or phrase, "the art of good behavior" in chapter titles, or subtitles in their books. For instance, one manual had a chapter title "The Proper Conduct of Life, The Art of Pleasing: The True Lady and the True Gentleman" (*The Household Encyclopedia* 1896:2). Other relevant book titles in this genre include *Art, Society, and Accomplishments: A Treasury of Artistic Homes, Social Life and Culture* (Blackburn 1891), *The Ladies and Gentlemen's Etiquette Book . . . and the Art of Making One's Self Agreeable* (Ater 1881) and *The Art of Entertaining* (Sherwood 1893). This transition of everyday behavior into an art form is probably related to the Victorians' propensity toward "theatrical culture" (Hemphill 1988:566).

However, the Victorian etiquette literature also catered to the new business class, and learning proper decorum in specific social interactions amounted to more than creating smooth social relations. Knowing proper decorum meant power, and power meant success. The advice writer of *The Manners That Win* (1880:11) observed:

> In business affairs the secret of power is manners. The basis of manners is self-reliance, the source of real power. Self-possession begets confidence, and is the free-masonry which puts men at once on dealing terms. Men measure each other when they meet, and every time they meet, and the superior in manners is master of the situation. . . . He who is master of the best way in the matter in hand is victor at the outset.

By the turn of the 20th century, etiquette books grappled with incorporating the ideas of scientific management into everyday decorum. One author in 1912 remarked:

> Efficiency in life is our watchword to-day. It is an indisputable point in the complicated machinery of business and social life, that wheel that are successfully coordinated and well oiled run the smoothest, and good manners combined with ability, make the most pleasing combination in the accomplishment of the day's work. (Cushing 1926:ii)

The author emphasized etiquette was not instinctive, but needed to be learned, repeated, and practiced. When they are practiced, the manners of the day become "automatic," and in time they become "instinctive" (Cushing 1926:ii).

Simplicity and symmetry were the rules for setting an early 19th-century table. The rules for setting the Victorian table became even more complex. Different types of settings were developed for the breakfast, the formal luncheon (also known as the lady's luncheon), the formal dinner, the wedding breakfast, the afternoon tea, and the chafing dish supper (*Alvin Manufacturing Co.* 1917). The utensils also became very specialized.

> It is also necessary to have two, better three, carving sets, two large and one small. The largest one will be used for roast and turkey; the second size for fowls; the smallest for steaks and birds. We have, in these days, many special pieces of silver, dainty and convenient, as butter picks, cheese knives, asparagus tongs, cake knives, pie and ice cream servers, Saratoga chip servers, jelly spoons, cold meat forks, and salad sets. (Roper 1901:5)

A formal dinner would have between five and ten courses (Roper 1901).

The Art of Doing Without

Before the 20th century, middle-class households could conceivably spend at least part of their lives in boardinghouses, although some stigma developed with this living situation. Boardinghouse life, for the most part, was a product of the industrial revolution, under which families would move from place to place, depending upon the work available for the household head.

The 20th century brought a concerted effort to create self-sufficient middle-class households (see for instance *Harper's Household Handbook*, 1913; Herrick 1900). In one scenario created by household management author Christine Herrick, a young bachelor promised not to start his new married life in a boardinghouse. He claims,

> "I made up my mind I would have a home of my own at once," he said, with the antenuptial decisiveness of a very young man. "I am tired of a

boardinghouse, and poor Mabel has never had any home but a hotel or a foreign pension." (Herrick 1900:2)

To show how to create the self-sufficient middle-class house, household management literature relied upon scientific management principles, although some areas of concern remained the same. Cooking and recipes were still the focus of these manuals. Issues related to water supplies and self-medication were replaced with ideas on how to keep a sanitary household and how to equip the kitchen. The latter included the types of furnishings, and quantities and types of kitchen utensils and dishes necessary for the household (see Jones 1946; Morse 1903; Van Rensselaer et al. 1920). In some ways, this may have been a conscious, or unconscious effort by industrialists to stabilize a transient workforce. By allowing the wage laborer to be able to afford to purchase a home and settle in an area, the industrialist had to worry less about finding and training new laborers. A workforce rooted in a community meant steady and uninterrupted work flow and a stable wage. Thus, a stable workforce mitigated some uncertainties of a free market system.

While trying to create a stable workforce with a minimum outlay of cash, many of the new 20th-century household manuals also focused on economics and frugality. Social workers of the early 20th century believed the cost of living was generally too high for an unskilled laborer to support an average family of five. About that time the average unskilled worker in New York City received about $825 per year (based on a sample of 500); in the Chicago Stock Yard District, the wage was closer to $800 per year (based on a sample of 200). Within that same decade the Board of Estimate and Apportionment of New York City estimated a salary of $980.41 per year was sufficient for a working-class family to live comfortably. To put these numbers in perspective, a moderate income was calculated at $1,500–$2,500 per year and 88 percent of the American population lived below this level (Abell 1927:1–4). Nesbitt (1918:10) believed a salary of about $980 was necessary in both smaller towns and rural areas. Although residents were closer to food sources, the cost of many consumer goods would be greater due to their distance from market.

A growing literature catered to families considered on the edge of "making it." Maria Parloa in *The Ladies Home Journal* addressed some strategies on how a family could survive on $1,000 per year, and on $1,500 per year (Parloa 1893b:15). In some sense this literature may have justified to their readers that they should be content to live on the cusp.

One book is explicitly titled *The Story of John and Rose who Began Married Life on an Income of $900.00 a Year* (Schuette 1914). The story is set in an industrial urban area, surrounded by a countryside whose timber had been recently harvested. The image is titled "Their Home Town," and it seems inevitable that "industrial progress" will march into the hinterlands. Wealth does not bring happiness, explained the author. In a created scenario he explains:

> When I asked him (a friend) how he felt, he replied, "never better in my life, content from A to Z." "Well, well, then you are a millionaire?" "Oh no," he replied, "I have not much of the world's goods—just enough to keep me comfortab)].

Success was up to the individual. Those who did not flourish economically were usually to be considered individually at fault. This attitude, found in many household management guide books, is best summed up by Mary Abel (1927:4) who stated; "Doors of opportunity are ajar, but they are to be pushed open only by that energy and initiative which is best developed by difficulties . . . "

CONSUMPTION PATTERNS: ENTREPRENEURS AND BOARDERS IN VICTORIAN HARPERS FERRY

Rules of behavior found in etiquette books and household management guides provide the standards people are expected to follow in order to belong to a group. Although these guidelines furnish expected standards of behavior, the archaeological record shows how people responded to and followed these expectations. This information—a comparison between the expected and the actual evidence—provides a basis for interpreting the contradictions found in the everyday life of Harpers Ferrians.

The new Victorian etiquette, and the growing factions found in society, affected the redevelopment of Harpers Ferry. By the 1880s, Harpers Ferry had recovered from the devastation of the war. Local newspaper accounts detail the optimism about the town's new growth and revival. Tourism, relying upon the memory of the Civil War and industrial manufacturing, replaced the large-scale industry at the armory, although smaller industries, such as flour, paper, and pulp mills, existed for several decades. Some were profitable into the 20th century. Many working-class families rented houses or space in a boardinghouse. By being surrounded by the preserved armory and mill ruins, Harpers Ferrians were continually reminded of the prowess of the once mighty industrial community.

Although the exact demographic composition of residents in the McGraw boardinghouse is not known, a census survey of Harpers Ferry suggests that in the early 20th century, many of the town's boarders originally emigrated from Germany, England, and Ireland. Women operated close to 90 percent of the documented Harpers Ferry boardinghouses. After 1880, women operated all of the boardinghouses.

A comparison of ceramic functional forms between the Hurst and boardinghouse assemblages shows the entrepreneur's family had a much greater proportion of tableware ceramic vessels than any other form (Table 17). This proportion was twice as large as the proportion found in the boardinghouse assemblage. This pattern suggests a far greater ritualization of the meal and entertainment among the entrepreneur's family.

Tea and coffee vessels make up the largest functional category in the boardinghouse assemblage and the size of the proportion is similar to that found at the Boott Mills boardinghouse in Lowell, Massachusetts (Dutton 1988:92). By the late 19th century coffee had become a major component of the working-class diet (Levenstein 1988:100; Lucas 1993:14.24; 1994:89). The Hursts' assemblage contained a much larger proportion of glass tumblers and berry dishes than the boardinghouse (Table 17), although both assemblages had about the same proportion of stemware.

Previous archaeological investigations in other regions of the country have produced large quantities of undecorated china related to boarders' occupation (i.e., Dutton 1988). These undecorated wares, often called "thrashers' china," could be purchased from mail order catalogs and were ideal for hotels and boardinghouses since they were durable and cheap. The

Table 17. Ceramic and Glassware Vessel Count from the McGraw Boardinghouse and the Hurst Privies

| | Boarding house | | Hurst | |
| | Feature 32 (1890S–1907) | | Feature 99 (1890–1900) | |
Ceramic	Percent	N	Percent	N
Tableware	25	20	55	17
Tea/Coffee	33	26	26	8
Storage	8	6	6	2
Personal	13	10	3	1
Other	23	18	10	3
Glassware				
Tumbler	34	12	52	1
Stemware	17	6	14	3
Pitcher	6%	2	0	0
Handled cup	3	1	0	0
Shot glass	3	1	0	0
Berry dish	9	3	24	5
Bowl	0	0	0	0
Butter dish	0	0	0	0
Unidentified	11	4	0	0
Other	11	4	10	2

(Percent) percentage of vessels; (N) total number of vessels.

boardinghouse assemblage at Harpers Ferry was a relatively more expensive assemblage than the Hursts' assemblage. It contained fine tableware sets and some ceramics that also fit into the category of "thrasher's china." The sets included transfer prints, gilded, and decal decorated wares. The Hursts had undecorated china, along with ceramics with transfer print, gilded, and decal-decoration, although none of these ceramics could be considered "thrashers' china." Although boarders are often perceived as landless and poor, part of the ceramic assemblage shows a relatively higher status of material goods than found at workers' housing elsewhere. This outcome may be an attempt of a boardinghouse keeper trying to establish the image of a first-class boardinghouse that McGraw advertised in the early 1890s.

The faunal assemblage from the Hurst household and the boarders also defies 20th-century conventional wisdom of Victorian ritualized behavior. Hurst was a well-respected entrepreneur and a community leader in Harpers Ferry. Even though he declared bankruptcy at the turn of the 20th century, the *Accounts of Fiduciary* report (1921:6–7) suggests that by the time of their deaths in 1920, the Hursts had a substantial amount of wealth. At the Hurst household pigs feet (i.e., foot, wrist, and ankle elements) comprise most of the biomass remains (see Burk 1993c:16.5–16.8), an item not proposed in etiquette books for upper class dining. Cow and sheep/goat are less than 5 percent of the biomass. Although Hurst owned a farm with livestock that included pigs, but he also raised a substantial number of cows and sheep. The high quantities of pig remains may reflect the families' bias toward the consumption of this animal, even though it runs counter to Victorian expectations for an upper-class family. Historical archaeologists are quick to decide rank based on cuts of meat (see Schulz and Gust 1980), however the Hurst household is one case where these assumptions do not hold true. These findings show that it is important not to impose our 20th-century biases when interpreting these materials and risk incorrectly associating certain cuts of meat with specific social status.

There are four different domestic species, but only one wild species is present in the Hurst zooarchaeological findings. Apparently the Hursts relied heavily on the market for their meat consumption.

In the boardinghouse assemblage, there is a relatively higher cow biomass (35 percent) than in the Hursts', although pig and sheep/goat account for less than 7 percent of the biomass. About 75 percent of the cow biomass consists of cranial elements. A review of late 19th-century cookbooks reveals dozens of recipes for preparing calf skulls (Tyree 1879; Hall 1855; see Burk 1993a:15.2–15.3). One recipe shows calf skull served as a good substitute for a delicacy of the era—turtle soup (Tyree 1879:77).

The large number of recipes for calf skulls suggests this cut was a valued food item.

I would have expected the boardinghouse keeper to acquire most of the foods from a market, since a considerable amount of time would have been spent cooking and cleaning the facility. Most of the identifiable faunal biomass are domesticates (45.5 percent), with wild species making up only 1 percent. Only one wildlife species could be identified in the Hursts' assemblage, however the boarders consumed a greater variety of wildlife species (5) which accounts for ten times more biomass (1.0 percent) than the entrepreneurs' assemblage. Identified fish from the Hurst and the boardinghouse assemblages are similar. Apparently, the boardinghouse keeper spent some time acquiring wild species to consume with family, or to serve boarders and thus make ends meet.

Both contexts contain evidence of raspberry, tomato, strawberry, and grape in the form of seeds, while the Hurst context exclusively had black huckleberry, celery, cantaloupe, mustard, watermelon, apple, plum, and cherry (see Cummings 1993:7.21–7.40; 1994:99–101). By the late 19th-century, fruit had become an essential component of the American diet, not because of its nutritional value, but because it was regarded "as an agreeable stimulant to digestion" (Peltz 1883:201). A jelly bag was prescribed for every kitchen, and recipes for various jellies were also described (Peltz 1883:201). Many canned fruits and vegetables became available after the mid-19th century as canning developed into a leading industry (Ward 1882:32–33). From 1890 to the first decade of the 20th century, the output of canned goods increased by almost 10 times (Powell 1917:11). Many fruits in both privies could have been eaten fresh or as jellies and preserves. In either case, the consistent distribution of these elements suggests equal concern for proper digestion, although the Hursts apparently had greater access to these foods.

HEALTH, SANITATION, AND TOURISM

Sanitation Reform in Harpers Ferry

Attempts to improve health and sanitation conditions in Harpers Ferry were closely tied to the development of tourism. Prominent entrepreneurs in Harpers Ferry believed a cleaner and more sanitary town would attract visitors and industry. Making Harpers Ferry a clean and healthy place became an economic necessity. In many ways, their portrayal of the past also became sanitized. Industrial might and great military maneuvers took precedent over labor and the struggle between labor and capital.

Changes in health and sanitation conditions are often regarded now as natural and inevitable when, in fact, health and medical campaigns often struggled against people's resistance to change. While health and reform movements established themselves in many urban communities by the late 19th century, residents still relied on traditional methods of sanitation. Although indoor plumbing replaced outhouses and legislation restricted hogs from roaming the streets, such changes did not come quickly to Harpers Ferry. Residents did not follow sanitary reform policies until well into the 20th century. Most citizens still relied on privies. Municipal balloting in 1873 and 1891 condoned having hogs run free in town.

After the Civil War, state legislators enacted few regulations to develop better health and hygiene conditions in West Virginia. The bulk of this responsibility fell upon local governments and individual initiative. The Jefferson County Board of Health, which was established in 1885, oversaw Harpers Ferry. The board proclaimed that each year before June 1 all streets, alleys, pig pens, cesspools, and privy vaults should be cleaned and disinfected to improve community health. The Board of Health was supposed to perform home inspections to enforce these laws (Ford 1993:12:18).

Businessmen, such as J. Garland Hurst, founded the Harpers Ferry General Improvement Company in 1884 to encourage manufacturing, community hygiene, and beautification. The organization wanted to promote Harpers Ferry as a summer resort and a permanent residence. By creating a healthy and clean town, Hurst believed Harpers Ferry could cater to tourists who visited Civil War sites as well as attract new industrialists who would settle in town with their families.

Late 19th-century household management guidebooks were concerned about the placement and construction of cesspools and privies. One author noted they should be constructed of good substantial brickwork and built so they were perfectly impervious to leaks, to prevent the possibility of escape of liquid sewage. They should be far removed from the nearest point of any dwelling—"at least, a hundred feet—to allow the cesspool being periodically opened for the purpose of cleansing and emptying" (Cassell's 1875:247). The author also warned against constructing them near a well in case water percolated from the cesspool. Hurst may have been a major proponent of sanitary reform, but his privy was not totally pargetted. Liquid wastes easily percolated from his privy vault to surrounding properties.

Sanitation reformers of the 1880s unanimously condemned privy vaults, claiming they were dangerous and unsafe. They recommended water closets as one remedy for this malady. Those who needed an outdoor privy should set it on piers or posts. "[A] strong box coated on the inside with hot coal tar, should be used to receive the compost, which must be kept as dry as possible, and removed often" (King 1886:16). The author went on to instruct that the privy should be ventilated by an air-shaft, from the privy seat to a height of six to ten feet above the roof. Contemporary authorities agreed that if people would follow these instructions, then much of the stench associated with privies would disappear (King 1886:17). Many other contemporary authors wrote about their concerns related to proper sanitation (Eassie 1874; Heller 1882; Talbot 1913; Waring 1885). Harpers Ferry residents could have installed indoor plumbing in the 1890s, yet they continued to use the outdoor privy vault system.

Apparently some Harpers Ferrians, like the Hursts and the McGraws, ignored the county Board of Health's requirement for annual cleaning of streets and privies. For example, the earliest privy deposits associated with the Hursts date to the early 1890s. The Hursts may have periodically cleaned their privy for several years in the 1880s, but they had abandoned this practice by 1891. The privy remained open until the beginning of the 20th century. This behavior, the use of privy vaults as well as not cleaning them out for over a decade, runs counter to the prescribed household management literature and contemporary etiquette on cleanliness.

The boardinghouse privy, constructed in 1893, apparently was never cleaned. Around 1907, the Dorans capped the vault with lime and covered it with clay. Even though plumbing existed in the boardinghouse just after the turn of the century, and the boardinghouse privy was capped in about 1907, there were other privies on the property were kept until past the first quarter of the 20th century. When the National Park Service took control of the town in 1954, the few remaining occupants in Lower Town Harpers Ferry still used the privy vault system.

Victorian Harpers Ferry residents signaled to the outside world about their willingness to improve health and sanitation conditions, but individuals often failed to act. No municipal-wide water service existed in Harpers Ferry until the turn of the 20th century. In 1895, the *Spirit of Jefferson* said J.C. McGraw piped the "finest and purest" spring water from Loudoun Heights across the Shenandoah River for his brewery (*SoJ* 16 April 1895:1). He may have soon after piped some water to nearby domiciles. This distribution of water by private individuals was a common practice in the United States at the turn of the century. Waterworks in more than 40 percent of the cities of America were privately owned (Ford 1993:12.20, 1994:52). A 1906 deed for the brewery mentions the water pipes laid in the street. This form of private entrepreneurship supplied water to a large segment of Harpers Ferry's population. Connecting the water to the house became the responsibility of the property owner.

Even though the 1906 deed of sale for the brewery provides the impression of an equal distribution of water pipes laid throughout the streets, this may not have been the case. A 1907 Sanborn Fire Insurance map shows that several "water plugs" existed in Lower Town Harpers Ferry, but they all clustered around the brewery and Market Street. J.C. McGraw's (later the Doran's dwelling), businesses, and boardinghouse were next to this brewery, and the "water plugs." Archaeologists found many sewer and water lines in the backyard areas running to the boardinghouse and the McGraw/Doran dwelling. The waterlines did not connect to Shenandoah Street, but ran toward Market Street and Hamilton Alley. This evidence suggests McGraw, rather than originally laying the water lines down Shenandoah Street, piped water to his dwelling, making his buildings among the first to acquire indoor plumbing in Lower Town. Between 1911 and 1922 waterlines were laid in the streets of Lower Town Harpers Ferry (Sanborn Fire Insurance Map 1922). Water pipes are often found in the backyard excavations of many early 20th-century Harpers Ferry sites (see for instance Pousson 1986), but these lines are connected to major water lines in the streets.

By the turn of the 20th century, indoor plumbing was no longer considered a novelty in small towns. Their construction and maintenance became a standard in household management guides (Morse 1903:442). In Harpers Ferry, however, indoor plumbing and bathing appear to have been a luxury until the beginning of the 20th century. Doran installed a bathtub in the boardinghouse after 1903, even though plumbing and running water had been available in Lower Town almost a decade earlier. Public baths did not exist in Harpers Ferry. The lack of personal hygiene, although not surprising, also runs counter to national trends and Victorian etiquette.

In the Victorian era specific rules for cleanliness became much more specific and demanding:

> Some persons can bathe once a day, others less frequently; but no one should be content with less than two baths a week. This is the minimum number for cleanliness. (McCabe 1870:389)

Another author wrote:

> Primarily speaking, the first and most important hygienic affect of the bath in health is cleanliness. In these days of diffused knowledge all men and women know that the skin contains millions of little orifices called pores, through which a part of the waste of the body escapes. . . . [Therefore] healthy skin is like a healthy body; it is far less liable to contract disease.
>
>   . . . A tub bath, with the water between 60 and 70 degrees Fahrenheit, may be taken every other day on rising from the bed, and if the person

be in very robust health, and he or she likes this bath, it may be taken daily. In place of it a shower bath for two or three minutes, with the water at 60 degrees Fahrenheit, may be substituted.

Everyone knows the delicious feeling of cleanliness, the glow of the skin, and the general sense of robust health which follow a good bath. (Edson 1896:19)

Progress, we are often taught, is natural and part of our human nature. This so-called natural progression was far from fact in Harpers Ferry. Piped water became available in late 1890s, and the Dorans introduced running water to their boardinghouse almost ten years later. Although plumbing had been installed in the boardinghouse, occupants continued to use the privy vault system for several more years. Even Hurst, a proponent of sanitarianism as a vehicle to promote tourism, kept his privy into the 20th century. Economics may partially explain the lack of a modern sanitary system. However, residents had the means for sanitary systems. The boardinghouse had a water closet, but many of the occupants continued to use a privy. This circumstance leads one to question a natural desire for "progress" and ask whether such desire needs to be created like other phenomena in industrial society, such as time discipline and mass-produced goods.

Comparative Health in Harpers Ferry

Larsen (1993:11.11–11.12, 1994:76) notes that medicinal practices changed dramatically with the development of industrial society. Many of these changes can be seen in Harpers Ferry. Many reform movements in 19th-century medicine challenged the earlier treatments of blood-letting and purgatives. As a systematic study of diseases progressed in the mid-19th century, Grahams's diet, hydropathy, and proprietary medicines challenged the course of scientific medicine practices. Scientific medicines made slow progress through the 1840s, 1850s, and 1860s, and proprietary medicines became increasingly popular. By the turn of the 20th century, professional medicines had become the dominant form of medication.

The use of the Hurst and the boardinghouse privies occurred during America's transition from proprietary medicines to professional medicines. A comparison of these features provides information about the dramatically different lifestyles between the two households and how they both perceived medical treatment. It is probably no coincidence that proprietary medicines, with their high alcohol content, flourished with the growth of America's industrialization. Proprietary medicines created and reinforced the first step away from self reliance. Larsen (1993: 11.22) implies that proprietary medicine use may have served to create an ideology of self reliance when in fact it took the control away from the individual. Much like the armory craftsman in Harpers Ferry who lost control of his means of production, with the industrialization process (see for example Smith 1977; Shackel 1996) the individual lost control of self-healing with the advent of professional medicine. The patient's participation in diagnosis and therapy diminished as each individual became more dependent upon a specialist's knowledge and technology.

Proprietary medicines provided immediate and visible effects during an era when machinery-related injuries and poor work conditions persisted. It is no coincidence that about 76 percent of the containers found at the boardinghouse were medicinal/prescription bottles as opposed to 20 percent at the business entrepreneur's house. General health conditions, addiction rates, and the means to acquire good health varied between these two groups. About a fourth (n = 12) of the identifiable medicinal bottles found in the boardinghouse privy were pain killers; the Hurst household had none (Table 18). The boarders also used proportionately almost twice as many digestive remedies.

The use of any material item, including proprietary medicine, can be examined not only for understanding economic conditions, but also for its creation of group solidarity and cohesion. Although the dominant culture chose to participate in professional medicines, lower-level groups (such as boarders), who were increasingly excluded from middle and upper groups as the new Victorian ideology developed may have opted for self-medication in an attempt to gain some control over their lives.

Working-class boardinghouses were sometimes single sex residences, but there were women and children present at the turn-of-the century McGraw boardinghouse in Harpers Ferry. The boardinghouse assemblage included both a nursing bottle and a whooping cough remedy bottle. The presence of marbles, toy saucers, and doll parts, also suggest children at the site. In the boardinghouse assemblage were proprietary medicines,

Table 18. Types of Identified Medicine Bottles found in the Hurst and Boardinghouse Privies

	Hurst		Boardinghouse	
Medicine type	N	Percent	N	Percent
Pain killers	0	0	12	24
Prescription	2	22	5	10
Natural cures	3	3	14	28
Digestive remedies	1	11	9	18
Other	3	33	9	18

(N) number of bottles; (Percent) percentage of identifiable bottles.

such as Lydia Pinkham's Vegetable Compound or Fletcher's Castoria, developed for female consumers. Advertisements for these products often show women as nurturing. These advertisements were one form of media that allowed for defining gender relations and, along with etiquette guidebooks, established the new and changing roles of women in the industrial era, emphasizing their nurturing nature (Larsen 1993:11.50–11.51, 1994:72-73; Little 1993).

Social differences may also account for the differences between the two assemblages. Townspeople saw the Hursts as progressive because they were involved in health reform for the development of tourism (*SoJ* 24 June 1884:3). This profile of the Hursts makes it likely that they would accept professionally controlled medicine. In a small sample size of identified bottles, 22 percent are professional prescription bottles. In contrast, less than half (10 percent) of this proportion was found in the boardinghouse assemblage. The boarders showed a greater reliance upon a variety of proprietary medicines, including a substantial amount of pain killers (Larsen 1993:11.50).

An analysis of medicine use creates only a partial picture of comparative health conditions between boardinghouse dwellers and a wealthy entrepreneur's family. A parasite analysis of the privies also challenges conventional wisdom that general health conditions among the higher socioeconomic groups might be better than the lower groups. Reinhard (1993:13.2–13.4,1994:63–65) found parasite eggs, such as intestinal roundworm and whipworm, in both privies. These eggs must be consumed to initiate infection. Poor personal, household, and community sanitation contributed to the spread of these parasites. One possible route of infection is through consumption of poorly washed vegetables grown in contaminated soils. Whipworm had some degree of protection from soil chemistry, while roundworm trichiura needs densely shaded, warm and moist areas (Reinhard et al. 1986:34).

A late 19th-century boardinghouse privy deposit from Lowell, Massachusetts revealed a count of 500–1,999 eggs/grams. In comparison the Harpers Ferry boardinghouse privy samples had up to 5,000 eggs/millileters, and a Hurst privy sample netted more than 21,000 eggs/millileters. The relatively high concentration of parasites among the Hursts seems at odds with Hurst's position as cofounder of the Harpers Ferry Rural Improvement Company, which encouraged community hygiene, beautification, and tourism. The different infection rates at Harpers Ferry may be an indication of the different households' dependance on larger markets. Most of the boarders' food was probably imported from the larger markets where such practices as using human sewage decreased with the rise of health and sanitation concerns in the east. Meanwhile, the Hursts, who had a large and varied supply of fruits and vegetables (see Cummings 1994:99–101), may have relied heavily on local markets for their food. If the suppliers to the market still used night soil to fertilize their crops, this process would have greatly influenced the Hursts' health.

PROSPECTS FOR AN ARCHAEOLOGY OF A PEOPLE WITHOUT HISTORY

Charles Henderson (1897), writing for the Chautauqua Literary and Scientific Circle in the late 19th century, commented on the conditions of industrial labor and its effects on the household. He said that, in general, the wages of the working class fathers did not always support the family, and because of the cycles of industry these fathers often found themselves unemployed. At times families turned to other sources of income, such as child labor:

> [V]isit great department stores and shops where child labor can be used and where rigid law has not counteracted the merciless progress of machine industry, and you will be distressed to find that many children who ought to be in school are fixed in the unpitying mills of manufacture and trade. Their pittance of earnings is necessary to sustain the family. One may often find a child tending a machine while his father is seeking in vain for occupation—the babe the successful competitor for a place against his natural supporter. That is cheap labor at war with the home. Such homes turn out thieves, tramps, and abandoned girls. They fill insane asylums and prisons. The coroner's list of suicides is full of horrors, and reveals the tragedies of our imperfect industrial arrangements. (Henderson 1897:162)

There are those, Henderson (1897:162) noted, who believe "legislation should not be invoked to protect adults from the neglect, greed, and cruelty of employers. But few intelligent and humane persons will object to laws on behalf of helpless children." During the 1890s, girls under the age of 16 had a 33 times greater chance of injury in the factory than those over the age of 16; boys had an accident rate twice that of the men, and a seven times greater chance of fatal accidents (Henderson 1897:163).

Child labor is difficult to document in Harpers Ferry oral histories show that children worked at various occupations, including factory work. Edna Brashear Farmer, a local Harpers Ferrian, said her sisters worked as servants for the well-off families of Camp Hill. At age 13, Mrs. Farmer worked in a local restaurant. One year later she joined her sisters, only a couple of years older, at the Harpers Ferry Interwoven Mill to help with the family income (Farmer 1995).

Henderson commented on the paradox of "progress":

> The very inventions which are the marks and means of social progress
> turn into the cold street many men who are too old to learn to use the
> new machinery. Progress moves forward in its triumphant chariot and
> crushes its own ministers under its pitiless wheels. . . . The period of
> transition to better things is full of horrors. The cost of general progress
> is too often borne by a part of society. It is not strange and pitiful that
> men with strong arms and stout hearts should go hungry, cold, and
> ragged, driven to suicide by the cries of hungry children. (Henderson
> 1897:107)

The idea of a free market for the wage earner is somewhat of a mockery
since salary, hours, and conditions are often dictated by the relative competition in the market.

> The wage-earner has no direct and tangible interest in the product, save
> as it affects his rate of wages; and the interests of his employer frequently
> seem in antagonism to his own. The disputes relating to the rate of
> wages, the length of hours, the regulations of the work shop, and the
> competition with outsiders have been so bitter as to endanger and
> sometimes destroy the social peace. (Henderson 1897:134)

The new machinery of the industrial revolution was a political construct which imposed a wage labor and a factory discipline. This new
system benefited the manufacturer and came at the expense of the craftsman. Harpers Ferrians have a long history of workers' resistance to industry that dates to the early 19th century (see Smith 1977; Shackel 1996).
Work slowdowns, pilfering, and sabotage were all part of the labor scene
at Harpers Ferry. Beyond overt reactions to imposed industrialization,
one Harpers Ferry resident complained about the infiltration of industrial
culture into the daily lives of merchants and townspeople. Tired of the
monotonous repetitive motions of industry, the resident complained about
the ways time pieces in a jewelry store window affected the everyday lives
of townspeople. An article in the *Spirit of Jefferson* (5 November 1878:2)
observed:

> Mr. Burton, the jeweler of Harpers Ferry, has a singular sort of mechanical
> contrivance in his store window, from which hangs half a dozen
> watches . . . —like little babies following their fat papas, and this contrivance
> keeps continually going round at the same solemn, blind horse rate—no
> variation, no check, no change of time. Citizens are beginning to complain
> of this; they say it is having a bad effect on the brain of people who are
> obliged to look into the window. We certainly think that Mr. Burton, if
> he cannot give some variety to the movements of this machine of his,
> [he] ought to remove it. What would Mr. Burton think and say, and do,
> if—after paying his five cents for a look at a short panorama, that instead
> of ever changing views, the same old Mount Vesuvius, or Gen. Scott on
> his white charger, was revolving round? Why! he'd smash the show, and
> knock down the dirty-faced Italian that managed it . . . [W]e really think
> that if Mr. Burton cannot give some variety to the movements of this
> machine of his that we have described, he ought incontinently remove it.

REMAKING HARPERS FERRY'S HISTORY

Until the late 1980s, visitors who came to Harpers Ferry National Historical Park left with the impression the town had died after the Civil War. Some sporadic and inconsequential industry occurred, but it seems as though the town had essentially disappeared. This interpretation grew out of local traditions and local histories that developed at the turn of the 20th century.

Tourism that developed during the Harpers Ferry's Victorian era highlighted the achievements of the town's early industry and the strategic role it played during the Civil War. Tourists came mostly from the Middle Atlantic states to view and commemorate this past. While the battered town lay in ruins after the war, visitors came to see these sights. The Baltimore & Ohio Railroad outlined the foundations of the armory and erected a monument to John Brown's Fort. They placed iron tablets that conveyed the story of Stonewall Jackson's siege and capture of Harpers Ferry. People also visited the Civil War fortifications on the surrounding Maryland Heights and Loudoun Heights. Many photographs also exist that show tourists posing next to a cannon and in front of John Brown's Fort. The Herr flour mill ruins on Virginius Island were allowed to remain after several redevelopment and beautification projects. By the late 19th century, however they became mistaken for the Rifle Factory, which existed several hundred feet upriver and lay under six to ten feet of fill.

As Harpers Ferrians became more aware of their rural and rustic setting, they promoted the town as a healthy place to live and visit to stimulate tourism and industry. The Baltimore & Ohio Railroad took advantage of the town's attempt to beautify and sanitize. They built and maintained Island Park, an amusement park developed on a Potomac River island. Boardinghouses and hotels sprang up, restaurants thrived, and many merchants profited from the new tourist industry during the early 20th century.

Many early 20th-century histories of the town do not discuss the new industries and commercial achievements of the town's Victorian era. When the town became a national park, the National Park Service believed that restoring the town to only its 1859–1865 appearance was appropriate. They did not recognize the rich Victorian history of the town. The development, construction, and rehabilitation plans for the park came during an era in the National Park Service's history known as "Mission 66." The federal government devoted large sums of money to support development, preservation, and interpretive programs. Not only was Harpers Ferry National Monument developing during this surge of capital into the National Park Service Mission 66 program, it also occurred on the heels of the Civil War Centennial when the nation needed props and educational tools to help quell growing civil strife in the United States (Blight 1989; Bodner 1992). Commemorating the Civil War and the meaning of heroism—obedience and dedication to a higher authority—became an important and overriding concept in the park's early development. To some extent, it still remains an important theme today as the park's staff interprets the Confederate Victory of Stonewall Jackson's capture of Harpers Ferry in September 1862. Consequently, many other histories, such as the town's Victorian era, remain uncovered.

Recent historical and archaeological research sponsored by the National Park Service has been fruitful and has shed some light on the everyday life in this postwar town. The story of Victorian Harpers Ferry is about the consumer patterns, health, wealth, and hygiene practices of its residents in a revitalizing industrial and tourist town. It is a story about contradictions found in the expectations associated with wealth and class. It is also a story about what people choose to remember and choose to forget. The archaeology reveals a lifestyle among Harpers Ferry's Victorian population that we could not predict from solely reading the primary documentation, etiquette books, and the household management literature. Leading townspeople may have proposed a new code in health and sanitation procedures, but they violated much of what they preached. While national social reformers decried boardinghouse living, Harpers Ferrians continued to construct and operate these enterprises. An archaeology of Harpers Ferry's postbellum era sheds new light on some alternative ways to interpret the town's past and to understand how the town's history has been created. Some of these stories are making their way into the interpretive displays at the national park, especially in the form of permanent exhibits. I believe that still more can be done to make this history part of the national memory, but I also believe it is important to recognize that the Lower Town archaeology project, with its broader and more inclusive questions, has begun to change the landscape and memory of the town's postbellum era.

References

Abel, M.H., 1927, *Successful Family Life on the Moderate Income: Its Foundations in a Fair Start, the Man's Earnings, the Woman's Contributions, The Cooperation of the Community*. J.B. Lippincott Company, Philadelphia.

——, 1921, *Accounts of Fiduciary*. Book P:6-7. On file, Jefferson County Court House, Charlestown, West Virginia.

Adams, J.P., 1917, *The Business of Being a Housewife: A Manual to Promote Household Efficiency and Economy*. Armour and Company, Chicago.

Adams, S.H., 1905 and 1906, *The Great American Fraud: Articles on the Nostrum Evil and Quacks, in two series*. Reprinted from *Colliers Weekly*, P.F. Collier and Son.

Addams, J., 1972 [1909], *The Spirit of Youth and the City Streets*. University of Illinois Press, Urbana.

Addams, J., 1990 [1910], *Twenty Years at the Hull House*, with autobiographical notes. University of Illinois Press, Urbana.

Allen, H.B., 1878, *The Useful Companion and Artificer's Assistant: A Complete Encyclopaedia of Valuable Information, including Thousands of Valuable Recipes, Formulas, Processes, Trade Secrets, Mathematical Calculations, Tables, &c., of Great Service to Inventors, Model-Makers, Machinists, Mechanics, Engineers, Artisans, Apprentices, Farmers, Gardners, and the Household*. Empire State Publishing Company, New York.

Alpern, A., 1975, *Apartments for the Affluent: A Historical Survey of Buildings in New York*. McGraw-Hill, New York.

Alvin Manufacturing Co., 1917, *Setting the Table Correctly by Oscar of the Waldorf*. The Alvin Manufacturing Co., Sag Harbor, New York.

——, 1886, *The American Potter and Illuminator*. (reprint.) A. & P. Shimko, Aurora, Oregon.

Anonymous, 1910, Hilltop House brochure. HFB 305. On file, Harpers Ferry National Historical Park, Harpers Ferry, West Virginia.

——, N.d., *In John Brown's Country*. McDonald Collection. On file, Harpers Ferry National Historical Park, Harpers Ferry, West Virginia.

Anthony, K.J., 1891, *Storer College, Harpers Ferry, W.Va: Brief Historical Sketch*. Morning Star Publishing House, Boston.

——, 1848, *The Art of Good Behavior, and Letter Writer on Love, Courtship, and Marriage: A Complete Guide for Ladies and Gentlemen, Particularly Those Who Have Not Enjoyed the Advantage of Fashionable Life*. C.P. Huestis, New York.

Ater, Mrs. J., 1881, *The Ladies and Gentlemen's Etiquette Book of the Best Society. Information and Instruction for Those about Entering, and Those Who Desire to Become Educated and Polished in General Society. Containing Nice Points of Taste, Good Manners and the Art of Making One's Self Agreeable. A Manual of Manners and Customs, Parties, Balls, Dinners and Sociables, with Forms for Invitations, Balls, Regrets, Marriages, Funerals, Etc.* G.W. Carlton & Co., Publishers, New York.

Atwood, A.W., 1945, Potomac, River of Destiny. *National Geographic Magazine* (July):49.

Austin, G.L., 1885, *Dr. Austin's Indispensable Hand-Book and General Educator. Useful and Practical Information Pertaining to the Household, the Trades, and the Profes-sions*. George Stinson & Company, Portland, Maine.

Bailey, T.A., 1973, *Probing America's Past: A Critical Examination of Major Myths and Misconceptions*, Vol. I., D.C. Heath and Company, Lexington, Massachusetts.

Bales, K., 1999, *Disposable People: New Slavery in the Global Economy*. University of California Press, Berkeley.

Ball, H., N.d., Horace Ball 34th Massachusetts Regiment: Civil War Letters. Typescript. On file, Harpers Ferry National Historical Park, Harpers Ferry, West Virginia.

Baron, S., 1962, *Brewed in America: A History of Beer and Ale in the United States*. Little, Brown and Company, Boston.

Barry, J., 1988, *The Strange Story of Harpers Ferry with Legends of the Surrounding Country*. Reprint of 1903 edition. Shepherdstown Register, Inc., Shepherdstown, West Virginia.

Bayles, J.C., 1879, *House Drainage and Water Service in Cities, Villages, and Rural Neighborhoods*. David Williams, New York.

Bee, The [newspaper, Washington, D.C.]
    1884, Clara to Louise. 2 August:3.
    1885, Louise to Clara. 1 August:2.
    1888, Harpers Ferry. 16 June:1.
    1888, Harpers Ferry. 30 June:1.

Beecher, C.E., and Stowe, H.B., 1994 [1869], *The American Woman's Home, or Principles of Domestic Science; Being a Guide to the Formation and Maintenance of Economical, Healthful, Beautiful, and Christian Homes*. The Stowe–Day Foundation, Hartford, Connecticut.

Beverly, J.H., Jr., 1992, Civil War Era Harpers Ferry, 1861–1865; An Examination for Public Interpretation: The Civil War Occupation Material Culture Recovered during the Package 116 Archaeological Excavations. M.A.A. Project. Anthropology Department, University of Maryland, College Park.

Blackburn, B., 1891, *Art, Society, and Accomplishments: A Treasury of Artistic Homes, Social Life and Culture*. The Blackburn Company, Chicago.

Blee, C.H., 1978, *Archaeological Investigations of the Wager Block Buildings 1977-1978: Harpers Ferry National Historical Park, West Virginia*. Denver Service Center, National Park Service, Department of the Interior, Denver, Colorado.

Blight, D.W., 1989, "For Something beyond the Battlefield": Frederick Douglass and the Struggle for the Memory of the Civil War. *Journal of American History* 75(4):1156-1178

Bodner, J., 1992, *Remaking America: Public Memory, Commemoration, and Patriotism in the Twentieth Century*. Princeton University Press, Princeton, New Jersey.

Bond, K.H., 1989, The Medicine, Alcohol, and Soda Vessels from the Boott Mills. In *Interdisciplinary Investigations of the Boott Mills, Lowell, Massachusetts, Vol.3, The Boarding House System as a Way of Life*, edited by M.C. Beaudry and S.A. Mrozowski, pp.121–140. Cultural Resources Management Study 21. United States Department of the Interior, National Park Service, North Atlantic Regional Office, Boston.

Brands, H.W., 1995, *The Reckless Decade: America in the 1890s*. St. Martin's Press, New York.

Browne, J.H., 1869, *The Great Metropolis: A Mirror of New York*. American Publishing, Hartford.

Bryant, W.C., 1872, *Picturesque America or the Land We Live In*. Appleton and Company, New York.

——, 1877, *Buckeye Cookery and Practical Housekeeping: Compiled from Original Recipes*. Buckeye Publishing Company, Marysville, Ohio.

Burk, B.J., 1993a, Calves' Heads on a Platter: A Late Nineteenth-Century Boardinghouse Privy Faunal Analysis. In *Interdisciplinary Investigations of Domestic Life in Government Block B: Perspectives on Harpers Ferry's Armory and Commercial District*, edited by P.A. Shackel, pp. 15.1–15.12. Occasional Report No. 6, National Park Service, Department of the Interior, Washington, D.C.

Burk, B.J., 1993b, "Hotel de Stipes" Faunal Assemblage: A Civil War Boardinghouse in an Occupied Town. In *Interdisciplinary Investigations of Domestic Life in Government Block B: Perspectives on Harpers Ferry's Armory and Commercial District*, edited by Paul A. Shackel, pp. 10.1–10.28. Occasional Report No. 6, National Park Service, Department of the Interior, Washington, D.C.

Burk, B.J., 1993c, Pigs' Feet in a Politician's Privy. In *Interdisciplinary Investigations of Domestic Life in Government Block B: Perspectives on Harpers Ferry's Armory and Commercial District*, edited by Paul A. Shackel, pp. 16.1–16.16. Occasional Report No. 6. National Park Service, Department of the Interior, Washington, D.C.

Busch, J., 1987, Second Time Around: A Look at Bottle Reuse. *Historical Archaeology* 21(1):67–80.

Cameron, A., 1993, *Radicals of the Worst Sort: Laboring Women in Lawrence, Massachusetts, 1860–1912*. University of Illinois Press, Urbana.

Cameron, A., 1996, Comments on "Cleansing History." *Radical History Review* 65:91–97.

Campbell, H., 1881, *The Easiest Way in Housekeeping and Cooking: Adapted to Domestic Use, or Study in Classes*. Fords, Howard, and Hulbert, New York.

Campbell, H., 1889, Woman's Work and Wages. *Good Housekeeping* 14 September 9(10):237–238.

Campbell, H., 1890a, Woman's Work and Wages. *Good Housekeeping* 1 February 10(7):159–162.

Campbell, H., 1890b, Woman's Work and Wages. *Good Housekeeping* 15 February 10(8):183–185.

Campbell, H., 1890c, Woman's Work and Wages. *Good Housekeeping* 11 October 11(12):279–281.

Campbell, H., 1897, *Household Economics: A Course of Lectures in the School of Economics of the University of Wisconsin*. G.P. Putnam's Sons, New York.

Cassell, Petter, and Galpin, 1875, *Cassell's Household Guide: Being a Complete Encyclopedia of Domestic and Social Economy, and Forming a Guide to Every Department of Practical Life. Volume I*. Cassell, Petter, and Galpin, New York.

Chickering, P. with Jenkins, M.A., 1994, HAFE Package 116, Historic Structures Report, History Section, Block B, Lots 2 and 3 Shenandoah Street, Park Buildings 32, 33, 33A, 34/35, 34A and 36, Harpers Ferry National Historical Park, Harpers Ferry, West Virginia. National Park Service/University of Maryland Cooperative Agreement. On file, Harpers Ferry National Historical Park, Harpers Ferry, West Virginia.

Collard, E., 1984, *Nineteenth-Century Pottery and Porcelain in Canada*. McGill University Press, Montreal.

Cotter, J.L., 1959, Preliminary Investigations at Harpers Ferry: Harper House Garden and Building 23, Arsenal Area at Shenandoah and High Streets, April 8, 1959. Harpers Ferry National Monument. On file, Harpers Ferry National Historical Park, Harpers Ferry, West Virginia.

Cotter, J.L., 1960, Completion of Archaeological Test at Corner of Arsenal Building, June 7, 1960. Harpers Ferry National Monument. On file, Harpers Ferry National Historical Park, Harpers Ferry, West Virginia.

Cowen, R.S., 1979, From Virginia Dare to Virginia Slims: Women and Technology in American Life. *Technology and Culture* 17(January):51–63.

Cowen, R.S., 1983, *More Work for Mother: The Ironies of Household Technology from the Open Hearth to the Microwave*. Basic Books, Inc., New York.

Cook, L.J., 1989, Descriptive Analysis of Tobacco-Related Material from the Boott Mills Boardinghouses. In *Interdisciplinary Investigations of the Boott Mills, Lowell, Massachusetts. Volume III: The Boardinghouse System as a Way of Life*, edited by M.C. Beaudry and S.A. Mrozowski, pp. 209–230. Cultural Resource Management Study 21. United States Department of the Interior, National Park Service, North Atlantic Regional Office, Boston.

Cromley, E.C., 1989, *Alone Together: A History of New York's Early Apartment*. Cornell University Press, Ithaca.

Cullen, M.O., 1976, *How to Carve Meat, Game, and Poultry*. Dover, New York.

Cummings, L.S., 1993, Pollen and Macrofloral Analysis of Material for Package 116, The Late Nineteenth-Century Privies and Possible Garden Areas Associated with the Early Nineteenth-Century Old Master Armorer's House at Harpers Ferry National Historical Park, West Virginia. In *Interdisciplinary Investigations of Domestic Life in Government Block B: Perspectives on Harpers Ferry's Armory and Commercial District*, edited by P.A. Shackel, pp. 7.1–7.46. Occasional Report No. 6., National Park Service, U.S. Department of the Interior, Washington, D.C.

Cummings, L.S., 1994, Diet and Prehistoric Landscape during the Nineteenth and Early Twentieth Centuries at Harpers Ferry, West Virginia: A View from the Old Master Armorer's Complex. In An Archaeology of Harpers Ferrys' Commercial and Residential District, edited by P.A. Shackel and S.E. Winter. *Historical Archaeology* 28(4):94–105.

Cushing, E.F., 1926, *Culture and Good Manners, Consist of Thorough and Practical Knowledge of Rules, Customs and Laws Governing the Niceties of Modern Etiquette*. Students Educational Publishing Co., Memphis, Tennessee.

Davis, A., 1967, *Spearheads for Reform: The Social Settlement and the Progressive Movement, 1890–1914*. Oxford University Press, New York.

Devner, K., 1968, *Patent Medicine Picture*. The Tombstone Epitaph, Tombstone, Arizona.

Drickamer, L.C. and Drickamer, K.D. (editors), 1987, *Harpers Ferry: On the Boarder of North and South with "Rambling Jour," a Civil War Soldier: The Civil War Letters and Newspaper Dispatches of Charles H. Moulton (34th Mass. Vol. Inf.)*. White Mane Publishing Co., Inc., Shippensburg, Pennsylvania.

Du Bois, W.E.B., 1962 [1909], *John Brown*. International Publishers, New York.

Duncan, R. (editor), 1992, *Blue-eyed Child of Fortune: The Civil War Letter of Colonel Robert Gould Shaw*. University of Georgia Press, Athens, Georgia.

Dunning, W.A. 1907. *Reconstruction, Political and Economic*. Harper, New York.

Dutton, D.H., 1988, "Thrashers China" or "Colored Porcelain": Ceramics From the Boott Mills Boarding House and Tenement. In *Interdisciplinary Investigations of the Boott Mills, Lowell, Massachusetts. Volume III: The Boardinghouse System as a Way of Life*, edited by M.C. Beaudry and S.A. Mrozowski, pp. 83–120. Cultural Resources Management Studies 21. United States Department of the Interior, National Park Service, North Atlantic Regional Office, Boston.

Eassie, W., 1874, *Sanitary Arrangements for Dwellings: Intended for the Use of Officers of Health Architects, Builders, and Householders*. Smith, Elder, & Co., London.

Edson, C., 1896, When and How to Bathe. *The Ladies' Home Journal*. June 13(7):19.

Everhart, W.C., 1952, A History of Harpers Ferry. On file, Harpers Ferry National Historical Park, Harpers Ferry, West Virginia.

Fairbairn, C.J., 1961, John Brown's Fort: Armory Engine and Guard House 1848-1961. Harpers Ferry, West Virginia. On file, Harpers Ferry National Historical Park, Harpers Ferry, West Virginia.

Farmer, E., 1995, Interviews with Mrs. Edna Brashear Farmer: Resident of Virginius Island, 1914–1924. Interviews conducted on September 2, 1992 (Eric Larsen), May 19, 1994 (John T. Eddins and Anna Marie York), June 14, 1994 (John T. Eddins and Anna Marie York). On file, Harpers Ferry National Historical Park, Harpers Ferry, West Virginia.

Farmers Advocate [Charlestown, West Virginia. Newspaper on microfilm, Harpers Ferry National Historical Park].

1900, No title. 2 May:3.

1900, No title. 5 May:3.

1900, No title. 12 May:2.

1902, No title. 15 February:3.

1903, No title. 31 October:2.

1908, No title. 2 May:2.

1909, No title. 16 January:2.

1909, No title. 25 December:2.

Fenicle, D.L., 1993, The Ties that Bind: A Social History of Block B, Lots 2 and 3. In *Interdisciplinary Investigations of Domestic Life in Government Block B: Perspectives on Harpers Ferry's Armory and Commercial District*, edited by P.A. Shackel, pp. 3.1–3.22. Occasional Report No. 6., National Park Service, Department of the Interior, Washington, D.C.

Fike, R., 1987, *The Bottle Book: A Comprehensive Guide to Historic, Embossed Medicine Bottles*. Peregrine Smith Books, Salt Lake City, Utah.

Fisher, P.G., 1989, Historic Structures Report, Package 116, 1865–1910, Lots 2 and 3, Block B Shenandoah Street, Park Buildings 32, 33, 33A, 34–35, 34A, and 36. Harpers Ferry National Historical Park, Harpers Ferry, West Virginia. National Park Service–University of Maryland Cooperative Agreement, History Research Project. On file, Harpers Ferry National Historical Park, Harpers Ferry, West Virginia.

Fisher, P.G., Chickering, P., and Jenkins, M., 1991, Historical Structures Report, Package 116, History Section, 1865–1952, Lots 2 and 3, Block B, Shenandoah Street, Park Buildings 32, 33, 33A, 34–35, 34, and 36, Harpers Ferry National Historical Park, West Virginia. National Park Service–University of Maryland, Cooperative Agreement, Historical Research Report.

Ford, B.P., 1993, Health and Sanitation in Nineteenth-Century Harpers Ferry. In *Interdisciplinary Investigations of Domestic Life in Government Block B: Perspectives on Harpers Ferry's Armory and Commercial District*, edited by P.A. Shackel, pp. 12.1–12.38. Occasional Report No. 6., National Park Service, Department of the Interior, Washington, D.C.

Ford, B.P., 1994, The Health and Sanitation of Postbellum Harpers Ferry. In An Archaeology of Harpers Ferry's Commercial and Residential District, edited by P.A. Shackel and S.E. Winter. *Historical Archaeology* 28(4):49–61.

Fonner, E., 1988, *Reconstruction: America's Unfinished Revolution, 1863–1877*. Harper and Row, New York.

Foner, P.S. (editor), 1970, *W.E.B. Du Bois Speaks: Speeches and Addresses, 1890–1919*. Pathfinder, New York.

Foote, K. E. 1997, *Shadowed Ground: America's Landscapes of Violence and Tragedy*. University of Texas Press, Austin.

Friedrich, M., and Bull, D., 1976, *The Register of United States Breweries: 1876–1976*. Donald Bull, Trumbull, Connecticut.

Frye, D.E., 1987, Stonewall Attacks! The Siege of Harpers Ferry. *Blue and Gray Magazine*, August-September:8–27,47–54.

Frye, S.W., and Frye, D.E., 1989, *Maryland Heights Archaeological and Historical Re-*

sources Study. Occasional Report No. 2. National Capital Region, National Park Service, Department of the Interior, Washington, D.C.

Frye, S.W. and YoungRavenhorst, C., 1988, Archeological Investigations on Virginius Island, Harpers Ferry National Historical Park, 1986–1987. On file, Harpers Ferry National Historical Park, Harpers Ferry, West Virginia.

Galishoff, S., 1976, Drainage, Disease, Comfort and Class: A History of Newark's Sewers. *Societas: A Review of Social History* 6:121–135.

Gardner, W., 1974, Excavation–Harpers Ferry, Backyards and Paymaster's Yard, 1973–1974. On file, Harpers Ferry National Historical Park, Harpers Ferry, West Virginia.

Gee, C.S., 1958, John Brown's Fort. *West Virginia History* XIX(2):93–100.

Geier, C.R. Jr., 1994, Toward a Social History of the Civil War: The Hatcher-Cheatham Site. In *Look to the Earth: Historical Archaeology and the American Civil War*, edited by C.R. Geier, Jr. and S. Winter, pp. 191–214. The University of Tennessee Press, Knoxville.

Geier, C., Andrews, S., Buchanan, R., Cromwell, J.R., Jr., Mullins, P.R., and Rebar, J., 1989, The Hatcher–Cheatham Site (44CF258): A Multicomponent Historic Site in Chesterfield County, Virginia. Volume IV. Ceramic, Toys, Pipes, Glass, Buttons, Metal, and Faunal Analysis. James Madison University, Archaeological Research Center, Harrisonburg, Virginia. Submitted to Virginia Department of Transportation, Richmond, Virginia. Project #0288-020-102,PE-101.

Giglierano, G., 1976, The City and the System: Developing a Municipal Service, 1800–1890. *The Cincinnati Historical Society Bulletin* 34:223–246.

Gilbert, C., Joseph, M.D., and Wheelock, P.C., 1993, *Cultural Landscape Report: Lower Town, Harpers Ferry National Historical Park*. National Park Service, Department of Interior, Harpers Ferry National Historical Park, National Capital Region.

Gilbert, D., 1984, *Where Industry Failed: Water-Powered Mills at Harpers Ferry, West Virginia*. Pictorial Histories Publishing Co., Charles Town, West Virginia.

Gilbert, D., 1999, *Mills, Factories, Machines & Floods at Harpers Ferry, West Virginia, 1762–1991*. Harpers Ferry Historical Association, Harpers Ferry, West Virginia.

Godden, G.A., 1964, *Encyclopedia of British Pottery and Porcelain Marks*. Bonanza Books, New York.

Goldmark, J., 1953, *Impatient Crusader: Florence Kelley's Life Story*. University of Illinois Press, Urbana.

Goodholme, T.S. (editor), 1877, *A Domestic Cyclopaedia of Practical Information*. Henry Holt and Company, New York.

Griscom, J.H., 1970 [1854], *The Sanitary Condition of the Laboring Population of New York*. Arno Press, New York.

Halchin, J.Y., 1992, The Island of Virginius, 1800–1936, Harpers Ferry National Historical Park, Harpers Ferry, West Virginia. On file, Harpers Ferry National Historical Park, Harpers Ferry, West Virginia.

Halchin, J.Y., 1994, *Archaeological Views of the Uppers Wager Block, A Domestic and Commercial Neighborhood in Harpers Ferry*. United States Department of the Interior, National Park Service, Washington, D.C.

Hale, S.J., 1844, *The Good Housekeeper, or The Way to Live Well, and to Be Well While We Live*. Otis, Broaders, & Co., Boston.

Hall, E.M., 1855, *Practical American Cookery and Domestic Economy*. C. M. Saxton, Miller, New York.

Hannah, D.H., 1969, *Archaeological Investigations of Virginius Island, Harpers Ferry, National Historical Park, 1966–1968*. Harpers Ferry National Historical Park, Harpers Ferry, West Virginia.

Harcourt, Mrs. C., 1907, *Good Form for Women: A Guide to Conduct and Dress on All Occasions*. The John Winston Co., Philadelphia.

Hardesty, D.L., 1988, The Archaeology of Mining and Miners: A View from the Silver State. *Special Publication Series*, No. 6. Society for Historical Archaeology, California, Pennsylvania.

Harland, M., 1899, *Household Management*. Home Topics Publishing Co., New York.

——, 1913, *Harper's Household Handbook: A Guide to Easy Ways of Doing Woman's Work*. Harpers & Brothers Publishers, New York.

Harpers Ferry Times, [Harpers Ferry, West Virginia. Newspaper on microfilm, Harpers Ferry National Historical Park, Harpers Ferry, West Virginia.
   1906, No Title. 14 September:5.
   1907, No Title. 4 January:5.

Harpers Ferry Town Records, 1907, Harpers Ferry Town Records, 1 July. On file, Harpers Ferry Town Hall, Harpers Ferry, West Virginia.

Harris, N., 1970, Introduction. In *The Land of Contrasts: 1880–1901*, edited by N. Harris, pp.1–28. George Braziller, New York.

Harrison, Mrs. B., 1898, *The Well-Bred Girl in Society*. Doubleday & McClure Co., New York.

Hartley, C., 1860, *The Gentlemen's Book of Etiquette and Manual of Politeness*. G.W. Cottrell, Publisher, Boston.

Hawes, E., 1993, *New York, New York: How the Apartment House Transformed the Life of the City*. Knopf, New York.

Hawthorne, N., N.d., Extracts from "The Conflict of Conviction." On file, Harpers Ferry National Historical Park, Harpers Ferry, West Virginia, HFB-216.

Hearn, C.G., 1996, *Six Years of Hell: Harpers Ferry during the Civil War*. Louisiana State University Press, Baton Rouge.

Heller, S., 1882, *The Plumber and Sanitary Houses*. B.T. Batsford, London.

Hemphill, C.D., 1988, *Manners for Americans: Interaction Ritual and the Social Order*. Ph.D. dissertation, Department of History, Brandeis University. University Micro films, Ann Arbor, Michigan.

Henderson, C.R., 1897, *The Social Spirit in America*. The Chautauqua Century Press, New York.

Herrick, C.T., 1900, *First Aid to the Young Housekeeper*. Charles Scribner's Sons, New York.

Hershey, W.D., 1964, Arch1eological Survey of the Lockwood House (Paymaster's House) Harpers Ferry, West Virginia. On file, Harpers Ferry National Historical Park, Harpers Ferry, West Virginia.

Hobsbawm, E., 1983, Mass-producing Tradition: Europe, 1870–1914. In *The Invention of Tradition*, edited by E. Hobsbawm and T. Ranger, pp. 263–307. Cambridge University Press, New York.

Holt, F., 1890, Climbing the Social Ladder. *The Ladies' Home Journal* February 7(3):4.

——, 1889, House Service: Why Do Capable Girls Shun It for Harder Callings. *Good Housekeeping* 17 August 9(8):180.

——, 1863, *Household Work; or, The Duties of Female Servants, Practically and Economically Illustrated, Through the Respective Grades of Maid-of-all-Work, House and Parlor-Maid, and Laundry Maid: With Many Valuable Recipes for Facilitating Labour in Every Department*. Joseph Masters, London.

——, N.d., *The Household Encyclopaedia of Business and Social Forms, Containing the Rules of Etiquette for All Occasions*. Desmond Publishing Co., Boston.

Hull-Walski, D. A. and F.L. Walski, 1993, Brewing and Bottling in Harpers Ferry, West

Virginia. In *Interdisciplinary Investigations of Domestic Life in Government Block B: Perspectives on Harpers Ferry's Armory and Commercial District*, edited by P.A. Shackel, pp. 17.1–17.53. Occasional Report No. 6., National Park Service, U.S. Department of the Interior, Washington, D.C.

Hull-Walski, D. A. and Walski, F.L., 1994, There's Trouble a-Brewin: The Brewing and Bottling Industries at Harpers Ferry, West Virginia. In An Archaeology of Harpers Ferry's Commercial and Residential District, edited by P.A. Shackel and S.E. Winter. *Historical Archaeology* 28(4):106–121.

Inashima, P., 1981, Archaeological Monitoring: Park Repair: Lateral-Sag-Failure Section along the Northern Portion of the First Terrace "Harpers" Gardens' Wall. On file, Harpers Ferry National Historical Park, Harpers Ferry, West Virginia. National Park Service, Denver Service Center, National Capital Team, Washington, D.C.

——, 1986, *1986 Information Please Almanac*. Houghton Mifflin, Boston.

Irving, T., 1878, *More Than Conqueror, or Memorials of Col. J. Howard Kitching*. Hurd and Houghton, New York.

Jefferson County Birth and Death Records (*[JCBD]*. On file, Jefferson County Court House, Charleston, West Virginia). 1866–1905 Birth and Death Records of Jefferson County, West Virginia. Jefferson County Courthouse, Charles Town, West Virginia.

Jefferson County Deed Book (*[JCDB]*. On file, Jefferson County Court House, Charleston, West Virginia).
   1894, 25 April 77:47.
   1895, 26 October 80:112.
   1896, 27 July 81:475-476.
   1897, 1 October 98:21.
   1903, 17 February 92:506.
   1906, 27 October 98:21.

Jeffries, B.G., 1902, *The Household Guide: or Safe Treatment at Home*. J.L. Nichols, Naperville, Illinois.

Johnson, M. and Barker, J., 1993, Virginius Island Community: Preliminary Social Analysis, 1800–1936. On file, Harpers Ferry National Historical Park, Harpers Ferry, West Virginia.

Johnson, M., 1996, *An Archaeology of Capitalism*. Blackwell, Cambridge, Massachusetts.

Jones, G.B., 1946, *Manual of Smart Housekeeping*. Chester R. Heck, Inc., New York.

Joseph, M.D., Wheelock, P.C., Warshaw, D., and Kriemelmyer, A., 1993, *Cultural Landscape Report, Virginius Island: Harpers Ferry National Historical Park*. Harpers Ferry National Historical Park, National Capital Region, National Park Service, Department of the Interior, Washington, D.C.

Juravich, J., 1985, *Chaos on the Shop Floor*. Temple University Press, Philadelphia.

Kamm, M.W., 1951, *Old China*. Mrs. Oliver Kamm, Grosse Pointe Farms, Michigan.

Kelley, W.J., 1965, *Brewing in Maryland: From Colonial Times to the Present*. William J. Kelley, Baltimore, Maryland.

King, D.W. (editor), 1886, *Homes for Home-Builders, or Practical Designs for Country, Farm and Village*. O. Judd Co., New York.

Kitchen-Garden Association, 1882, *Household Economy: A Manual for Use in Schools*. Ivison, Blakeman, Taylor, and Company, New York.

Kovel, R., and Kovel,T., 1986, *Kovels' New Dictionary of Marks*. Crown Publishers, Inc., New York.

——, 1889, *Ladies' Home Journal*. October 6I(2):23.

Landon, D.B., 1987, Zooarchaeological Remains from the Kirk Street Agent's House. In *Interdisciplinary Investigations of the Boott Mills Lowell, Massachusetts Vol II: The*

Kirk Street Agent's House, edited by M.C. Beaudry and S.A. Mrozowski, pp. 131–142. Cultural Resource Management Study 19. United States Department of the Interior, National Park Service, North Atlantic Regional Office, Boston.

Landon, D.B.,1989, Domestic Ideology and the Economics of Boardinghouse Keeping. In *Interdisciplinary Investigations of the Boott Mills, Lowell, Massachusetts. Volume III: The Boardinghouse System as a Way of Life,* edited by M.C. Beaudry and S.A. Mrozowski, pp. 37–47. Cultural Resources Management Studies 21. United States Department of the Interior, National Park Service, North Atlantic Regional Office, Boston.

Lanigan, F.E., 1896, Progressive Dinner-Parties. *The Ladies' Home Journal* January 12(2):21.

Larrabee, E.M., 1960a, Report of Archaeological Investigation of the Arsenal Square at Harpers Ferry National Monument, Harpers Ferry West Virginia, From July 20 through September 5, 1959. On file, Harpers Ferry National Historical Park, Harpers Ferry, West Virginia.

Larrabee, E.M., 1960b, Report of Exploratory Archaeological Excavations Conducted on the Lower Hall Island Rifle Factory, Harpers Ferry National Monument, Harpers Ferry, West Virginia, from August 25 through August 29, 1959. On file, Harpers Ferry National Historical Park, Harpers Ferry, West Virginia.

Larrabee, E.M.,1961, Rifle Works Archaeological Report: Report of the Second Season of Exploratory Archaeological Excavations Conducted at the U.S. Rifle Works, Lower Hall Island, Harpers Ferry National Monument, Harpers Ferry, West Virginia, from June 23 through July 6, 1960. On file, Harpers Ferry National Historical Park, Harpers Ferry, West Virginia.

Larrabee, E.M., 1962, Report of the Third Season of Exploratory Archaeological Excavations Conducted at the U.S. Rifle Works Lower Hall Island, Harpers Ferry National Monument, Harpers Ferry, West Virginia, from 25 August through 10 November 1961. On file, Harpers Ferry National Historical Park, Harpers Ferry, West Virginia.

Larsen, E.L., 1993, "That Trying Climate": Health and Medicine in Nineteenth Century Harpers Ferry. In *Interdisciplinary Investigations of Domestic Life in Government Block B: Perspectives on Harpers Ferry's Armory and Commercial District,* edited by P.A. Shackel, pp. 11.1–11.64. Occasional Report No. 6., National Park Service, Department of the Interior, Washington, D.C.

Larsen, E.L., 1994, A Boardinghouse Madonna—Beyond the Aesthetics of a Portrait Created through Medicine Bottles. In An Archaeology of Harpers Ferry's Commercial and Residential District, edited by P.A. Shackel and S.E. Winter. *Historical Archaeology* 28(4):68–79.

——, 1836, *The Laws of Etiquette, or Short Rules and Reflections for Conduct in Society.* Carey, Lea, & Blanchard, Philadelphia.

Learner, Mrs. F., 1906, *The Etiquette of New York To-day.* Frederick A. Stokes Company, New York.

Lears, T.J., 1981, *No Place of Grace: Antimodernism and the Transformation of American Culture, 1880–1920.* Pantheon Books, New York.

Leone, M.P., 1988, The Georgian Order as the Order of Mercantile Capitalism in Annapolis, Maryland. In *The Recovery of Meaning: Historical Archaeology in the Eastern United States,* edited by M.P. Leone and P.B. Potter, Jr., pp. 235–262. Smithsonian Institution Press, Washington, D.C.

Leone, M.P., 1995, A Historical Archaeology of Capitalism. *American Anthropologist* 97(2):251–268.

Letters [On file, Harpers Ferry National Historical Park, Harpers Ferry, West Virginia]. Andrews, Matthew Page to Hon. Jennings Randolph. HAFE microfilm, reel 117. Frederickson, Fred to his wife, 7 May 1863, HFD-390.

Fritz to Pete, 25 April 1954. On file, Historian's office.

Griffith, Mary Jane Coates to her sister, 20 July 1864, HFD-364.

Mauzy, George to J.H. Burton, 19 April 1861, HFD-388.

Powell, Sally Lee to Jennings Randolph. HAFE microfilm, reel 117.

Ramsey to Dyer, 27 July 1865. HAFE microfilm, reel 117.

Shewbridge, J. to D. Shewbridge, April 23, 1861, HFD-581.

Young, D.J. to Mr. James McGraw, 16 September 1878, HAFE microfilm, reel 238:1025-26

Levenstein, Harvey, 1988, *Revolution at the Table: The Transformation of the American Diet*. Oxford University Press, New York.

Lief, A., 1965, *A Close-up of Closures: History and Progress*. Glass Container Manufacturers Institute, New York.

Lincoln, William Seyer, 1879, *Life with the Thirty-Fourth Massachusetts Infantry in the War of the Rebellion*. Noyes, Snow, & Co., Worcester.

Little, Barbara J., 1995, *National Capital Area Archeological Overview and Survey Plan*. Occasional Report 13, National Capital Area, National Park Service, Department of the Interior, Washington, D.C.

Loewen, James, 1995, *Lies My Teacher Told Me: Everything Your American History Textbook Got Wrong*. Simon and Schuster, New York.

Lowenthal, David, 1985, *The Past is a Foreign Country*. Cambridge University Press, New York.

Lowenthal, David, 1998, *The Heritage Crusade and the Spoils of History*. Cambridge University Press, New York.

Lucas, Michael T., 1993, Late Nineteenth-Century Material Goods from Lower Town Harpers Ferry: The Ceramic and Glass Evidence from Features 99, 132, and 21. In *Interdisciplinary Investigations of Domestic Life in Government Block B: Perspectives on Harpers Ferry's Armory and Commercial District*, edited by P.A. Shackel, pp. 14.1-14.36. Occasional Report No. 6. National Park Service, Department of the Interior, Washington, D.C.

Lucas, Michael T.,1994, A la Russe, a la Pell-Mell, or a la Practical: Ideology and Compromise at the Late Nineteenth-Century Dinner Table. In An Archaeology of Harpers Ferry's Commercial and Residential District, edited by P.A. Shackel and S.E. Winter. *Historical Archaeology* 28(4):80-93.

Majewski, T., and O'Brien, M.J., 1987, The Use and Misuse of Nineteenth-Century English and American Ceramics in Archaeological Analysis. In *Advances in Archaeological Method and Theory*, Volume 11, edited by M.R. Schiffer, pp. 97-209. Academic Press, Orlando.

——, 1880, *The Manners That Win. Compiled from the Latest Authorities*. Buckeye Publishing Co. Minneapolis, Minnesota.

Marmion, A.P., 1959, *Under Fire: An Experience in the Civil War*. Compiled and edited by W.V. Marmion, Jr.. William Marmion, Harpers Ferry.

Martin, E.W., 1942, *The Standard of Living in 1860: American Consumption Levels on the Eve of the Civil War*. University of Chicago Press, Chicago.

Matthews, G., 1987 *"Just a Housewife": The Rise and Fall of Domesticity in America*. Oxford University Press, New York.

McCabe, J.D., 1881, *The National Encyclopaedia of Business and Social Forms*. M.R. Gately & Co., New York.

Miller, S.C., 1969, *The Unwelcome Immigrant: The American Image of the Chinese, 1785-1882*. University of California Press, Berkeley.

Montgomery, D., 1996, Bread and Carnations Maybe? *Radical History Review* 65:98-102.

Moore, W.P., 1962, Union Army Provost Marshals in the Eastern Theater. In *Military Affairs* 26:120–26.

Morse, S., 1903, *Household Discoveries: An Encyclopedia of Practical Recipes and Processes*. The Success Company, New York.

Mrozowski, S.A., Ziesing, G.H., and Beaudry, M.C., 1996, *Living on the Boott: Historical Archaeology at the Boott Mills Boardinghouses, Lowell, Massachusetts*. University of Massachusetts Press, Amherst, Massachusetts.

Mueller, J.W., Fischler, B., and Frye,S.W. 1986, Preservation and Discovery along the Shenandoah Canal at Harpers Ferry National Historical Park in 1983 and 1984. On file, Harpers Ferry National Historical Park, Harpers Ferry, West Virginia.

Mumford, L., 1961, *The City in History: Its Origins, Its Transformations, and Its Prospects*. Harcourt, Brace & World, Inc., New York.

Murfin, J.V., 1989, *From the Riot & Tumult: Harpers Ferry*. Harpers Ferry Historical Association, Harpers Ferry, West Virginia.

Nassaney, M.S., and Abel, M.R., 1993, The Political and Social Contexts of Cutlery Production in the Connecticut Valley. *Dialectical Anthropology* 18:247–289.

National Park Service, N.d., Achieving Excellence in Interpretation: Compelling Stories. Pamphlet. National Park Service, Department of Interior, Washington, D.C.

Nesbitt, F., 1918, *Household Management*. Social Work Series. Russell Sage Foundation, New York.

Noffsinger, J.P., 1958, Harpers Ferry, West Virginia: Contributions toward a Physical History. On file, Harpers Ferry National Historical Park, Harpers Ferry, West Virginia.

Oates, S.B., 1970, *To Purge this Land with Blood: A Biography of John Brown*. Harper and Row, New York.

——, 1889, Occasional Lapses of Manner. *The Ladies' Home Journal* 1889 November 6(12).20.

Parloa, M., 1893a, Division of Household Work. *The Ladies' Home Journal* January 10(2):19.

Parloa, M., 1893b, Division of the Family Income, Part 1. *The Ladies' Home Journal* February 10(3):19.

Parloa, M., 1893c, Division of the Family Income, Part 2. *The Ladies' Home Journal* February 10(3):19.

Parloa, M., 1993d, When Cleaning House. *The Ladies' Home Journal* April 10(5):31.

Parsons, M.T., 1995, Archaeological Investigation of the Harper Terraces: A Nineteenth-Century Domestic Yard and Garden, Harpers Ferry National Historical Park. U.S. Department of the Interior, National Park Service, Harpers Ferry National Historical Park, Harpers Ferry, West Virginia.

Paynter, R., 1989, The Archaeology of Equality and Inequality. *Annual Review of Anthropology* 18:369–399.

Paul, J.R., and Parmalee, P.W., 1973, *Soft Drink Bottling: A History with Special Reference to Illinois*. Illinois State Museum Society, Springfield, Illinois.

Peirce, M.F., 1884, *Co-Operative Housekeeping: How Not to Do It and How to Do It; A Study in Sociology*. James R. Osgood and Company, Boston.

Peltz, G.A., 1883, *The House Wife's Library (many volumes in one) Furnishing the very Best Help in all the Necessities, Intricacies, Emergencies, and Vexations that Puzzle a Housekeeper in Every Department of Her Duties in the House*. Hubbard Brothers Publishing Co., New York.

Pousson, J.F., 1985, *Archeological Investigations, Harpers Ferry National Historical Park, Package No. 110A, Wager Block Backyards*. National Park Service, Northeastern Team, United States Department of the Interior, Denver, Colorado.

Powell, O., 1917, *Lippincott's House Manuals: Successful Canning and Preserving, Practical Hand Book for Schools, Clubs, and Home Use*, edited by Benjamin Andres. J.B. Lippincott Company, Philadelphia.

Quarles, B., 1974, *Allies for Freedom; Blacks and John Brown*. Oxford University Press, New York.

Register (Newspaper, Rockingham, Virginia)
1861, No title. 24 May:2.

Reinhard, K.J., 1993, Parasitology Analysis of Latrine Soils from Harpers Ferry, West Virginia. In *Interdisciplinary Investigations of Domestic Life in Government Block B: Perspectives on Harpers Ferry's Armory and Commercial District*, edited by P.A. Shackel, pp. 13.1–13.8. Occasional Report No. 6. National Park Service, Department of the Interior, Washington, D.C.

Reinhard, K.J., 1994, Sanitation and Parasitism of Postbellum Harpers Ferry. In *An Archaeology of Harpers Ferry's Commercial and Residential District*, edited by P.A. Shackel and S.E. Winter. *Historical Archaeology* 28(4):63–67.

Reinhard, K.J., Mrozowski, S.A., and Orloski, K.A., 1986, Privies, Pollen, Parasites and Seeds: A Biological Nexus in Historical Archaeology. *MASCA Journal* 4(1):31–36.

Report, 1863, Report of United States Agent Daniel J. Young to Colonel H.K. Craig, On file, Harpers Ferry National Historical Park, Harpers Ferry, West Virginia.

——, 1863, *Revised United States Army Regulations of 1861*. Government Printing Office, Washington, D.C.

Riley, J.J., 1972 [1958], *A History of the American Soft Drink Industry: Bottled Carbonated Beverages: 1807–1957*. Arno Press, New York.

Roberts, B., 1960, *Harpers Ferry in Pictures*. Heritage Printers, Charlotte, North Carolina.

Roper, Mrs. S.T., 1901, *How to Set the Table: Being a Treatise Upon This Important Subject*. R. Wallace & Sons Mfg. Co., New York.

Rovner, I., 1993, Phytolith Analysis: Archaeological Soils from Lower Town Harpers Ferry, West Virginia. In *Interdisciplinary Investigations of Domestic Life in Government Block B: Perspectives on Harpers Ferry's Armory and Commercial District*, edited by P.A. Shackel, pp. 6.1–6.13. Occasional Report No. 6, National Capital Region, National Park Service, Washington, D.C.

Rovner, I., 1994, Floral History by the Back Door: A Test of Phytolith Analysis in Residential Yards at Harpers Ferry. In *An Archaeology of Harpers Ferry's Commercial and Residential District*, edited by P.A. Shackel and S. E. Winter. *Historical Archaeology* 28(4):37–48.

Sanborn Map Company, 1922, *Sanborn Fire Insurance Map of Harpers Ferry, West Virginia*. On file, Harpers Ferry National Historical Park, Harpers Ferry, West Virginia.

Schlesinger, A.M., 1968, *Learning How to Behave*. Cooper Square Publishers, Inc., New York.

Schuette, J., 1914, *The Story of John and Rose Who Began Married Life on an Income of $99.00 a Year Shows the Comforting Results Attained by Strict Economy Systematic House and Bookkeeping and Their Accumulation to Their Olden Age*. The Lakeside Press, R.R. Donnelly & Sons Company, Chicago.

Schulter, H., 1910, *The Brewing Industry and the Brewery Workers' Movement in America*. International Union of United Brewery Workmen of America, Cincinnati, Ohio.

Schulz, P.D. and Gust, S.M., 1980, Faunal Remains and Social Status in 19th Century Sacramento. *Historical Archaeology* 17(1):44–53.

Schuyler, Mrs. V.K., 1893, Correct Service at Table. *The Ladies' Home Journal* February 10(3):26.

Scott, J., 1985, *Weapons of the Weak: Everyday Forms of Peasant Resistance*. Yale University Press, New Haven, Connecticut.

Scott, J.,1990, *Domination and the Arts of Resistance: Hidden Transcripts.* Yale University Press, New Haven, Connecticut.

Sears, Roebuck and Co., 1929, *The Sears Roebuck Catalog.* Originally published 1902. Bounty Books, New York.

Sears, Roebuck and Co., 1970, *The Sears, Roebuck and Co. Catalog.* Originally published 1900. DBI Books, Inc., Northfield, Illinois.

Seidel, E.M., 1986, Archaeological Investigation on Virginius Island 1977-1981. Harpers Ferry National Historical Park, Harpers Ferry, West Virginia. On file, Harpers Ferry National Historical Park Harpers Ferry, West Virginia.

Sellars, R., 1987, Vigil of Silence: The Civil War Memorials. *Courier.* March:18-19.

Shackel, P.A., 1993a, *Personal Discipline and Material Culture: An Archaeology of Annapolis, Maryland, 1695-1870.* University of Tennessee Press, Knoxville.

Shackel, P.A., 1994, Memorializing Landscapes and the Civil War in Harpers Ferry. In *Look to the Earth: An Archaeology of the Civil War,* edited by C. Geier and S. Winter, pp. 256-270. The University of Tennessee Press, Knoxville.

Shackel, P.A., 1995, Terrible Saint: Changing Meanings of the John Brown Fort. *Historical Archaeology* 29(4)11-25.

Shackel, P.A., 1996, *Culture Change and the New Technology: An Archaeology of the Early American Industrial Era.* Plenum Press, New York.

Shackel, P.A., in press, John Brown's Fort: A Contested National Symbol. In *John Brown: An Interdisciplinary Approach,* edited by Paul Finklemann and Peggy Russo. University of North Carolina Press.

Shackel, P.A. (editor), 1993b, *Interdisciplinary Investigations of Domestic Life in Government Block B: Perspectives on Harpers Ferry's Armory and Commercial District,* Occasional Report No. 6, National Capital Region, National Park Service, Washington, D.C.

Shackel, P.A., and Winter, S.E., (editors), 1994, An Archaeology of Harpers Ferry's Commercial and Residential District. *Historical Archaeology* 28(4):16-26.

Shackel, P.A., YoungRavenhorst, C.C., and Winter, S.E., 1993, The Archaeological Record: Stratigraphy, Features, and Material Culture. In *Interdisciplinary Investigations of Domestic Life in Government Block B: Perspectives on Harpers Ferry's Armory and Commercial District,* edited by P.A. Shackel, pp. 4.1-4.85. Occasional Report No. 6, National Park Service, Department of the Interior, Washington, D.C.

Sherwood, M.E.W., 1893, *The Art of Entertaining.* Dodd, Mead and Company, New York.

Sider, G.M., 1996, Cleansing History: Lawrence Massachusetts, the Strike for Four Loaves of Bread and No Roses, and the Anthropology of Working-Class Consciousness. *Radical History Review* 65:48-83.

Simkhovitch, M.K., 1938, *Neighborhood: My Story of Greenwich House.* W.W. Norton, New York.

Sklar, K.K., 1985, Hull House in the 1890s: A Community of Women Reformers. *Signs: Journal of Women in Culture and Society* 10(4):658-677.

Smith, H.N. (editor), 1967, *Popular Culture and Industrialism, 1865-1890.* New York University Press, New York.

Smith, M.R., 1977, *Harpers Ferry Armory and the New Technology: The Challenge of Change.* Cornell University Press, Ithaca, New York.

Snell, C.W., 1958, A History of the Island of Virginius, 1751-1870. Harpers Ferry National Historical Park, Harpers Ferry, West Virginia. On file, Harpers Ferry National Historical Park, Harpers Ferry, West Virginia.

Snell, C.W.,1959, Harpers Ferry becomes a Fortress, September 21, 1862-October 6, 1863. On file, Harpers Ferry National Historical Park, Harpers Ferry, West Virginia.

Snell, C.W., 1960a, The Fortifications at Harpers Ferry, VA, in 1861 and Jackson's Attack, May 1862. On file, Harpers Ferry National Historical Park, Harpers Ferry, West Virginia.

Snell, C.W., 1960b, Harpers Ferry Repels an Attack and Becomes the Major Base of Operations for Sheridan's Army, July 4, 1864, To July 27, 1865. On file, Harpers Ferry National Historical Park, Harpers Ferry, West Virginia.

Snell, C.W., 1973, A Compendium of the Commercial and Industrial Advertisements of the Business and Manufacturing Establishments of Harpers Ferry and the Island of Virginius, 1824–1861, Virginia. On file, Harpers Ferry National Historical Park, Harpers Ferry, West Virginia.

Snell, C.W., 1979, The Acquisition and Disposal of Public Lands of the U.S. Armory at Harpers Ferry, West Virginia, 1796–1885: A Narrative History. National Park Service. On file, Harpers Ferry National Historical Park, Harpers Ferry, West Virginia.

——, 1883, *Social Etiquette of New York*. D. Appleton and Company, New York.

Spencer-Wood, S., 1987, A Survey of Domestic Reform Movement Sites in Boston and Cambridge, ca. 1865–1905. *Historical Archaeology* 21(2)7–36.

Spencer-Wood, S., 1991, Toward an Historical Archaeology of Materialistic Domestic Reform. In *The Archaeology of Inequality*, edited by Randall H. McGuire and Robert Paynter, pp. 231–286. Basil Blackwell, Cambridge, Massachusetts.

Spirit of Jefferson (SoJ) [Charles Town, West Virginia]. Newspaper on microfilm, Harpers Ferry National Historical Park, Harpers Ferry, West Virginia.

    1861, No title. 4 May:2.
    1873, No title. 17 January:3.
    1878, No title. 5 November:2.
    1880, No title. 6 July.
    1883, No title. 27 March:3.
    1884, No title. 22 January:3.
    1884, No title. 12 June:3.
    1884, No title. 24 June:3.
    1885, No title. 28 April:2.
    1885, No title. 22 May:2.
    1887, No title. 15 November:3.
    1888, No title. 26 June:2.
    1888, No title. 14 August:1.
    1889, No title. 4 June:1.
    1889, No title. 17 September:3.
    1890, No title. 28 January:3.
    1890, No title. 13 May:3.
    1890, No title. 21 October:3.
    1891, No title. 6 January:2.
    1891, No title. 28 July:3.
    1892, No title. 22 March:2.
    1892, No title. 17 May:3.
    1892, No title. 5 July:3.
    1992, No title. 7 November:2.
    1894, No title. 10 June:3.
    1895, No title. 16 April:1.
    1895, No title. 7 May:3.
    1895, No title. 26 May:2
    1895, No title. 4 June:2.
    1895, No title. 1 October:2.

  1895, No title. 8 October:1.
  1896, No title. 16 May:2.
  1896, No title. 17 November:3.
  1897, No title. 23 November:3
  1897, No title. 7 December:3.
  1898, No title. 12 July:1.
  1900, No title. 22 February:3.
  1900, No title. 25 February:2.
  1900, No title. 6 March:3.
  1902, No title. 11 February:2.
  1902, No title. 25 November:2.
  1903, No title. 5 September:3.
  1910, No title. 17 May:2.
  1916, No title. 16 May:2.
  1981, No title. 11 June:2.

Stern, P.V.D., 1961, *Soldier Life in the Union and Confederate Armies*. Indiana University Press, Bloomington.

Strasser, S., 1982, *Never Done: A History of American Housework*. Pantheon Books, New York.

Strother, D.H., 1861, No title. Unpublished manuscript. On file, Harpers Ferry National Historical Park, Harpers Ferry, West Virginia. July 22.

——, 1854, *Table Observances: Including the Arrangement of the Table, with Hints on Carving, on the Room, the Service, the Duties of the Host and His Guests; and Kitchen Arrangements*. Wm. S. Orr and Co., London.

Taft, G.J., 1898, A Trip to Harpers Ferry. On file, Harpers Ferry National Historical Park, Harpers Ferry, West Virginia.

Talbot, M., 1913, *House Sanitation: A Manual for Housekeeping*. Whitcomb and Barrows, Boston.

Taylor, J.E., 1989, *The James E. Taylor Sketchbook*. The Western Reserve Historical Society. Morningside House, Inc., Dayton, Ohio.

Thelen, D., 1989, Memory and American History. *Journal of American History* 75 (4):1117–1129.

Trowbridge, J.T., 1866, *The South: A Tour of its Battle-Fields and Ruined Cities, A Journey Through the Desolated States, and Talks with the People*. L. Stebbibs, Hartford, Connecticut.

Trowbridge, J.T.,1870, *Lawrence's Adventure*. Porter and Crates, Philadelphia.

Tyree, M.C., 1879, *Housekeeping in Old Virginia*. John P. Morton and Company, Louisville, Kentucky.

United States Bureau of Census, 1900, *Population Statistics*. Harpers Ferry, Virginia. Microfilm, Harpers Ferry National Historical Park, Harpers Ferry, West Virginia.

United States War Department (USWD), 1880–1901, *The War of the Rebellion: A Compilation of the Official Records of the Union and the Confederate Armies*. The War Department. Government Printing Office, Washington, D.C., vol 2.

Van Rensselaer, M., Rose, F., and Canon, H., 1920, *A Manual of Home-Making*. The MacMillan Company, New York.

Villard, O.G., 1910, *John Brown, 1800–1859; A Biography Fifty Years After*. Houghton Mifflin, New York.

Virginia Free Press (*VFP*) (Charles Town, West Virginia). Newspaper on microfilm, Harpers Ferry national Historical Park.)
  1831, No title. 15 September:3.

1867, No title. 19 December:1

1869, No title. 15 November:2.

1872, No title. 17 December:3.

1896, No title. 26 August:3.

1911, No title. 13 April:3.

1912, No title. 19 December:5.

1913, No title. 9 October:2.

Wallerstein Company, 1950, *Forty Years A-Brewing. A Record of Wallerstein Service To the Brewing Industry.* Wallerstein Company, Inc., New York.

Ward, A., 1882, *The Grocers Handbook and Directory for 1883.* Philadelphia Grocer Publishing Company, Philadelphia.

Ward, Mrs. H. O., 1878, *Sensible Etiquette of the Best Society, Customs, Manners, Morals, and Home Culture.* Porter & Coates, Philadelphia.

Ward, J., 1985, Civil War Letters of J.F. Ward 34th Regiment, Massachusetts Volunteers, Company B. Unpublished typescript. On file, Harpers Ferry National Historical Park, Harpers Ferry, West Virginia.

Waring, G.E., Jr., 1867, *Draining for Health and Draining for Profit.* Houghton Mifflin, New York.

Waring, G.E., Jr., 1876, *The Sanitary Drainage of Houses and Towns.* Houghton Mifflin, New York.

Waring, G.E., Jr., 1885, *How to Drain a House: Practical Information for Householders.* Henry Holt and Company, New York.

Wentzell, V, 1957, History Awakens at Harpers Ferry. *National Geographics* 61(3):402–408.

Western Brewer, 1974, *One Hundred Years of Brewing: A Complete History of the Progress Made in the Art, Science and Industry of Brewing in the World, Particularly during the Nineteenth Century.* Arno Press, New York.

——, 1880, *Whitall and Tatum &Co.* Reprinted for the American Historical Catalog Collection. The Pyne Press, Princeton, N.J.

Wiley, B.I., 1971, *The Life of Johnny Reb: A Compilation of the Official Records of the Union and Confederate Armies.* Doubleday, Garden City, New York.

Winter, S.E., and Frye, D.E., 1992, *Loudoun Heights Archaeological and Historical Resources Study. Harpers Ferry National Historical Park,* Occasional Report No. 8, Harpers Ferry National Historical Park, National Capital Region, National Park Service, U.S. Department of the Interior, Washington, D.C.

Wirka, S.M., 1996, The City Social Movement: Progressive Women Reformers and Early Social Planning. In *Planning the Twentieth-Century American City,* edited by M.C. Sies and C. Silver, pp. 57–75. The Johns Hopkins University Press, Baltimore.

Wright, H.E., 1982, *Handy Book for Brewers.* Crosby Lockwood and Sons, London.

Writer's Program, 1941, *West Virginia: A Guide to the Mountain State.* Compiled by workers of the Writer's Program of the Work Project Administration in the State of West Virginia. American Guide Series. Oxford University Press, New York.

Index

CONTRIBUTIONS TO GLOBAL HISTORICAL ARCHAEOLOGY
Chronological Listing of Volumes

A HISTORICAL ARCHAEOLOGY OF THE MODERN WORLD
Charles E. Orser, Jr.

CULTURE CHANGE AND THE NEW TECHNOLOGY
An Archaeology of the Early American Industrial Era
Paul A. Shackel

ARCHAEOLOGY AND THE CAPITALIST WORLD SYSTEM
A Study from Russian America
Aron L. Crowell

BETWEEN ARTIFACTS AND TEXTS
Historical Archaeology in Global Perspective
Anders Andrén

AN ARCHAEOLOGY OF SOCIAL SPACE
Analyzing Coffee Plantations in Jamaica's Blue Mountains
James A. Delle

HISTORICAL ARCHAEOLOGIES OF CAPITALISM
Edited by Mark P. Leone and Parker B. Potter, Jr.

RACE AND AFFLUENCE
An Archaeology of African America and Consumer Culture
Paul R. Mullins

AN ARCHAEOLOGY OF MANNERS
The Polite World of the Merchant Elite of Colonial Massachusetts
Lorinda B. R. Goodwin

MEANING AND IDEOLOGY IN HISTORICAL ARCHAEOLOGY
Style, Social Identity, and Capitalism in an Australian Town
Heather Burke

LANDSCAPE TRANSFORMATIONS AND THE ARCHAEOLOGY
OF IMPACT
Social Disruption and State Formation in Southern Africa
Warren R. Perry

THE HISTORICAL ARCHAEOLOGY OF BUENOS AIRES
  A City at the End of the World
Daniel Schávelzon

DOMESTIC ARCHITECTURE AND POWER
  The Historical Archaeology of Colonial Ecuador
Ross W. Jamieson

A HISTORICAL ARCHAEOLOGY OF THE OTTOMAN EMPIRE
  Breaking New Ground
Edited by Uzi Baram and Lynda Carroll

ARCHAEOLOGY AND CREATED MEMORY
  Public History in a National Park
Paul A. Shackel